ART THERAPY FOR PSYCHOSIS

Art Therapy for Psychosis presents innovative theoretical and clinical approaches to psychosis that have developed in the work of expert clinicians from around the world. It draws on insights that have emerged from decades of clinical practice to explain why and how specialised forms of art therapy constitute a particularly appropriate psychotherapeutic approach to psychosis.

The contributors present a diverse range of current theoretical perspectives on the subject, derived from the fields of neuroscience, phenomenology and cognitive analytic theory, as well as from different schools of psychoanalysis. Collectively, they offer insights into the specific potentials of art therapy as a psychotherapeutic approach to psychosis, and describe some of the specialised approaches developed with individuals and with groups over the past twenty years. Throughout the book, the meaning and relevance of art-making as a medium for holding and containing unbearable, unthinkable and unspeakable experiences within the psychotherapeutic setting becomes apparent. Several of the chapters present detailed illustrated case studies which show how making visual images with an appropriately trained art psychotherapist can be a first step on the path into meaningful relatedness. Full colour versions of these illustrations can be viewed on the ISPS website (see p. ix for details of how to access these).

This book offers fresh insights into the nature of psychosis, the challenges encountered by clinicians attempting to work psychotherapeutically with people in psychotic states in different settings, and the potentials of art therapy as an effective treatment approach. It will be essential reading for mental health professionals who work with psychosis, including psychiatrists, psychoanalysts, psychotherapists and arts therapists, and those in training.

Katherine Killick trained as an art therapist and a psychoanalytic psychotherapist. She is a Training Analyst of the Society of Analytical Psychology and a Training and Supervising Analyst of the British Jungian Analytic Association working in private practice. She developed a specialised art-psychotherapeutic approach to psychosis and has published widely in this area. She is co-editor of *Art, Psychotherapy and Psychosis* with Joy Schaverien and contributes to various clinical trainings in art psychotherapy and Jungian psychoanalysis.

THE INTERNATIONAL SOCIETY FOR PSYCHOLOGICAL AND SOCIAL APPROACHES TO PSYCHOSIS BOOK SERIES

Series editors: Alison Summers and Anna Lavis
Series advisor for the monograph strand: Andrew Moskowitz

ISPS (The International Society for Psychological and Social Approaches to Psychosis) has a history stretching back more than five decades, during which it has witnessed the relentless pursuit of biological explanations for psychosis. This tide has been turning in recent years and there is growing international interest in a range of psychological, social and cultural factors that have considerable explanatory traction and distinct therapeutic possibilities. Governments, professional groups, people with personal experience of psychosis and family members are increasingly exploring interventions that involve more talking and listening. Many now regard practitioners skilled in psychological therapies as an essential component of the care of people with psychosis.

A global society active in at least twenty countries, ISPS is composed of a diverse range of individuals, networks and institutional members. Key to its ethos is that individuals with personal experience of psychosis, and their families and friends, are fully involved alongside practitioners and researchers, and that all benefit from this collaboration.

ISPS's core aim is to promote psychological and social approaches to understanding and treating psychosis. Recognising the humanitarian and therapeutic potential of these perspectives, ISPS embraces a wide spectrum of therapeutic approaches from psychodynamic, systemic, cognitive, and arts therapies, to need-adapted and dialogical approaches, family and group therapies and residential therapeutic communities. A further ambition is to draw together diverse viewpoints on psychosis and to foster discussion and debate across the biomedical and social sciences, including establishing meaningful dialogue with practitioners and researchers who are more familiar with biological-based approaches. Such discussion is now increasingly supported by empirical evidence of the interaction of genes and biology with the emotional and social environment especially in the fields of trauma, attachment, social relationships and therapy.

Ways in which ISPS pursues its aims include international and national conferences, real and virtual networks, and publication of the journal *Psychosis*. The book series is intended to complement these activities by providing a resource for those wanting to consider aspects of psychosis in detail. It now also includes a monograph strand primarily targeted at academics. Central to both strands is the combination of rigorous, in-depth intellectual content and accessibility to a wide range of readers. We aim for the series to be a resource for mental health professionals of all disciplines, for those developing and implementing policy, for academics in the social and clinical sciences, and for people whose interest in psychosis stems from personal or family experience. We hope that the book series will help challenge excessively biological ways of conceptualising and treating psychosis through the dissemination of existing knowledge and ideas and by fostering new interdisciplinary dialogues and perspectives.

CBT FOR PSYCHOSIS
A Symptom-based Approach
Edited by Roger Hagen, Douglas Turkington, Torkil Berge and Rolf W. Gråwe

EXPERIENCING PSYCHOSIS
Personal and Professional Perspectives
Edited by Jim Geekie, Patte Randal, Debra Lampshire and John Read

PSYCHOSIS AS A PERSONAL CRISIS
An Experience-Based Approach
Edited by Marius Romme and Sandra Escher

MODELS OF MADNESS
Psychological, Social and Biological Approaches to Psychosis 2nd Edition
Edited by John Read and Jacqui Dillon

SURVIVING, EXISTING, OR LIVING
Phase-specific Therapy for Severe Psychosis
Pamela Fuller

PSYCHOSIS AND EMOTION
The Role of Emotions in Understanding Psychosis, Therapy and Recovery
Edited by Andrew Gumley, Alf Gillham, Kathy Taylor and Matthias Schwannauer

INSANITY AND DIVINITY
Studies in Psychosis and Spirituality
Edited by John Gale, Michael Robson and Georgia Rapsomatioti

PSYCHOTHERAPY FOR PEOPLE DIAGNOSED WITH SCHIZOPHRENIA
Specific techniques
Andrew Lotterman

CREATIVITY AND PSYCHOTIC STATES IN EXCEPTIONAL PEOPLE
The work of Murray Jackson
Murray Jackson and Jeanne Magagna

ART THERAPY FOR PSYCHOSIS
Theory and Practice
Edited by Katherine Killick

MONOGRAPHS
PSYCHOSIS, PSYCHOANALYSIS AND PSYCHIATRY IN POSTWAR USA
On the borderland of madness
Orna Ophir

MEANING, MADNESS AND POLITICAL SUBJECTIVITY
A study of schizophrenia and culture in Turkey
Sadeq Rahimi

ART THERAPY FOR PSYCHOSIS

Theory and Practice

Edited by Katherine Killick

Routledge
Taylor & Francis Group

LONDON AND NEW YORK

First published 2017
by Routledge
2 Park Square, Milton Park, Abingdon, Oxon OX14 4RN

and by Routledge
711 Third Avenue, New York, NY 10017

Routledge is an imprint of the Taylor & Francis Group, an informa business

British Library Cataloguing-in-Publication Data
A catalogue record for this book is available from the British Library

Library of Congress Cataloging-in-Publication Data
Names: Killick, Katherine, editor.
Title: Art therapy for psychosis: theory and practice / [edited by] Katherine Killick.
Other titles: International Society for Psychological and Social Approaches to Psychosis book series.
Description: Abingdon, Oxon; New York, NY: Routledge, 2017. | Series: International Society for Psychological and Social Approaches to Psychosis book series | Includes bibliographical references.
Identifiers: LCCN 2016039521 | ISBN 9781138792098 (hardback: alk. paper) | ISBN 9781138792104 (pbk.: alk. paper) | ISBN 9781315762340 (ebook)
Subjects: | MESH: Psychotic Disorders—therapy | Art Therapy—methods
Classification: LCC RC489.A7 | NLM WM 200 | DDC 616.89/1656—dc23
LC record available at https://lccn.loc.gov/2016039521

ISBN: 978-1-138-79209-8 (hbk)
ISBN: 978-1-138-79210-4 (pbk)
ISBN: 978-1-315-76234-0 (ebk)

Typeset in Times New Roman
by codeMantra

CONTENTS

CONTENTS

ILLUSTRATIONS

Full colour versions of the illustrations can be viewed at http://isps.org/index.php/publications/book-series/publication-photos The password is ArTPerspectives8

CONTRIBUTORS

Jean-Jacques Bonneau came from a fine art background and moved from Paris to London in 1987 to train as an art therapist, which he did at both postgraduate and advanced levels. He worked in NHS mental health settings as an art therapist for 25 years and is currently developing his private practice as an art therapist and clinical supervisor.

Rafael Cohen is an art therapist, psychotherapist, and supervisor in two settings: private practice and an inpatient psychiatric unit. He works psychoanalytically with a focus on Freud and Lacan. He is committed to bringing a rigorous psychoanalytic perspective to art therapy. He has also previously worked as an art teacher and arts organiser.

Simone Donnari is an art therapist. He is vice-president of the Italian Association of Art Therapists (APIArt), Educational Director of Art-Therapy School in Assisi and a co-founder of Istituto Gaetano Benedetti, a school of psychotherapy. He has developed an innovative video integration form of art therapy. In 1995, he co-founded 'Sementera onlus', an association dedicated to the social rehabilitation of psychotic and autistic patients. In 2011, he co-founded ISPS Italy. Since 2013, he and Maurizio Peciccia have been in charge of a research project, "Sensory Motor Integration Therapies", in cooperation with Vittorio Gallese. He regularly gives seminars, lectures and supervisory sessions in Mental Health Centres in Italy, University of Perugia and New York University Steinhardt.

Helen Greenwood has 30 years experience employed as an art therapist in NHS adult mental health services in the UK. Since then, self-employed, she has provided supervision and teaching. She is an associate of the Art Therapy Northern Programme. Her areas of interest have been working with people diagnosed with psychotic illness or psychotic thought processes, and also those adults who have endured abuse, deprivation or early trauma in childhood. She has published a number of papers and chapters based on this work.

Eleanor Hagert is a licensed creative arts therapist who is registered and board certified in the United States of America. She specialises in utilising creative expression to support and empower individuals who are in recovery from substance abuse. She is currently employed at New Directions, an Outpatient Alcoholism and Substance Abuse Treatment Program in Brooklyn, NY, USA.

Katherine Killick trained as an art therapist and Jungian analyst (Society of Analytical Psychology, London). She worked at Hill End Hospital, St Albans, UK, in the 1980s and 90s, and developed a specialised art-psychotherapeutic approach to people in psychotic states. She has published a number of papers and chapters in books about that subject. She co-edited the book *Art, Psychotherapy and Psychosis* (Routledge 1997) with Joy Schaverien. She currently works in private practice as a psychotherapist, clinical supervisor, trainer and consultant, and maintains a specialised interest in working with states of mind in which psychotic anxieties predominate. She is a Training Analyst for the Society of Analytical Psychology, and a Training and Supervising Analyst for the British Jungian Analytic Association. She contributes to various clinical trainings in art psychotherapy and Jungian psychoanalysis.

Johannes Lehtonen is Professor of Psychiatry Emeritus at the University of Eastern Finland and a psychoanalyst at the Finnish Psychoanalytical Society. His research has recently focused on the embodied nature of the matrix of the mind and its relation to the formation of mental images both from psychophysiological and psychoanalytic perspectives.

Maurizio Peciccia is a psychiatrist, psychoanalyst (IFPS), art therapist, President of the Italian branch of ISPS; Professor of psychotherapy of the psychoses and Scientific Director of the Gaetano Benedetti Institute of Existential Psychoanalytic Psychotherapy. Together with Gaetano Benedetti he developed the method of progressive mirror drawing, a psychodynamically oriented audio-visual integration therapy for psychoses. He is the author of over 140 publications concerning psychotherapy of the psychoses. He is currently conducting research on multisensory integration therapy for psychoses in collaboration with the Department of Social and Human Sciences of Perugia University, the Mental Health Department of Perugia and the Neuroscience Department of Parma University.

Mimmu Rankanen is a registered art therapist and cognitive-analytic psychotherapist, who has long experience of teaching art therapy at university level and of clinical work with adults in private practice in Finland. She has written several articles and co-edited a book of arts based art therapy. Additionally, she has exhibited her art both in Finnish and international galleries and worked as artist in residence both in Ireland and Ecuador. Currently, she is finishing her doctoral research into clients' art therapy experiences in Aalto University Department of Art.

Hanne Stubbe Teglbjaerg works as a consultant psychiatrist specialising in psychotherapy in the Department of Psychosis, Aarhus University Hospital, in Risskov, Denmark. She is educated in expressive arts therapy with a Certificate of Advanced Graduate Studies from the European Graduate School in Switzerland and wrote her PhD thesis on the subject of art therapy for psychiatric patients with a special focus on schizophrenia. She is the author of a book in Danish (*Skabende Kunstterapi*) and several articles about art therapy and is a regular guest teacher in the expressive arts educations in Scandinavia.

ACKNOWLEDGEMENTS

The image 'Marble Figurine of a Woman' in Chapter One appears by permission of The British Museum.

Parts of Chapter Seven are republished by permission of Aalto Art Books.

The editor and chapter authors gratefully acknowledge the permissions granted by those who created the images used as illustrations in Chapters Two, Three, Five, Seven and Eight for their use in this book; and the permissions granted by all those whose personal journeys in art therapy are referred to within the written text for the use of this material.

INTRODUCTION

Places for the mind to heal

Katherine Killick

The title of this Introduction refers to the final paragraph of a chapter I con-tributed to the book *The Changing Shape of Art Therapy* (Gilroy and McNeilly 2000) in which I quoted a person who had spent many years as a patient in art therapy and who had sustained a commitment to working with me over years of multiple inpatient admissions—including some to the locked ward in the hospi-tal, day hospital attendance, and outpatient treatment. The words 'People like me need places like that art room—places that allow the mind to heal' were part of the patient's expression of gratitude in our final session (Killick 2000). This book bears witness to the meaning and relevance of 'places like that art room' for people who, like my patient, experience psychosis.

The eight chapters in this book can each be read as an individual 'standalone' essay. The book as a whole aims to develop the reader's understanding of the appropriateness of art therapy as a treatment medium, both for people in acute psychotic states and for those who historically have a proneness to psychosis. It presents innovative theoretical and clinical approaches that were developed in a range of different treatment settings in Denmark, Finland, Italy, the UK, and the USA, and some of the chapters use illustrated case material to amplify the reader's understanding of the complexities of this subject. The diverse ap-proaches in theory and in practice that the book's eight chapters present offer the reader common understandings of the key issues involved in working with people who are prone to psychosis, and of the potentials of specialised forms of art therapy in bringing about fundamental and lasting psychological healing.

The specialised field of art therapy as a psychotherapeutic treatment approach to psychotic states of mind has matured since the publication of the book that Joy Schaverien and I co-edited in 1997, *Art, Psychotherapy and Psychosis*. At that time, there was a need for a book to define this field of clinical practice within the art therapy profession, and to introduce the approaches that had developed at that stage. This book continues that process, presenting a range of theoretical and technical approaches that evolved within the field over the ensuing twenty years in different clinical settings and in different countries. Its presence in the ISPS series is in itself a sign of the increased recognition that the field of art therapy for psychosis has earned over the years. It is my hope that this book will offer its reader an understanding of the specific potentials that art therapy offers to people experiencing the ravages of psychosis, and that it will provide the basis for further research into this subject.

In my opinion, one of the most significant developments in the field since 1997 was the ground-breaking research undertaken over a number of years by Goldsmiths College, University of London and Oxleas NHS Trust, which developed an evidence-based 'Clinical Practice Guideline' (Brooker *et al.* 2007) for art therapists to refer to when working with people prone to psychosis. This collected all the existing published work on the subject and distilled the understanding of expert specialist practitioners and the experiences of service users, identifying the adaptations of art psychotherapy technique that are most significant when working with people who are prone to psychosis. Many of those findings resonate with the approaches presented in this book, and to date, as far as I know, there have been no clinical trials of art therapy in which the research design was informed by these key issues that emerge as specific to art therapy for psychosis. Accordingly, the effectiveness of art therapy as a treatment approach remains a matter of opinion.

The theoretical basis of the work that I and other practitioners presented in *Art, Psychotherapy and Psychosis* (Killick and Schaverien 1997) was predominantly informed by various traditions within psychoanalytic thinking, which prevailed within the profession at that time in the UK. However, the chapters by Maclagan, Wood and Henzell reminded the reader that art therapy evolved from, and is informed by, a diverse background of theoretical and philosophical traditions, within which psychoanalytic theory and practice is one element amongst many. This is reiterated by the diversity of theoretical and philosophical approaches that underpin the various chapters in this book. These include original perspectives derived from neurophysiology (Lehtonen and Peciccia and Donnari), phenomenology (Teglbjaerg), ontology (Bonneau) and cognitive analytic theory (Rankanen), as well as those derived from different psychoanalytic traditions. In Chapter Five, Cohen introduces the reader to Lacanian psychoanalysis and to the unique perspectives that this offers to thinking about psychosis and working with psychosis in art therapy. Chapters Two (Peciccia and Donnari), Four (Bonneau), Six (Greenwood) and Eight (Hagert) include thinking derived from Freudian and Kleinian schools of psychoanalysis. In Chapter Six, Greenwood introduces the concept of *mentalisation* that has evolved within current psychoanalytic thinking, and applies the concept to art therapy theory and practice.

Some of the chapters in the book are written from the perspective of the therapist, whereas others include reflections from patients. The chapters written by Teglbjaerg (Chapter Three), who introduces artwork-focused art therapy, and Rankanen (Chapter Seven), who introduces dialogical art therapy, each include material contributed by the authors' patients about the meaning and relevance of the art therapy process described. The necessity for patients to provide informed consent for the use of their material in this book, and the effect that seeking consent could have on the therapeutic relationship, has been managed by different authors in different ways. Bonneau (Chapter Four), Cohen (Chapter Five) and Greenwood (Chapter Six) make use of imaginary 'vignettes' based on, but not descriptive of, the authors' clinical experiences to illustrate the approaches being described, whereas Peciccia and Donnari (Chapter Two), Rankanen (Chapter Seven), and Hagert (Chapter Eight) sought consent from patients for the therapist to present images made by their patients, and verbatim accounts of therapeutic interactions. The detailed, illustrated case studies presented in Chapters Two (Pecicia and Donnari), Seven (Rankanen), and Eight (Hagert) vividly convey experiences that are characteristic of art therapy process with people in psychotic states of mind in different settings.

Each chapter presents aspects of what is involved in working in art therapy, both individually and in groups, with people experiencing the vulnerabilities deriving from psychosis. The nature of psychosis is considered in each chapter, and by implication, theories of primitive, pre-verbal states of mind. Common understandings of the profound anxieties pervading these states of mind, and of their role in psychotic states, emerge from different theoretical perspectives. These understandings form a basis for appreciating the traumatic threat that the relationship with the therapist presents, and, accordingly, this threat is taken into account in the therapist's approach.

The chapters present a range of different approaches, through which common understandings of the role that art-making can play in psychotherapeutic work with psychosis emerge. Both individual and group treatment settings are considered. Chapters Four (Bonneau), Seven (Rankanen) and Eight (Hagert) focus on work with individuals, whereas Chapter Three (Teglbjaerg) focusses on work with groups. Chapters Two (Peciccia and Donnari) and Six (Greenwood) discuss the use of the approaches presented in the chapters in both individual and group settings.

Throughout the book, art-making and transactions surrounding the making of images and the presence of art objects form a field of experience within the therapeutic relationship that is considered from the different theoretical perspectives presented to be of specific value when working with psychosis. Lehtonen (Chapter One) and Teglbjaerg (Chapter Three) both present rigorously researched arguments identifying art-making as a healing agent in psychotic states when this takes place within a specialised therapeutic relationship. This resonates with the approach that the pioneer of art therapy for psychosis in the UK, Edward Adamson, developed in his work at Netherne Hospital, described in his seminal book, *Art as Healing* (1984), which placed emphasis on the art-making process as healing in itself. Lehtonen presents this argument in relation to an original neuroscientific and developmental theory of mind and of psychosis, and Teglbjaerg presents it from the perspective of phenomenology, introducing the reader to the original form of art therapy practice that she has developed, named 'artwork-focused art therapy'. Peciccia and Donnari (Chapter Two) extend the concept of art-making to include ways of working with images that are facilitated by modern technologies.

The book as a whole identifies issues that need to be considered when developing therapeutic relations with people prone to psychosis if the therapeutic potentials of art-making and of other elements within the art therapy setting are to be maximised. To a greater or lesser extent, all the chapters discuss the fragmentation of the sense of the experienced, embodied self and the breakdown in the capacity to use words as symbols as aspects of psychotic states that necessitate specialised therapeutic approaches. The concepts presented by Peciccia and Donnari (Chapter Two), Bonneau (Chapter Four) and Cohen (Chapter Five), which are drawn from Freudian, Kleinian, Lacanian and existential schools of psychoanalysis, lay theoretical foundations for understanding the way the therapist may be experienced by the patient when mediating the experiences of symbolic realities that cannot be engaged with in psychotic states of mind. Teglbjaerg's phenomenologically based approach (Chapter Three) and Rankanen's cognitive-analytic approach (Chapter Seven) contribute similar understandings from very different philosophical and theoretical traditions.

The potential for the balance of institutional power to exacerbate the suffering of the patient emerges in several chapters and is discussed in depth from different perspectives by Cohen (Chapter Five) and Greenwood (Chapter Six), who also draw the reader's attention to the significance of the power differential within the art therapy setting and the necessity for attending to its effect on the therapeutic relationship. Some of these issues are highlighted in Chapter Eight (Hagert), which discusses the particular challenges and complexities of psychotherapeutic work with people in psychotic states within 'correctional' settings.

The need for a specifically structured psychotherapeutic relationship that respects and accommodates the extreme anxiety that lies at the core of psychotic states formed the subject of my own published work (Killick 1991, 1993, 1997, 2000), and this is described and discussed in some detail by Bonneau (Chapter Four), who demonstrates the adaptation of the principles of my approach to a setting more characteristic of present-day art therapy practice. The vignettes presented by Bonneau illustrate the issues involved in engaging with psychosis and establishing therapeutic relations within the art therapy setting. At this early stage, the psychotic patient's use of imagery and setting is often primarily self-protective. The therapist's understanding and acceptance of the patient's profound anxiety, and of the consequent use of the setting for self-protection, enables a particular form of primitive therapeutic alliance to develop. This exerts no pressure on the patient to engage prematurely in symbolic ways of relating, but it maintains a constant invitation to do so if and when he or she is able and willing.

The different approaches presented in the book all make use of specific potentials of the art therapy setting to protect the patient's fragile sense of self, whereas the unintrusive yet consistent presence and attitude of the therapist maintains the possibility of engaging in an interpersonal relationship. The detailed, illustrated case study in Chapter Two (Peciccia and Donnari) illustrates the way in which a psychotic patient's sense of self can gradually strengthen through repeated experience of the art therapy setting, to the point where he or she may dare to risk engaging affectively with the therapist. At this point, the images can begin to serve communicative purposes and, accordingly, to develop the potential to be used as symbols. The case study presented by Rankanen (Chapter Seven) includes the dimension of relatedness that becomes possible when patient and therapist engage in reflective discussion in relation to images that have acquired symbolic meaning within the relationship. At this point, the patient can potentially engage in forms of art psychotherapy that rely on the capacity to use words as symbols, as well as in other forms of psychotherapy that do so.

The specific value of art therapy for psychosis as presented in this book lies in its capacity to offer structured psychotherapeutic approaches that minimise the requirement for forms of interpersonal relating that are to a greater or lesser extent impossible in psychotic states. The various approaches presented in the chapters reveal ways in which art-making in itself can become a healing agent, and in which the interpersonal context within which this happens can become another. The presence of art objects in the setting and the transactions surrounding the making of images and their presence can be employed by the therapist to form therapeutic alliances with people in psychotic states, and to undertake work by means of which fundamental change is possible. Returning to the memory of my patient's words, quoted at the start of this piece of writing, it is my hope that individually and collectively the chapters in this book demonstrate that 'places' that enable 'the mind to heal' can be developed within a diverse range of treatment settings. They evolve through the particular forms of relatedness that can develop between therapist and patient in specialised forms of art therapy, and they rely on the therapist's appreciation of and respect for the particular form of suffering experienced in psychosis.

References

Adamson, E. (1984). *Art as healing*, London: Coventure.

Brooker, J., Cullum, M., Gilroy, A., *et al.* (2007). *The use of art work in art psychotherapy with people who are prone to psychotic states*, University of London: Goldsmiths.

Gilroy, A. and McNeilly, G. (eds.) (2000). *The changing shape of art therapy: New developments in theory and practice*, London: Jessica Kingsley.

Henzell, J. (1997). 'Art, madness, and anti-psychiatry: A memoir' in Killick, K. and Schaverien, J. (1997) *Art, psychotherapy and psychosis,* London: Routledge.

Killick, K. (1991). 'The practice of art therapy with patients in acute psychotic states', *Inscape*, Winter 1991.

Killick, K. (1993). 'Working with psychotic processes in art therapy', *Psychoanalytic Psychotherapy*, 7 (1): 25–38.

Killick, K. (1997). 'Unintegration and containment in acute psychosis', *British Journal of Psychotherapy*, 13 (2).

Killick, K. (2000). 'The art room as container in analytical art psychotherapy with patients in psychotic states', in Gilroy, A. and McNeilly, G. (eds.) *The changing shape of art therapy: New developments in theory and practice,* London: Jessica Kingsley.

Killick, K. and Schaverien, J. (1997). *Art, psychotherapy and psychosis*, London: Routledge.

Maclagan, D. (1997). 'Has "psychotic art" become extinct?' In Killick, K. and Schaverien, J. (1997) *Art, psychotherapy and psychosis*, London: Routledge.

Wood, C. (1997). 'The history of art therapy and psychosis 1938–95' in Killick, K. and Schaverien, J. (1997) *Art, psychotherapy and psychosis*, London: Routledge.

1

THE MATRIX OF THE MIND, THE NETWORKS OF THE BRAIN, AND THE PRINCIPLE OF TRANSFORMATION IN ART THERAPY FOR PSYCHOSIS

Johannes Lehtonen

Introduction

Art therapy is historically closely related to the treatment of people suffering from psychosis (Kennard 2009). In this chapter it will be argued that a psychotic state of mind creates the need for psychotherapeutic methods, such as art therapy, that are able to focus on mental *imagery* in ways that are not experienced as threatening. In this approach, it is implicit that a person in psychosis is overwhelmed by threats and anxieties that deeply disorganise the cohesion of the mind. It will, moreover, be proposed that the capacity to work on 'scenic mental images' is a significant aspect of art therapy in its aim to transform anxious, psychotic mental imagery to forms that are psychologically more adaptive and reality-oriented.

Following an increasing need to combine biological findings with clinical and psychosocial aspects in the research of mental illness (Akil *et al.* 2010; Portin *et al.* 2010), this chapter studies mental transformations in two parallel frameworks. The principles of neurophysiological functioning of the networks of the brain and the psychological matrix-like organisation of the unconscious layers of the mind will, respectively, be outlined, and a perspective for their integration will be presented. For an introduction to the theme of mental transformation and its relevance to art therapy, the nature of scenic mental images will be presented in a developmental context by describing their early forms in infancy and their organisation into primary awareness of mental functioning.

How to read this chapter

The aim of the chapter is to bring together clinical and neuroscientific views of the development and nature of the unconscious functions that support mental cohesion, and to this end, an approach using multiple dimensions is necessary.

The nature of psychosis is understood in terms of loss of mental organisation and the benefits of art therapy are illuminated in the regaining of the lost cohesion. Although several different approaches need to be integrated, it follows that only a tentative picture can be portrayed in this chapter. The multidimensional approach also involves the use of parallels and analogies between developmental, clinical and neuroscientific aspects. This approach should not be confused with the presentation of causal relationships.

Because psychological and neuroscientific knowledge cannot directly be translated from one to the other, the use of modelling is necessary. Here we deal with a general scientific problem about which Hawking and Mlodinow (2010: 46) write: 'We make models in science, but we also make them in everyday life. Model-dependent realism applies not only to scientific models but also to the conscious and subconscious mental models we all create in order to interpret and understand the everyday world.'

As Hawking and Mlodinow remind us, facts need a frame or model within which their significance is evaluated. There are no absolutely plain facts in science. A helpful frame for the understanding of observations is always necessary. To compare the subject area of this chapter with an example from another topical research area may be illuminating. Complicated computational models are required for making prognoses of long-term climate evolution, and the models created are only approximations that are accompanied with uncertainty, and they are in constant need of revision, testing and retesting. Problems in credulity and differences in opinion are therefore often aroused. This two-layered structure (facts and models/theories) of science is implicit in the nature of scientific research.

The same tentative pattern of a dialogue between observations and theories also applies to the creating of frameworks for the understanding of mind and brain function. As in other fields, proven facts are the corner stones of the science of the mind and the brain. However, without a wider model that allows a perspective to understand the meaning of facts simultaneously at different levels, research cannot make use of the facts. The theories of Freud, or Damasio and Edelman, to be shortly reviewed, are models that have been created to aid understanding of how explanations grow from observations. Even physics, the most precise of the natural sciences, cannot bypass the necessity of modelling to create the corpus of its theories (Hawking and Mlodinow 2010: Chapter 3).

The model-building relevant for this chapter will start with a delineation of early mental development after birth and its significance for the developing organisation of the mind. Next the principles of neural networks will be presented with the aim of describing them as a background for the understanding of mental functions, especially of the capacity for mental transformation that is crucial in maintaining and restoring of mental health.

Thereafter the concept of the 'mental canvas' is presented grounded in an assumption of a cohesive principle in the unconscious mind.[1] Towards the end of the chapter, clinical features that characterise psychotic disorganisation are introduced and the capacity of the cohesive function of art and art therapy will be presented.

Neurophysiological maturation and the multimodal sensory world of the infant

The time during the first few weeks and months of extra-uterine life is connected with more profound developmental changes in brain organisation than will be seen at any time later. Brain regions associated with more basic functions such as sensory and motor processes including the limbic and striatal structures mature first, followed by association areas involved in top-down control of behaviour (Chugani 1998; Casey et al. 2005). At birth, the brain of the newborn is functional at the levels of the brain stem, midbrain, diencephalon and the posterior sensory areas of the cortex. The myelination[2] of the motor cortex and the prefrontal areas starts proceeding at the age of two-to-three months to continue its development until early adulthood. A balance between the development of new synapses and the pruning out of redundant ones (Casey et al. 2005) leads to the consolidation of those neural networks that are functionally important.

After birth, the continuity of life is based on radically different biological conditions compared to the sensory world prevailing in the foetal period. After delivery, the infant is compelled to adapt to the new extra-uterine conditions. Breathing has to be initiated and reflexive sucking established for gaining nutrients from their provider. During the foetal period, the sensory stimuli impinging on the infant, such as taste, smell, auditory signals, movements and thumb sucking, do not yet have vital implications. The placental supply of oxygen and nourishment is automatic and relatively independent of conditions outside the womb.

In contrast to the foetal period, the stimuli that prevail after delivery signal a formation of a fresh, vital bond between the newborn and its caretaker supported by several physiological and neuroendocrine markers (Uvnäs-Moberg 1996; Gordon et al. 2010). The experiential world of the neonatal infant becomes fuelled through all external senses together with the internal proprioceptive and physiological sensations (the 'coenesthetic dimension'; Spitz 1957). Repeated experience of satisfaction involves all external and internal modalities that allow the infant's experiential world to acquire its first organised and meaningful forms. They leave traces in the infant, which can also be observed on a neurophysiological plane (Lehtonen et al. 1998; Cheour et al. 2002; Rinaman 2004; Denton et al. 2009).

The emergence of the nascent mind during the first weeks and months of life can be compared with the creation of a multimodal artwork, and consists of parallel sensory modalities that become integrated. In this sense, the organisation of the experiential world is a product of the infant's primary psychobiological creativity that precedes the more psychological transitional creativity that emerges towards the end of the first year (Winnicott 1951). The building of 'networks' between the sensory channels and motor pathways allows the infant to respond to and form an attachment bond with the caretaker (Fonagy 2001).

9

The soothing imprints gain particular strength in the most intensive forms of repetition, such as in breastfeeding, in which a double sensation is aroused as the infant receives somatosensory stimulation from the perceptions of its own skin and from the one providing the feeding. The stimulation of the skin and mouth become connected with the effort of sucking and the ensuing experience of satiation, which ultimately link with the safety of being alive (e.g. Brenman 2006: 43; Lehtonen *et al.* 2006; Lappi *et al.* 2007). The merger between infant and caretaker helps to build a soothing and life-supporting internal image in the infant to which sensations coming from inside the body contribute.

In the embodied satiation that follows adequate care, the infant's own sensations and the image of the external caretaker cannot be fully separated by the infant as its cognitive capacities are still waiting to mature, as described by Spitz (1959) and Tyson and Tyson (1990). According to Polan and Hofer (1999), the infant-mother dyad develops into a self-organising unit. From the repeated interactions of care the image of the caretaker gradually consolidates into a sensory and procedural memory network (Kandel 2006), the traces of which can be observed with neurophysiological techniques such as, for example, by comparing the infant's responses to familiar (mother) and unfamiliar female voices (Purhonen *et al.* 2005).

Secure experiences of the interaction with the caretaker foster in favourable circumstances the development of the sense of continuity of life and an enduring attachment bond (Winnicott 1949; Schore 2003), accompanied by a sense of an embodied core self (Hägglund and Piha 1980; Stern 1985). At the age of around two to three months, the emerging capacity for goal-seeking sensorimotor coordination and social signalling, such as smiling and reciprocal vocalisation, indicate that an internal model of an external object is developing in the infant. This has led some clinical researchers to hypothesize that there is a process of internal primary identification with the caretaker going on (Hoffer 1981; Salonen 1989; Spitz 1957, 1959; Tyson and Tyson 1990).

The role of the gap between the infant and the caretaker

The changes brought about by birth make the infant familiar with hunger and the need for external provision for the first time, with an ensuing awareness of absolute dependence on the caretaker (Winnicott 1963). The baby cannot live on its own from the start, from which it follows that dependence on the caretaker who herself is not dependent on the infant implies a real danger of discontinuity of care after birth, even though this danger is not often realised. This fact tends to be hidden, however, by the normal and variable, more or less successful, procedures of care. Therefore, the point of view of 'the fear of breakdown' presented by Winnicott (1974) is important as it explicitly focuses on this always-present, though seldom realised fear. Ogden (2014), in joining with Winnicott, has pointed out that a break of the securing tie remains a real possibility after birth, and a fear of it never disappears completely. Therefore, exclusively pleasure-related conceptions of the effects of early care do not do justice to the fact that the experiential world of the newborn is always imbued with a basic psychobiological uncertainty of survival.

Clinical signs of the fear of breakdown are seen in disturbances of bonding in the infant-caretaker relationship such as avoidant, insecure-preoccupied or disorganised attachment behaviour (Fonagy 2001). Disturbed attachment is also followed by eating and sleeping disturbances, which are readily accompanied with homeostatic dysregulation and increase in stress hormone cortisol levels (Hofer 1987, 2014; Liu *et al.* 1997; Gerhardt 2004). The most serious consequences from disrupted attachment have been observed in institutionalised children. In spite of adequate physical milieu and care these children live in a lack of secure attachment and emotional contact. Besides affective apathy, they develop an increased disposition to all kinds of diseases, and their mortality rate is high, as found by Spitz (1945) in his study on the hospitalism syndrome.

Although a comparison of early postnatal stages of development with psychosis may appear far-fetched, an understanding of these dangers in infant development can help the clinician to empathise with a person in a psychotic state. In severe mental disturbances, especially in psychosis, poorly differentiated early forms of mental life can be seen as threatening once again to predominate over more organised mental activity (the infantile psychotic self; Volkan 1995). The sense of a collapse, fear of death and irreversible loss of the vitally important connection to the object world—such as in the space ship travelling forever with no return in Harry Martinson's 'Aniara'[3]—are experiences that are familiar to subjects in a psychotic state, and they resonate with very early and primitive forms of anxiety. The verbal expression of such anxieties, which have been described as organismic panic, is difficult, if not impossible (Pao 1977; Rosenfeld 1992; Volkan 1995; Jackson 2009). A plausible link to the background of such experiences in early infantile fears is therefore relevant to understanding the depth and intensity of the threats in psychotic disorganisation that are beyond words.

Neural networks and the matrix of the mind

In what follows is an attempt to put the development of mental images and art, and their transformation, into a context of the theory of neural networks. It is well known that the major sensory and motor functions of the brain connect to cortical association areas (Brodal 2010) and to subcortical brain structures that subsume affect (LeDoux 1996), and that a joint effect of cortical and subcortical structures is needed for the creation of salience to the sensory processes, i.e. to endow perceptions with affective meaning. The neural structures for visual, auditory and somatosensory experience have been accurately mapped already for some time, as well as the motor centres that control movement and speech. The limbic structures relating to emotion and the right parietal cortical area's role in mental image formation are also well known (Schore 2003; Brodal 2010).

Moreover, the various brain centres' roles in artistic creation have also been tentatively delineated, as reviewed by Lusebrink (2004). In a recent fMRI (functional magnetic resonance imaging) study by DiDio *et al.* (2011), it was shown that viewing sculptures with an aesthetical and harmonic (canonical) quality specifically activates a different brain region from those activated by viewing similar realistic, but non-aesthetic images. The relevant brain area, the insula, is known to respond to changes in the variation between pleasure, unpleasure and pain. These findings suggest that specific neurophysiological phenomena can parallel aesthetic experiences and lay a basis for their memorisation. In this respect, these findings bear a certain resemblance to phenomenological understanding of art. Wright (2014), for example, writes that 'art forms are so constructed that experience "inhabits" the created image (i.e. the memory trace of the experience in the relevant brain area; my addition) and lives with it; this gives such images the power to resurrect experience (i.e. retrieve the memory) within a domain of contemplation.'

The localised specific functions just delineated give, however, only one picture of the brain's way of handling information. The neurologist John Hughlings Jackson, as far back as the end of the nineteenth century, put forward a different idea, namely, that understanding of brain function also requires the role of the connecting pathways between different brain structures to be taken into account in addition to studying the localised centres. He created a view of the brain that diverted from the prevailing doctrine of the dominant role of the localised brain centres. He introduced the idea that the networking connections between the different brain centres, not only the centres as such, are important for making the brain function in a smooth and coordinated way. Jackson's findings also guided Freud to his discoveries when he was studying the mechanisms of aphasia (Jones 1972).

With advancing knowledge it has become apparent that *connectivity* between the brain centres is of special significance. This has lucidly been exposed, for example, by Weingarten and Strauman:

> The number of discrete, observable brain regions is vastly outnumbered by connections between brain regions. Connections can be structural representing direct tissue connections between brain regions or functional temporal correlations between activity in discrete brain regions. *The totality of all structural and functional connections in the brain is referred to as the connectome* [my italics]. Mapping brain connectivity shifts our attention from discrete brain regions to networks of brain regions that support psychological functioning and are involved in psychological dysfunction as well.
>
> Weingarten and Strauman (2015: 190)

Taking account of the organising role of brain connectivity also facilitates understanding how the brain is able to create mental images. The connectivity principle is intrinsic in the anatomy of the sensory pathways of the brain. Sensory pathways are connected with each other in the association areas and they link to neural areas which regulate alertness, sleep, emotional experience, hormonal balance and autonomic functioning (Magoun 1965; LeDoux 1996; Brodal 2010). Damasio (2003) distinguishes a form of alertness that he calls *primary consciousness* and suggests that it forms the background feeling that colours all of our mental existence. He sees this as based on the activity of brain stem structures such as the reticular formation, which is known to function in wide, non-specific connections across the brain (Moruzzi and Magoun 1949) and is able to affect the background to other and more differentiated mental experiences.

Seung (2013) has recently suggested that the connectome plays a central role in how the human self image is created. However, in my opinion, this hypothesis needs to be coupled with another hypothesis that suggests that an additional factor is required for perceiving unity between the different functions. To enable the brain to create unity in our self experience instead of multiple separated fragments a synchronous factor is needed that ties the different networks together (the so-called *binding factor*; Singer 2001). In the context of art and art therapy, we don't know, however, whether the same or a different binding principle is concerned for the impression that gives sense to artistic creation and enables the colour pigments on the canvas to be turned into a piece of art, but we may assume that it is the same.

The principle of transformation

The process that turns external perceptions to internal mental images entails a significant *transformation* from raw perceptual stimuli to mental processes. Though general in nature, the concept of transformation, as defined by Bion (1965), makes the complex processes of mental image formation more understandable by underlining the meaning of a change from pure perception to psychological understanding of reality. Sensory perceptions, when elaborated to mental images proper, can be used in a flexible way in the adaptation to, and active engagement with, the external world, whereas raw perceptual material and unintegrated mental transformation cannot be easily modified.

In his book *Transformations*, Bion put it in the following way:

> Suppose a painter sees a path through a field sown with poppies and paints it: at one end of the chain of events is the field of poppies, at the other a canvas with pigment disposed on its surface. We can recognize that the latter represents the former, so I shall suppose that despite the differences between a field of poppies and a piece of canvas, despite the transformation that the artist has effected in what he saw to make it take the form of a picture, *something* has remained unaltered and on this *something* recognition depends. The elements that go to make up the unaltered aspect of transformation I shall call invariants.
>
> Bion (1965: 1)

While describing how the mind makes art from perceptions, Bion's definition of transformation also sets up a more general scene for understanding how external perceptions can be moulded into internal processes in the mind (and the brain) that ultimately create the mental images that we have.

That art is a more truthful representation of reality than an accurate photographic reproduction is also a view proposed by artists, such as for example Henri Matisse in whose work the body and strong colours on the surface of the canvas were used as central means for expression (Schneider 1984). In his 'Notes of a Painter' (1908; quoted in Flam 1978: 37) he wrote: 'There are two ways of expressing things; one is to show them crudely, the other is to evoke them through art. By removing oneself from literal *representation* of movement one attains greater beauty and grandeur.' Thinking with Matisse, it can be suggested that the transformation from perception to a painting, based on the internal transformation in the mind of the painter, depicts something essential about our way of seeing reality. Transformation is therefore not an isolated aspect of human experience but something that touches a basic and necessary function that nature has allotted to the human mind.

Another quote from Henri Matisse may illuminate the meaning that a painter attributes to transformation. In a letter to his son Pierre in 1942, Matisse wrote

> When I attain unity, whatever it is that I do not destroy of myself which is still of interest—I am told that it is transformed, sublimated—I am not absolutely certain. I do not find myself there immediately, the painting is not a mirror reflecting what I experienced while creating it, but a powerful object, strong and expressive, which is as novel for me as for anyone else. When I paint a green marble table and finally have to make it red[4] I am not entirely satisfied, I need several months to recognize that I created a new object just as good as what I was unable to do and which will be replaced by another of the same type when the original which I did not paint as it looked in nature will have disappeared—the eternal question of the objective and the subjective.
>
> Henri Matisse (quoted in Flam 1978: 90)

The example given here by Matisse illuminates how the process of making art is going on in the unconscious and follows its own pace and time. The process has a compelling nature and the object of working is experienced more like a thing than a cognitive construction. A similar relation between truth and aesthetic experience has also been conceived from a developmental and psychological perspective. Wright (2014) writes: 'The aesthetic concept of significant form acquires a new dimension of meaning: a form is "significant" when it *truthfully* portrays essential aspects of experience', and he suggests that a perception of significant form is already included in infantile experiences and that there is a similarity between the maternal impact on the infant's inner life and the later significant forms of art.

Transformation in neural networks

While attempting to transpose the developmental and clinical phenomena of transformation to a neuroscientific perspective, it is useful to remember that the activity of the living brain never ceases, day and night, and the updating of the state of the brain, and the mind, is a continuous process. Even though most of it takes place unnoticed, bringing about a change in the way reality is represented is something that the brain is specifically intended to do, as recently emphasised, for example, by Damasio (1999), Solms and Turnbull (2002) and Hari and Kujala (2009).

The networking organisation of the brain also ensures that brain activity does not remain chaotic. This is most obvious in the maturation and development of infant brain activity, which is poorly organised during the first postnatal weeks and lacks distinct rhythmical properties. Gradually, during the first months of life after the birth the organisation of brain activity begins to show topographical differentiation and acquires rhythmical properties, and this development continues over the years of childhood and adolescence. Synapses and networks that are used become stronger whereas unused networks wither away ensuring that the organisation of the brain becomes meaningful in relation to the real environment the subject lives in (Meaney and Szyf 2005; Kandel 2006).

In his theory of neuronal selection of groups (TNGS) Edelman (2006) describes how cross-talk occurs in interconnected groups of neurons and how, according to the re-entrant principle, the order of activation of the participating networks oscillates back and forth. Within a certain time period, re-entrant signalling strongly connects certain active combinations of neuronal groups in one map (circuit) to different combinations in another map (circuit). The re-entry property allows for recursive syntheses (new properties emerging in the course of time through successive and recursive re-entries). This means that at the level of neural networks it eventually becomes impossible to distinguish what activation came first and what next as the cross-talk goes on, which therefore may well change the way the brain creates pictures from the real world, and thereby *the meaning* carried on by the networks will also change, and different viewpoints of reality can be integrated when the cross-talk is stabilised. Rather than being entirely different from psychological reality, the properties of brain networks contain principles compatible with psychology that are familiar from the clinical realm, including the unconscious transformation of impressions, both in waking and dreaming states. The psychoanalyst André Green (2005: 270) has regarded Edelman's approach as the most promising among the recent neuroscience advances with regard to its psychoanalytic relevance.

The mental canvas

The first systematic approach to the transformative and symbol-creating capacity of the mind was given by Freud (1900) in his theory of dream work in which the

over-determined and condensed dream images function as models for unconscious representation. The nature of the template that may lay a basis for such
transformations has remained unclear, however. A thread to follow in search of
such a template (model) may be found in Freud's (1923: 26) later theory where he
expressed the often-quoted definition that 'the ego is first and foremost a bodily
ego'. Here he suggested that the mind originates from a projection of the body
surface to the psychic realm, i.e. through a process of transformation. By this he
was probably referring to the early development of the infant, which largely takes
place in a realm of bodily interactions such as skin caressing and oral nourishing.

In 1938, Otto Isakower recognised a special phenomenon in his clinical practice that seemed to suggest that there, indeed, is a connection between body surface experiences and sensory memories of early nursing. He wrote of patients
who described hypnagogic hallucinations (ie. hallucinations while falling asleep)
in which they experienced an amorphous mass moving towards the mouth and
filling it, sometimes accompanied by sour taste sensations, only to shrink back
again and disappear. Isakower assumed that such hallucinations were based on
a sensory memory of the mother's breast, which enters the mouth, comforts the
infant and leaves a lasting sensory memory from such very early stages of life.

Following Isakower's observations, Bertram Lewin (1946) came across a related clinical phenomenon. A female patient suffering from a psychotic disorder
told a dream to him, but at the moment of doing so she experienced the dream
scenery rolling off and disappearing as if it had been displayed on a screen like
a canvas. Lewin assumed that the phenomenon his patient described was of the
same origin as Isakower's description of hypnagogic experiences, and he suggested that in the background of dream images, there is a screen-like structure
that binds the dream images into scenery.

Although Lewin's original observations and the conclusions drawn from them
appear speculative, in modern neuroscience the mechanisms that connect the
different sensory functions into an integrated impression have become an important area of research (the binding problem; Singer 2001; Crick and Koch 2002).
A clinical hypothesis of a binding frame (a screen) for mental images therefore
appears relevant also in a modern neuroscience perspective, and it can be conceived like a canvas for mental images. Such a frame (also named as a matrix)
has been described by other authors as an ultimate safety principle of the mind,
also like an heir to the safety experienced in early infant-mother relationship
(Weil 1970; Pacella 1980; Ogden 1992) and as a site of primitive mental transformations (Glenn 1993). The association areas of the brain with their capacity for
amodal perception (Stern 1985) may play a role in such integrative and cohesive
functions, but brain structures deeper down in the diencephalon and the brain
stem are likely to be more important (Damasio 2003).

The nature of the clinical phenomena similar to those described by Isakower
and Lewin has further been illuminated by Kepecs (1952), Heilbrunn (1953),
Kanzer (1954) and Easson (1973). The undifferentiated nature of these phenomena is apparent in the clinical experiences of Michael, a patient of Easson (1973)

who experienced the therapy session as 'just being together' accompanied with sensations of floating, whirling and gently turning which were felt as 'fulfilment'. Moreover, Gammill (1980) has compared the function of the dream screen with the analytical attitude of listening with evenly hovering attention that intends to apprehend the layers behind the manifest contents of the mind. While experiencing one or another kind of derivative of this type of clinical phenomenon, the capacity for reality testing is retained and the subject is able to describe what is going on and to reflect on the ongoing experiences, as Easson's (1973) patient Michael did. In this respect, these phenomena do not have the character of a disturbing hallucination. They rather represent undifferentiated, intimately body-related mental images and effects of the sense of being, like those that Stern (1985) named 'vital affects' in contrast to more developed categorical affects. In the light of these clinical observations it seems that early bodily memories, alongside external reality, support the background awareness of the mind by taking the form of primitive mental scenery, much in the same way as, for example, Damasio (2003) depicts the role of the primary consciousness.

Relevant in this context also is Esther Bick's (1968) description of the psychological function of the skin, that is more or less in line with how body ego was defined by Freud (1923) as a projection of body surface. According to Bick, the skin has an organising container function, which protects early development and draws contours for the unlimited space of the mind. By this means, the mental representative of the skin participates in the creation of the intrinsic safety principle in the infant. When this important function remains deficient, replacement activities can occur that represent a kind of a secondary (psychological) skin, closely resembling Winnicott's (1963) notion of the 'false self'.

An example from art history suggests similarly that the surface of the body may have had a central role in the developmentally early self-image. During the late Stone Age culture of Cycladic art (3,000–1,000 BC), miniature sculptures were created that have come to be called the Cycladic Idols. The figurines were highly schematic images suggestive of an early artistic concept of man created during this prehistoric time. The sculptures had a minimum of details with the plain surface of the body dominating (Figure 1.1).

It was customary in the Cycladic culture to bury the Cycladic figurines together with a deceased person. This ancient tradition probably symbolised the continuity of the life of the buried person (Renfrew 1989). The enigmatic, often violin-shaped image of the body is the dominant feature of these sculptures, which have an aesthetically pleasing, abstract form.

The already mentioned fMRI study by Di Dio et al. (2011) has given indirect support to this hypothesis by showing that observing sculptures with distinct aesthetical qualities and symbolic meaning may evoke a specific response in the brain as compared to viewing realistic images of the human body. Such findings point to the brain's capacity to convert perceptions in the realm of early self-experience to mental images, which can eventually gain aesthetical qualities.

Figure 1.1 Marble Figurine of a Woman.
Source: By permission of the British Museum

The impact of mental illness

Psychotic phenomena can occur in a variety of different conditions that may have quite different clinical pictures. The common feature that is discussed here is a collapse of mental functions to a degree that the maintenance of an adequate relationship to reality is impaired.

Extensive neurobiological research has revealed a number of functional brain abnormalities in psychosis, especially in people diagnosed with schizophrenia, such as reduced sensory gating, decreased detection of differences in sensory stimuli and alterations in attention regulation. None of these has been found to be specific as similar observations have also been made in other clinical conditions (Salisbury *et al.* 2003). Morphological changes in the brain tissue of patients diagnosed with schizophrenia have also been revealed, such as smaller pyramidal neurons, less arborisation of dendrites and a decreased number of dendritic spines without, however, showing evidence of specificity (Harrison and Lewis 2003).

The current view of the role of neurobiological factors in psychosis is that disturbance in neurodevelopments during infancy and adolescence is likely to be crucial and more important than any neurodegenerative processes (Weinberger and Marenco 2003). Rather than being thought of as a state associated with specific local brain abnormalities, psychotic conditions, particularly those that are described as schizophrenic, are predominantly being characterised nowadays as a disconnection syndrome, i.e. a condition showing disorders in the connectivity of the neuronal structure of the brain (see also Andreasen 1999).

A suggestive finding of lowered activity of synchronising 40Hz gamma activity in the brain of psychotic patients supports this hypothesis especially with regard to the role of gamma activity in maintaining functional connectivity, i.e. a state of binding, in cortical circuits and also in cortico-thalamic networks (Salisbury et al. 2003). Given these findings, it seems likely that the perspective of the connectivity organisation of the brain offers a meaningful approach in the search for viable treatment methods for psychosis.

In the clinical picture of psychosis, the mind of the patient may appear to glide away from reality toward a poorly differentiated experience of the self with only weak verbal threads linking the self to reality (Rosenfeld 1992; Jackson 2009) and this can be seen as suggestive of a disconnection between representations of reality and affect. Moreover, psychotic mental contents are generally acknowledged to function in a concrete, thing-like manner, and less in ordinary symbolic language. Psychotic ideation may not be readily experienced as thinkable presentations, but rather as actualised, compelling contents of an unclear, non-conceptual kind, which may cause bewilderment and anxiety. When in a psychotic state, it may be inconceivable to reflect on the odd and threatening mental world, and reconsidering of the fears and threats that this world includes is then therefore avoided (Volkan 1995). Corollaries of these features are also found in the neurophysiological functions of subjects suffering psychosis (e.g. Valkonen-Korhonen et al. 2002).

In the early stages especially of severe, acute psychotic conditions, psychophysiological disturbances in the regulation of the biological rhythms such as the wake-sleep cycle, the heart rate and skin conductance are common. These indicate a psychophysiological disturbance in the homeostatic regulation of the body functions. A significant loss of the capacity to bind excitation and find a means of soothing prevails which results in the confusion and agitated anxiety often occurring in acute psychotic states (Valkonen-Korhonen et al. 2001, 2002, 2003).

Several different clinical perspectives have been applied to understanding the nature of psychotic states, such as the Kleinian concept of depressive and paranoid-schizoid positions (Klein 1946), the loss and regaining of cohesive self-representation (Boyer 1960), the primitive psychotic body image (Rosenfeld 1992; Lehtonen 1997) and the infantile and adult psychotic self (Volkan 1995; Volkan and Akhtar 1997). The role of a disturbance in the matrix of the mind has been emphasized among others by Boyer (1960) who puts the integrative effect of the dream screen in a central role in the recovery from disorganisation to cohesion. In an illuminating case report, Salonen (1979) has described the extinguishing of the aliveness of affects together with a fragmentation of the perceptual world of the patient as an outcome of disruption of the representative matrix of the mind. Thus, several different clinical viewpoints seem to lend support to the hypothesis that the symptoms of psychosis represent a disconnection syndrome in which the cohesive matrix of the mind no longer supports the integration of sensory functions with affects.

In fMRI studies psychotic states have been revealed to involve disturbances in large-scale neuronal circuits that include salience-generating structures such as the striatum (Hietala 2009). In a study by Raij *et al.* (2009), for example, the subjective reality of auditory hallucinations was correlated with the activity of Broca's speech area and the auditory cortices which, moreover, were positively and significantly connected with agency—and salience—generating activity in striatal, posterior temporal, parietal and cingulate areas and negatively with the activity of cortical midline regions that relate to self-monitoring.

It thus appears plausible that the fragmentation of the matrix, as seen both from a clinical and neuro-scientific point of view, may explain, at least partly, why the danger perceived by the patient in psychosis sometimes acquires intensities that the patient finds difficult to control. And conversely, a restoration of disturbed connectivity in psychosis has been suggested by several authors to have an integrative and soothing effect that increases the coherence of a mind drawn apart in a psychotic way (Boyer 1960; Volkan 1975; Rosenfeld 1992; Martindale 2003; Jackson 2009). Recognition of the signs of disruption of the matrix and appraisal of their waning during recovery, such as disappearance of restlessness and hallucinations, and decrease of paranoia, is therefore especially relevant in the treatment of psychotic states. A clinical course of to some extent similar nature can, however, also be found in post-traumatic psychosomatic conditions (Keinänen 2006; Leuzinger-Bohleber 2008).

The impact of art therapy

My discussion of the relevance of art therapy for psychosis is based on the view that art therapy using picture making or sculpting as a medium for therapeutic exchange can assist in the recreation of disconnected mental images by activating unconscious pictorial and scenic contents (Martindale 2003; Kennard 2009). Other forms of art therapy have their own characteristics but common to all forms is their ability to access the unconscious and use art media for the processing of unconscious mental ideation. This is particularly helped by a therapist who empathically assists indirect, artistic self-expression of a psychotic or prepsychotic subject and maintains a 'side-by-side' contact with the clinical reality of the patient, as described by Greenwood (2012). Engagement in art therapy is born from the clinical relationship to the therapist, and art therapy is an appropriate treatment method whether or not a person has the skill to paint and express unconscious ideation in art (Milner 1984).

Transformation of psychotic anxieties into tolerable forms by exclusively verbal exchange is difficult, however, as this focuses by its nature on more developed psychic layers than those prevailing in psychotic conditions. Psychotic mental contents have, using Ferro's (2002) metaphor, an indigestible quality. It is the very impossibility of certain mental impressions being digested, processed and understood that is at the core of why a psychotic person may abandon reality and resort to psychotic thinking. However the nature of the art therapy setting, in which the demand for logical expression and the pressure of time are minimised, can enable the subject to find a mental state that lends itself to the expression of dense affective and idiosyncratic material. Moreover, the scenic nature of unconscious mental functioning that arises from the activity of the networking matrix may be more readily expressed in a pictorial mode. The unconscious mental contents dwell, in the first place, on the canvas of the mind before being transformed to modes that can be verbalised. The experience of letting these emerge in pictures or in other forms of art may feel safe, and therefore be of great help to a person whose mind is locked in a state of psychotic anxiety.

Pictures created in art therapy are externalisations of the mental contents of the subject that can be viewed by anyone. Although these pictures originate from within the patient, after they are externalised in pictorial or other forms of art, the subject acquires the opportunity to view the mental contents from outside and with some distance. A special triangular (third party) constellation is thereby created in which the mental contents transformed to pictures can be observed and reflected in the interaction between the patient and the therapist. Schaverien (2012) describes it as triangularity that consists of two levels, life (mental life of the patient) in the picture and the picture's life. When they both function, a dynamic field in the setting arises, enhancing flexibility and subtlety in the triadic relationship between patient, therapist and picture compared with a relationship of a dyadic quality in which the acknowledgement of the reality of the third party tends to remain in the shadow. Viewing mental contents in the form of externalised pictures may in this way increase the neutrality and the experience of psychological safety for the patient and thereby foster the expression of warded-off mental contents.

One more aspect of art therapy that is relevant in the context of neuroscience is the role of the motor action required in the making of the artistic product. Artistic action can offer an alternative to other and more anxiety provoking forms of motor enactment especially with regard to aggressive themes. When mental pressures are expressed in a pictorial form and thereby externalised, reflection of their psychological character in relation to external reality becomes possible, i.e. the activation of reality testing. It is the motor behaviour that is, in the last analysis, *the factor* that gives mental ideation its final real meaning (Freud 1917; Spitz 1959: 20–21).[5] Motor behaviour is the ultimate part of the process of testing reality, i.e. of finding an answer to the question of what is really there and what is not. It is assumed to occur in a sensory-motor loop that connects perception to motor acting (Hari and Kujala 2009). When motor action is bound to the effort of creating an artistic product, behavioural pressures become channelled to indirect artistic means, which may reduce anxiety. Staying in touch with anxiety-provoking subjects can then become more tolerable and the sensitive contents of the psychotically disposed mind may be spared from being suppressed (Alanko 1984; Leijala-Marttila and Huttula 2012).

Conclusions

In early infant development basic forms of the mind take shape in an interplay between nature and nurture, the infant and the caretaking environment. The first images of external reality in the infant arise from everything that goes on between the newborn and the caring environment. It is only after birth that the infant becomes compelled to make efforts of sucking and actively expressing its needs by means of crying and other bodily signals.

Side by side with emerging cognition, affects that relate to bodily functions and interactions develop. According to the hypothesis of several authors mentioned earlier, embodied affects contribute to the formation of the primary background consciousness of the mind. The cohesion of such an early kind of consciousness is assumed to arise by means of the integrative capacity of the neural networks that bind together the different functions of the mind.

Although the phenomenon described as 'primary consciousness' has an undifferentiated nature, its functions manifest in all-over embodied states of mind that can be compared to a scenery often described as the matrix or a screen of the mind. Later emerging and more developed functions of consciousness are nested on top of this more primitive layer. The latter maintains the prevalent background feeling and indicates fluctuations between the degree of cohesion and well-being, and malaise and disintegration, of the current state of the mind.

Psychophysiological studies have shown that activation of a complex physiological 'orchestra' accompanies the neonatal interactions in which the caretaker is also deeply involved. It is empirically evident that successful care and the emerging attachment to the caretaker are merged in a complex homeostatic process that guarantees the survival of the infant. A secure attachment bond and a nucleus of the core self-enable the infant to express its internal state in a safe way, which can be assumed to contribute to the emerging capacity to create pictures and other art as several authors have suggested on the basis of observational and developmental phenomena.

Recent developments in the theories of neural networks have emphasised the role of the connections between different brain structures. A term 'connectome' has been introduced to denote the central role of the connectivity principle for the understanding of how the functions of the brain are integrated to create an all-over adaptation to the prevailing reality. In psychotic conditions, the cooperation between the different brain (and mind) functions is likely to fail and result in mental symptoms of psychosis such as loss of cohesion, failure in reality testing, fragmentation of the sensory world of experience, the threat of a fundamental catastrophe and fear of annihilation. All these are signals of ongoing psychotic disorder in the capacity for conceiving reality, and lack of integration in primary consciousness.

Recent findings in brain imaging studies have made it apparent that the neural networks of the connectome are involved in both normal and disturbed mental functions. A healthy brain monitors changes in internal and external conditions of the subject and updates the contents of the mind in response to whatever challenges are current. This function, which can be described as the transformation capacity of the mind, is likely to be impaired in psychosis.

According to Bion, the process of transformation has a central role in the elaboration of primitive mental contents to more tempered and nuanced forms. Bion describes the nature of transformation by comparing a visual scene of a landscape with a painting made of that landscape. The original vision and the painting made of it refer to the same scene, but the end product is different due to the transformation that the original impressions have undergone. Their difference is an indication of the elaboration that has taken place in the painter's mind. By using an artistic idiom Bion underlines the perceiver's idiosyncratic understanding and personal way of elaborating the impressions perceived.

When traumatic and anxiety-provoking experiences have occurred, they remain in the unconscious as a landscape of maladaptive memories. Their influence on the mind can be compared to potentially strong and powerful actors, who are not waiting to find expression, but are instead being warded off by defences. The elaboration of the remnants of severe traumas is therefore a challenge especially for a psychotically vulnerable subject due to the threatening and reality-distorting nature of such experiences.

As in any form of psychotherapy, successful art therapy requires addressing the patient's problems in the interaction with the therapist. Where psychotic states are concerned, the demanding nature of the clinical encounter needs to be carefully taken into account to find ways of working that are not threatening to the patient. In my opinion, the setting of art therapy has the capacity to alleviate anxiety by facilitating the expression of unconscious mental contents in disguised pictorial forms. Moreover, the triangular nature of the setting— the patient, the therapist and the externalised artistic product such as a painted picture—can increase the neutrality of the therapeutic dialogue. After recovery has started, the increasing cohesion of mental imagery can allow new and more meaningful expression of traumatic experiences to emerge.

The material presented here has introduced the ever-increasing understanding of the clinical meaning of transformation in psychic change. It is the author's hope that the presentation of neuroscientific and psychological aspects of transformation has added new perspectives to the prevailing concepts of psychosis and the place of art therapy in its treatment.

Acknowledgements

I thank Katherine Killick and Brian Martindale for generous help in revising the manuscript. Research funding is acknowledged from the Signe and Ane Gyllenberg Foundation, Helsinki, Finland.

Notes

1 The cohesive principle is often named as a matrix or a screen of mental images (e.g. Pacella 1980).
2 Myelination implies the development of a myelin shield to the efferent branch of a neuron that improves the speed of neural transmission (Brodal 2010).
3 Martinson Harry. *Aniara. Katsaus ihmiseen ajassa ja tilassa.* Finnish translation by Aila Meriluoto. (WSOY, Porvoo 1963).
4 The work Matisse refers to is probably *Nature morte rouge au magnolia* (Flam 1978: 90).
5 Freud (1917: 232) writes: '… we ascribed to the still helpless organism a capacity for making a first orientation in the world by means of its perceptions, distinguishing 'external' and 'internal' according to their relation to muscular action. A perception which is made to disappear by an action is recognised as external, as reality; where such an action makes no difference, the perception originates within the subject's own body—it is not real. It is of value to the individual to possess a means such as this of recognizing reality, which at the same time helps him to deal with it, and he would be glad to be equipped with a similar power against the often merciless claims of his instincts.'

References

Akil, H. *et al.* (2010). 'The future of psychiatric research: Genomes and neural circuits', *Science*, 327: 1580–81.

Alanko, A. (1984). *Taideterapia psykiatrisessa sairaalassa (Art therapy in a psychiatric hospital).* Monographs of Psychiatria Fennica No 11. Helsinki: Foundation for Psychiatric Research in Finland.

Andreasen, N.C. (1999). 'A unitary model of schizophrenia', *Archives of General Psychiatry,* 56: 781–87.

Bick, E. (1968). 'The experience of the skin in early object-relations', *International Journal of Psychoanalysis,* 49: 484–86.

Bion, W.R. (1965). *Transformations,* London: Karnac.

Boyer, B. (1960). 'A hypothesis regarding the time of appearance of the dream screen', *International Journal of Psychoanalysis,* 41: 114–22.

Brenman, E. (2006). *Recovery of the lost good object,* East Sussex: Routledge.

Brodal, P. (2010). *The central nervous system. Structure and function,* 4th ed. Oxford: Oxford University Press.

Casey, B.J., Tottenham, N., Liston, C. and Durston, S. (2005). 'Imaging the developing brain: What have we learned about cognitive development?', *TRENDS in Cognitive Science,* 9: 101–110.

Cheour, M. *et al.* (2002). 'Speech sounds learned by sleeping newborns', *Nature,* 415: 599–600.

Chugani, H.T. (1998). 'A critical period of brain development: Studies of cerebral glucose utilization with PET', *Preventive Medicine,* 27: 841–56.

Crick, F. and Koch, C. (2002). 'Why neuroscience may be able to explain consciousness', *Scientific American,* 12: 94–95.

Damasio, A.R. (1999). *The feeling of what happens: Body, emotion and the making of consciousness,* London: Vintage.

Damasio, A.R. (2003). *Looking for Spinoza. Joy, sorrow and the feeling brain,* London: Vintage.

Denton, D.A., McKinley, M.J., Farrell, M. and Egan, G.F. (2009). 'The role of primordial emotions in the evolutionary origin of consciousness', *Consciousness and Cognition,* 18: 500–14.

Di Dio, C., Canessa, N., Cappa, S.F. and Rizzolatti, G. (2011). 'Specificity of esthetic experience for art works: An fMRI Study', *Frontiers in Human Neuroscience,* 5: 139–52.

Easson, W.M. (1973). 'The earliest ego development primitive memory traces, and the Isakower phenomenon', *Psychoanalytical Quarterly,* 42: 60–72.

Edelman, G. (2006). *Second nature. Brain science and human knowledge,* New Haven: Yale University Press.

Ferro, A. (2002). *In the analyst's consulting room,* East-Sussex: Brunner-Routledge.

Flam, J.D. (1978). *Matisse on art,* New York: E.P. Dutton.

Fonagy, P. (2001). *Attachment theory and psychoanalysis,* New York: Other Press.

Freud, S. (1900). *The interpretation of dreams* in *Standard Edition,* 4 and 5, London: Hogarth Press (1963).

Freud, S. (1917). 'A metapsychological supplement to the theory of dreams' in *Standard Edition,* 14, London: Hogarth Press (1963), pp. 222–35.

Freud, S. (1923). 'The ego and the id' in *Standard Edition,* 19, London: Hogarth Press (1963), pp. 12–66.

Gammill, J. (1980). 'Some reflections on analytic listening and the dream screen', *International Journal of Psychoanalysis,* 61: 375–381.

Gerhardt, S. (2004). *Why love matters. How affection shapes a baby's brain,* New York: Brunner and Routledge.

Glenn, I. (1993). 'Developmental transformations: The Isakower phenomenon as an example', *Journal of the American Psychoanalytical Association,* 41: 1113–34.

Gordon, I., Zagoory-Sharon, O., Leckman, J.F. and Feldman R. (2010). 'Oxytocin and the development of parenting in humans', *Biological Psychiatry,* 68: 377–82.

Green, A. (2005). *Key ideas for a contemporary psychoanalysis,* London: Routledge.

Greenwood, H. (2012). 'What aspects of an art therapy group aid recovery for people diagnosed with psychosis', *ATOL: Art Therapy Online,* 1(4).

Hägglund, T.B. and Piha, H. (1980). 'The inner space of the body image', *Psychoanalytical Quarterly,* 49: 256–83.

Hari, R. and Kujala, M. (2009). 'Brain basis of human social interaction: From concepts to brain imaging', *Physiological Reviews,* 89: 453–79.

Harrison, P.J. and Lewis, D.A. (2003). 'Neuropathology of schizophrenia' in Hirsch, S.R. and Weinberger, D.R. (eds.) *Schizophrenia. Part two,* Oxford: Blackwell, pp. 310–25.

Hawking, S. and Mlodinow, L. (2010). *The grand design,* London: Bantam Press.

Heilbrunn, G. (1953). 'Fusion of the Isakower phenomenon with the dream screen', *Psychoanalytical Quarterly,* 22: 200–204.

Hietala, J. (2009). 'Challenges of antipsychotic drug treatment in schizophrenia' in Alanen, Y.O, González de Chávez, M., Silver A-L. S. and Martindale, B. (eds.) *Psychotherapeutic approaches to schizophrenic psychoses. Past, present and future*, East Sussex: Routledge, pp. 288–94.

Hofer, M.A. (1987). 'Early social relationships: a psychobiologist's view', *Child Development* 58: 633–47.

Hofer, M.A. (2014). 'The emerging synthesis of development and evolution: A new biology for psychoanalysis', *Neuropsychoanalysis*, 16: 3–22.

Hoffer, W. (1981). *Early development and education of the child*, London: The Hogarth Press.

Isakower, O. (1938). 'A contribution to the patho-physiology of phenomena associated with falling asleep', *International Journal of Psychoanalysis*, 19: 331–45.

Jackson, M. (2009). 'The contribution of Kleinien innovations to the treatment of psychotic patients' in Alanen Y.O., González de Chávez, M., Silver, A-L. S. and Martindale, B. (eds.) *Psychotherapeutic approaches to schizophrenic psychoses. Past, present and future*, East Sussex: Routledge, pp. 78–92.

Jones, E. (1972). *Sigmund Freud. Life and work, vol. 1*, London: The Hogarth Press.

Kandel, E.R. (2006). *In search of memory. The emergence of a new science of mind*, New York: W. W. Norton and Company.

Kanzer, M. (1954). 'Observations on blank dreams with orgasms', *Psychoanalytical Quarterly,* 23: 511–20.

Keinänen, M. (2006). *Psychosemiosis as a key to body-mind continuum: The reinforcement of symbolization-reflectiveness in psychotherapy*, New York: Nova Science Publishers.

Kennard, D. (2009). 'Psychological therapies for schizophrenic psychoses in the UK' in Alanen Y.O., González de Chávez, M., Silver, A-L.S. and Martindale, B. (eds.). *Psychotherapeutic approaches to schizophrenic psychoses. Past, present and future*, East Sussex: Routledge, pp. 93–107.

Kepecs, I.G. (1952) 'A waking screen analogous to the dream screen', *Psychoanalytical Quarterly*, 21: 167–71.

Klein, M. (1946). 'Notes on some schizoid mechanisms', *International Journal of Psychoanalysis*, 27: 99–110.

Lappi, H. *et al.* (2007). 'Effects of nutritive and non-nutritive sucking on infant heart rate variability during the first 6 months of life', *Infant Behavior and Development,* 30: 546–56.

LeDoux J. (1996). *The emotional brain*, New York: Simon and Schuster.

Lehtonen, J. (1997). 'On the origins of the body ego and its implications for psychotic vulnerability' in Volkan, V.D. and Akhtar S. (eds.). *The seed of madness. Constitution, environment, and fantasy in the organization of the psychotic core*, New York: International Universities Press, pp. 19–57.

Lehtonen, J. *et al.* (1998). 'The effect of nursing on the brain activity of the newborn', *Journal of Pediatrics,* 132: 646–51.

Lehtonen, J. *et al.* (2006). 'Nascent body ego. Metapsychological and neurophysiological aspects', *International Journal of Psychoanalysis,* 87: 1335–53.

Leijala-Marttila, M. and Huttula, K. (eds.) (2012). *Art psychotherapy from a psychoanalytical point of view.* (Published in Finnish as *Taidepsykoterapia. Psykoanalyyttinen näkökulma*). Helsinki: Duodecim.

Leuzinger-Bohleber, M. (2008). 'Biographical truths and their clinical consequences. understanding embodied memories in a third psychoanalysis with a traumatized patient recovered from severe poliomyelitis', *International Journal of Psychoanalysis*, 89: 1165–87.

Lewin, B.D. (1946). 'Sleep, the mouth, and the dream screen', *Psychoanalytical Quarterly,* 15: 419–34.

Liu, D. *et al.* (1997). 'Maternal care, hippocampal glucocorticoid receptors, and hypothalamic-pituitary-adrenal responses to stress', *Science* 277: 1659–62.

Lusebrink, V.B. (2004). 'Art therapy and the brain: An attempt to understand the underlying processes of art expression in therapy', *Journal of the American Art Therapy Association*, 21: 125–35.

Magoun, H.W. (1965). *The waking brain*, Springfield, Illinois: Charles C. Thomas.

Martindale, B., Mueser, K.T., Kuipers, E., Sensky, T. and Green, L. (2003). 'Psychological treatments for schizophrenia' in Hirsch, S.R. and Weinberger, D.R. (eds.) *Schizophrenia. Part four. Psychosocial aspects,* Oxford: Blackwell, pp. 657–87.

Meaney, M.J. and Szyf, M. (2005). 'Maternal care as a model of experience-dependent chromatin plasticity?', *Trends in Neuroscience,* 28: 456–63.

Milner, M. (1984). *On not being able to paint*, London: Heinemann.

Moruzzi, G. and Magoun, H.W. (1949). 'Brain stem reticular formation and activation of the EEG', *Electroencephalography and Clinical Neurophysiology*, 1: 455–73.

Ogden, T.H. (1992). *The matrix of the mind*, London: Karnac.

Ogden, T.H. (2014). 'Fear of breakdown and the unlived life', *International Journal of Psychoanalysis,* 95: 205–23.

Pacella, B.L. (1980). 'The primal matrix configuration' in Lax, R.F., Bach, S. and Burland, J.A. (eds.) *Rapprochement: The critical subphase of separation-individuation*, New York: Aronson.

Pao, P-N. (1977). 'On the formation of schizophrenic symptoms', *International Journal of Psychoanalysis,* 58: 389–401.

Polan, J.H. and Hofer, M.A. (1999). 'Psychobiological origins of infant attachment and separation responses' in Cassidy, J., Shaver, P.R. (eds.) *Handbook of attachment. Theory, research, and clinical applications*, New York: The Guilford Press, pp. 162–180.

Portin, P., Lehtonen, J. and Alanen, Y.O. (2010). 'Mental illness requires a multidisciplinary research plan', *Science*, 328: 1229.

Purhonen, M., Kilpeläinen-Lees, R., Valkonen-Korhonen, M., Karhu, J. and Lehtonen, J. (2005). 'Four-month-old infants process own mother's voice faster than unfamiliar voices— Electrical signs of sensitization in infant brain', *Cognitive Brain Research*, 3: 627–33.

Raij, T. *et al.* (2009). 'Reality of auditory verbal hallucinations', *Brain*, 132: 2994–3001.

Renfrew, C. (1989). *The cycladic spirit*, New York: Harry N. Abrams, Inc.

Rinaman, L. (2004). 'Postnatal development of central feeding circuits' in Stricker E. and Woods S. (eds.) *Neurobiology of food and fluid intake,* 2nd ed., vol. 14 of *Handbook of Behavioral Neurobiology*, New York: Plenum Publishers, pp. 159–94.

Rosenfeld, D. (1992). *The psychotic aspects of the personality*, London: Karnac.

Rycroft, C. (1951). 'A contribution to the study of the dream screen', *International Journal of Psychoanalysis,* 32: 178–84.

Salisbury, D.F., Krljes, S. and McCarley, R.W. (2003). 'Electrophysiology of schizophrenia' in Hirsch, S.R. and Weinberger, D.R. (eds.) *Schizophrenia. Part two*, Oxford: Blackwell, pp. 298–309.

Salonen, S. (1979). 'On the metapsychology of schizophrenia', *International Journal of Psychoanalysis*, 60: 73–81.

Salonen, S. (1989). 'The restitution of primary identification in psychoanalysis', *Scandinavian Psychoanalytical Review*, 12: 102–15.

Schaverien, J. (2012). 'The triangular relationship and the aesthetic countertransference in analytical art psychotherapy'. Translated into Finnish by Tuisku, K., Leijala-Marttila, M. and Huttula, K. In Leijala-Marttila, M. and Huttula, K. (eds.) (2002). *Taidepsykoterapia. Psykoanalyyttinen näkökulma*, Helsinki: Duodecim. (Originally published in Gilroy, A. and McNeilly, G. (eds.) (2002). *The changing shape of art therapy. New developments in theory and practice*, London and Philadelphia: Jessica Kingsley, pp. 55–8.

Schneider, P. (1984). *Matisse*, London: Thames and Hudson.

Schore, A. (2003). 'The seventh annual John Bowlby Memorial Lecture. Minds in the making: attachment, the self-organising brain, and developmentally-oriented psychoanalytic psychotherapy' in Corrigal, J. and Wilkinson, H. (eds.) *Revolutionary connections*, London: Karnac, pp. 7–51.

Seung, S. (2013). *Connectome. How the brain's wiring makes us who we are*, New York: Mariner Books.

Singer, W. (2001). 'Consciousness and the binding problem', *Annals of New York Academy of Sciences*, 929: 123–46.

Solms, M. and Turnbull, O. (2002). *The brain and the inner world*, London: Karnac.

Spitz, R.A. (1945). 'Hospitalism. An inquiry into the genesis of psychiatric conditions in early childhood', *The Psychoanalytic Study of the Child*, 1: 53–74.

Spitz, R.A. (1957). *No and yes. On the genesis of human communication*, New York: International Universities Press.

Spitz, R.A. (1959). *A genetic field theory of ego formation: Its implications for pathology*, New York: International Universities Press.

Stern, D. (1985). *The interpersonal worlds of the infant. A view from psychoanalysis and developmental psychology*, New York: Basic Books.

Tyson, P. and Tyson, R.L. (1990). *Psychoanalytic theories of development: An integration*, New Haven: Yale University Press.

Uvnäs-Moberg, K. (1996). 'Neuroendocrinology of the mother-child intraction', *Trends in Endocrinological Metabolism*, 7: 126–31.

Valkonen-Korhonen, *et al.* (2001). 'Loss of time-organised skin conductive responses in acute psychosis', *Journal of Nervous and Mental Diseases*, 189: 552–56.

Valkonen-Korhonen, M. *et al.* (2002). 'Cerebral signs of altered adaptability in females with acute psychosis', *Schizophrenia Research*, 55: 291–301.

Valkonen-Korhonen, M. *et al.* (2003). 'Heart rate variability in acute psychosis', *Psychophysiology*, 40: 716–26.

Volkan, V.D. (1975). 'Cosmic laughter: A study of primitive splitting' in Giovannini, P.L. (ed.) *Tactics and techniques of psychoanalytic psychotherapy, vol. 2: Countertransference*, North Vale, Jersey: Jason Aronson.

Volkan, V.D. (1995). *The infantile psychotic self and its fates. Understanding and treating schizophrenics and other difficult patients*, North Vale, Jersey: Jason Aronson.

Volkan, V.D. and Akhtar, S. (eds.) (1997). *The seed of madness*, New York: International Universities Press.

Weil, A. (1970). 'The basic core', *Psychoanalytical Study of the Child*, 25: 442–60.

Weinberger, D.R. and Marenco, S. (2003). 'Schizophrenia as a neurodevelopmental disorder' in Hirsch, S.R. and Weinberger, D.R. (eds.) *Schizophrenia. Part two*, Oxford: Blackwell, pp. 326–48.

Weingarten, C.P. and Strauman, T.J. (2015). 'Neuroimaging for psychotherapy research: Current trends', *Psychotherapy Research*, 25: 1,185–213.

Winnicott, D.W. (1949). 'Birth memories, birth trauma, and anxiety' in Winnicott, D.W. (1987). *Through pediatrics to psychoanalysis*, London: The Hogarth Press, pp. 174–93.

Winnicott, D.W. (1951). *Playing and reality*, London: Brunner and Routledge.

Winnicott, D.W. (1963). 'Ego distortion in terms of true and false self' in Winnicott, D. W. *The maturational processes and the facilitating environment*, London: The Hogarth Press, pp. 140–52.

Winnicott, D.W. (1974). 'Fear of breakdown', *International Review of Psychoanalysis*, 1: 103–107.

Wright, K. (2014). 'Maternal form in artistic creation', *Free Associations*, 15: 7–21.

2

PSYCHODYNAMIC ART THERAPY FOR PSYCHOSES

Progressive mirror drawing and other sensory integration techniques

Maurizio Peciccia and Simone Donnari

Introduction

In this chapter, we discuss the fragmenting effect of psychotic defences on verbal language and on dreaming, which presents a major obstacle to analytical verbal psychotherapy with people in psychotic states of mind. We propose that psychotic patients are in need of an inter-subjective experience where they can draw and 'dream' with a therapist, and we present the Progressive Mirror Drawing technique developed by Peciccia and Benedetti as means of establishing experiences of this kind. The potentials of new technologies have amplified the range of 'dreaming' experiences that are available to the therapist, and developments of the technique by Peciccia and Donnari, making use of these potentials, are described.

Many psychoanalysts working with psychotic patients, among whom are Abraham (1908), Freud (1924), Federn (1929), Bion (1957), Benedetti (1991), have presented the fragmentation of the experience of the self in relation to inner and outer reality in psychosis, and have seen a consequence of this as a difficulty for people experiencing psychosis to dream in the normal sense of the word. Bion (1962) wrote that the person suffering, incapable of dreaming, remains suspended in a state where he/she 'cannot go to sleep and cannot wake up'. He introduced the concept of 'alpha function' to psychoanalytic thinking to describe '... the unknown process involved in taking raw sense data and generating out of it mental contents which have meaning, and can be used for thinking.' (Hinshelwood 1991). His paper 'Differentiation of the Psychotic from the Non-Psychotic Personalities' (1957) differentiated the nature of fragmented states of mind characterised by the failure of alpha function, and those characterised by the presence of alpha function, such as dreaming. We propose that the psychotherapeutic approach that we introduce, which we call 'progressive mirror drawing,' enables the evolution of alpha function in states of psychotic fragmentation.

Progressive mirror drawing is based on the psychodynamic theory that connects the fragmentation of the primary process and dreamwork of people in psychotic states to a split between two states of the self. Peciccia and Benedetti (1996) define these split states as 'separate' and 'symbiotic'. We speculate that split states are correlated, at a neurophysiological level, to those neural circuits responsible for self-other identification (the putative mirror neuron system) and those responsible for self-other distinction (multisensory integration circuits). The approach aims at therapist and patient 'dreaming out together'. Racamier (1976), like the other psychoanalysts mentioned previously, pointed out the difficulty of dreaming, in the usual sense of the word, in psychotic states. He considered delusions to be an external 'dream' that realised the content of the undreamed internal dream in outer reality, and called them 'dreaming out'. In progressive mirror drawing the images are 'dreamed together' because patient and therapist move, displace and condense them outside, on the paper, using classical psychoanalytic dream mechanisms (Freud 1900).

We compare the 'progressive mirror drawing' approach to Winnicott's Squiggle game. The concept of the 'transitional subject' introduced by Gaetano Benedetti (1988), which is a key concept of the method, is discussed in relation to the concept of the 'analytic third', presented in the work of Ogden (1994). The transitional subject, co-constructed by the patient and the therapist, leads the healing process through dreams, images and drawings. These productions belong to the couple but are also a 'third'. That is, they have an independence from both the therapist and the patient.

The therapeutic images co-created in the transitional subject are placed in new associative sequences with symbolic connections that, in our opinion, can repair the associative links and networks that are fragmented by psychosis. These associative threads, made of images and emotions, eventually constitute a viable alternative to delusion, which can be understood to originate in a vain attempt to repair the tear between the ego and reality.[1]

We demonstrate the therapeutic approach and the potential of the method by presenting a clinical case study. The chapter concludes with a description of different audiovisual technological applications that can amplify the sensory integration that is typical of progressive mirror drawing. These innovations allow us to glimpse the possible future development of progressive mirror drawing and PaINTeraction System in the psychotherapy of psychosis.

The transitional subject

Peciccia and Benedetti (1992) propose that *transitional subjects* emerge in the drawings created in the progressive mirror drawing approach. These derive from the unconscious of the two partners and represent the patient's and the therapist's selves. They have the dual function of transmitting to the self both positive and negative affects and, at the same time, of protecting the patient's self from the disintegrating and disorganising action of emotions. Benedetti (1991) wrote:

> The term transitional subject is connected, to both Winnicott's transitional object and to Kohut's self-object. Using this term, however,

I describe phenomena that are not limited to childhood but occur strongly at a level which is completely unconscious, to the point of inducing, simultaneously, in the therapist and in the patient, the rise of what I call twin dreams.

Benedetti (1991: 281)

The transitional subject is an inter-subjective figure that is created in the common unconscious of the analytic couple and 'has roots both in the person of the analyst and the patient and completes the analytic duo with a figure of triangulation' (Benedetti 1991: 209). It is 'a figure that combines the two aspects of patient and analyst ... which can also be a visual projection of the patient, a hallucinated voice, a production of delusion, a work of art, but also an analyst's dream or fantasy ... The transitional subject, which sometimes acts independently of the therapist and the patient, is therefore the third subject, next to the patient and the analyst.' (Benedetti 1991: 110–111).

The theory concerning the transitional subject that was formulated by Benedetti at the end of the 1980s and in the early 1990s (Benedetti 1988; Benedetti and Peciccia 1989; Benedetti 1991) is very similar to Ogden's descriptions of the 'intersubjective analytic third', simply called 'the third analytic subject' or 'the analytic third' (Ogden 1994):

The analytic third is a concept that has become for me in the course of the past decade an indispensable part of the theory and technique that I rely on in every analytic session.

Ogden (2004a: 167)

The analytic situation, as I conceive of it, is comprised of three subjects in unconscious conversation with one another: the patient and analyst as separate subjects, and the intersubjective "analytic third" ... a subject jointly, but asymmetrically constructed by the analytic pair.

Ogden (2004b: 863)

Because the analyst's experience in and of the analytic third is predominantly unconscious, he must make use of indirect methods to gain greater conscious access to this aspect of the analytic relationship. The analyst's exploration of his reverie experience represents one such indirect method.

Ogden (1997: 161)

The analyst's dreams (his reveries in the analytic situation) are from the outset neither solely his own nor those of the patient, but the dreams of an unconscious third subject who is both and neither patient and analyst.

Ogden (2004b: 862)

Benedetti, like Ogden, thinks that the experience and awareness of the transitional subject in both the patient and the analyst are different and asymmetric. In conditions which are optimal for the psychotherapy of psychosis the most significant difference, defined by Peciccia and Benedetti (1996), is that the analyst has a symbiotic self which is integrated with his separate self, whereas, in the patient, these two self-states are split.

In these cases of splitting of the self, the transitional subject can manifest itself through hallucinations or delusions. Benedetti (1992) wrote:

> Often the transitional subject is perceived, by the psychotic patient, as an extra-psychic phenomenon, such as a voice, a hallucination, which still bears all the traits of a psychopathological third reality between patient and therapist, but, unlike the usual psychopathological phenomena, is already offering a healing process … This voice provides the patient with interpretations that are sometimes even better than those that come to mind to the therapist.
>
> Benedetti (1992: 79)

Both Benedetti and Ogden reported cases in which the transitional subject and the analytic third are also experienced in an extra-psychic space by the analyst as auditory hallucinations (Benedetti 1991) or somatic delusions (Ogden 1994). According to Benedetti, the transitional subject manifests itself not only through hallucinations or progressive delusions but also through daydreams, therapeutic dreams, associations, fantasies and drawings (Benedetti 1991). Benedetti's 'transitional subject' and Ogden's 'analytic third subject' are the protagonists of the field shared by the analytic couple, dreaming and drawing in the dual dimension in which the patient alone cannot dream and draw. The analyst makes the patient aware of the co-belonging, of the transitional subjects and of the mirror drawings, to the analytic couple, stressing their transforming and therapeutic role in the shared field. We propose that from this common ground the patient can absorb the ability to draw and to dream, i.e. the ability to oscillate between symbiosis and separation.

The symbiotic self and the separate self

Benedetti and Peciccia (1996) have hypothesised that the sense of identity of many people experiencing psychosis is threatened by a profound conflict between two states of the self that are characterised by opposing and highly intensive needs. In the same person, an extreme need to merge self and other can co-exist with the need to radically separate the subject and the object. These distinct aspects of the self can cooperate, be in conflict, or even attempt to destroy one another. Other authors, such as Stern (1985), Solan (1991), Mentzos (1991) and Ogden (1992), have described the coexistence in humans of different states of the self pushing towards union as well as towards separation. Benedetti and Peciccia referred to the psychic state that differentiates the self from objects as the 'separate self' while referring to the state that unites and blends the self with objects as the 'symbiotic self'. They think that these different states of the self are present in everyone, with varying degrees of integration. In some psychotic people, they are split to such an extent as to make cohesion and unity of the self fragile or impossible (Peciccia and Benedetti 1996). Neurophysiological research on the brain circuits responsible for self-other identification (the putative mirror neuron system) and those responsible for self-other distinction (multisensory integration circuits) offers an interesting neural basis for Benedetti and Peciccia's psychodynamic understanding of psychosis as lack of integration between the symbiotic and separate selves.

Gallese (2003) suggests that in psychosis a lack of integration occurs between an identity promoting social union (which he refers to as social identity or social self) and an identity (which he refers to as individual identity or individual self) based on self-object distinction. He put forward the hypothesis that the mirror neuron system[2] could be the neural basis of the social self that promotes union (Gallese 2003; Gallese and Ebisch 2013) whereas the multisensory integration circuits (involving many cortical and subcortical brain areas such as the ventral posterior premotor cortex and the posterior insula cortex) could be the neural underpinning of a bodily material sense of self which forms the individual identity (Gallese and Ebisch 2013).

Functional alterations of neural circuits responsible for self-other identification and self-other distinction had been previously demonstrated in psychosis. In a recent review, Metha et al. (2014) described several studies in which patients diagnosed with schizophrenia showed mirror neuron system dysfunctions. Alterations involving the multisensory integration circuits had been reported by Ebisch et al. (2013). Furthermore, an fMRI study on 24 patients with a diagnosis of schizophrenia illustrated abnormal connections between shared brain circuits of self-other identification and the multisensory circuits of self-other distinction (Ebisch et al. 2013). These neurophysiological studies confirm the data presented by several authors who describe alterations of sensory integration in people with a diagnosis of psychosis (for a review of the subject see Velasquez et al. 2011 and Postmes et al. 2014).

In the last thirty years, many researchers have been investigating sensory integration therapies for psychotic people (King 1974; Reisman and Blakeney 1991). For the last 20 years, Benedetti, Peciccia and Donnari have been working specifically with people with a diagnosis of psychosis using various techniques of sensory integration to restore the inner and outer boundaries of the self[3] and to integrate the symbiotic self and the separate self. One of these methods is 'progressive mirror drawing' where therapeutic communication takes place through the integration of three sensory channels: acoustic, visual and tactile (Peciccia and Benedetti 1998). More recently, new technological applications of progressive mirror drawing have introduced new forms of audio-visual sensory motor integration, which we will introduce later in this chapter.

Progressive mirror drawing

Progressive mirror drawing (Peciccia and Benedetti 1989) has similarities with the Squiggle game devised by Winnicott (1953, 1971) as well as some differences. In the Squiggle game Winnicott drew a scribble which a child then turned "into something"; at other times the child drew a shape which the analyst then developed or completed. Progressive mirror drawing is composed of an initial phase in which the patient and therapist simultaneously trace a spontaneous drawing on two different sheets of paper; and a second phase, in which, again simultaneously, the patient completes and transforms the therapist's drawing while the therapist completes and transforms the drawing of the patient.

This technique differs from the Squiggle game in that the patient's responses to the therapist's drawing and the therapist's responses to the patient's drawing do not occur on the same sheet, but on a transparent sheet which can be placed over (union) but remains separate (separation) from the underlying sheet of the other. This difference has some advantages over the Squiggle game for people in psychotic states. In our experience, when a person is in a psychotic state, they can easily experience their self as invaded or overwhelmed if the therapist changes the patient's drawing by acting directly on the sheet with his/her own projections. In progressive mirror drawing, transformations are performed on transparent sheets which are only temporarily superimposed, joined, and then separated from the patient's underlying drawing. In this way the drawings, and consequently the patient's internal world and his defensive need to maintain its fragmented state, are respected and kept untouched. This is, in the first phases of the therapy, significant because a therapist's requirement for non-psychotic functioning could be experienced by the patient as an impossible pressure.

In our view, the overlapping of the drawings, made possible by the transparency of the sheets, reflects the movements of union between the drawings of the patient and those of the therapist and of their inner worlds; whilst the separation of the drawings shows the distancing of the two worlds after the symbiotic contact, a sort of re-emergence to the surface after immersion in the inner reality of the other. The repetition of these movements of union and separation between patient and therapist is thought to facilitate the integration between the symbiotic and separate selves. The progressive mirror drawing expresses the therapist's attempt to integrate the symbiotic and separate selves in order to counteract the psychotic split. The alternation between union and separation of an indefinite number of transparent sheets creates a series of images.

In clinical practice, as the case study that follows will demonstrate, the therapist copies the drawings that the patient draws during the session and adds or removes small details. The patient, in turn, copies the therapist's responses, also adding or removing small details. These details are usually significant representations of the affective communication between patient and therapist. Because the drawings are each a slightly modified copy of the previous ones, a graphic sequence is created when they are put next to one another, and there is a clearly recognisable story-line with its own continuity and its own code of visual language, similar to that found in movies and dreams. The therapist's drawings mirror those of the patient and, at the same time, give them a progressive turn. Meanwhile the patient copies graphic elements of the therapist's drawings, and can then shift them, displace them and condense them with other elements that he or she provides by following spontaneous visual associations. In this way the therapist brings what Bion described as 'alpha function' to engage with the patient's fragmented state of mind.

As Peciccia and Benedetti have discussed (2006), one clinical consequence of psychotic fragmentation is that the psychotic person sometimes doesn't speak, or sometimes speaks using words as things. Freud (1915) proposed that in psychosis words undergo the same process which transforms verbal thoughts in dream images.[4] In the clinical case 'Anna', we will illustrate how, by exchanging drawings and by using the forms of communication described, it is possible to repair the mental processes fragmented by psychosis and to connect the split fragments of the unconscious of the patient.

In our experience, it is relatively easy for patients to enter this way of communicating and even patients who do not verbalise may go back to using verbal language communicatively while doing so. This happens when, in the dialogue carried out through images, the patient manages to build graphic representations of the 'transitional subjects' composed of parts of the therapist and parts of the patient. These figures entrust the other with emotions which may be expressed with far more intensity than the spoken word allows.

Anna (Therapist: Maurizio Peciccia)

The illustrated story of Anna's therapy will show the clinical application of the theory described so far, and its healing effects in the case of a young woman who was unresponsive to every other treatment.

Anna is a woman who had been diagnosed as psychotic. I met her in 1989 when I was working in the psychiatric clinic in Perugia. She looked very shabby, did not communicate verbally and would persistently repeat a stereotypic act: she continuously covered the area around her eyes with black using everything she had on hand: pencils, pens, paints, shoe polish. When stuck in this stereotypy, Anna demonstrated aggressive and violent behavior. Her sister reported a gradual autistic withdrawal[5] starting in 1979, at the age of 20, after having lived with a peer for a few months. She described how, over a period of 10 years, Anna had excluded herself from all social contacts, shut herself in her room and refused to eat and dine with other family members.

In 1989, when she was almost 30 years old, a colleague, who went on holiday to the Mediterranean island where she lived, heard by accident about a young woman who was kept hidden from social life by her parents, who were ashamed of her 'quirks'. The colleague suggested to one of Anna's sisters, who lived in Perugia, that she should be hospitalised at the department where I worked. There I began to meet her every day for only a few minutes because Anna could not tolerate my presence. Her very brief verbal formulations were incomprehensible and dominated by echolalia and neologism.[6] I too found the dialogue overwhelming because I had the painful impression that she did not understand the meaning of my words and I did not understand her words.

After fifteen days of hospitalisation, for the first time ever, she replied to my question:

'Do you know where you are?'

'In an eye clinic', she said.

I asked her: 'Why are you in an eye clinic?'

'For eye surgery', she replied.

Although in subsequent meetings she said nothing more that was comprehensible, I began to have confidence that beyond the autistic barrier Anna could understand me and talk. After a few days she answered my question:

'Why are you having eye surgery?'

'They are "pantischi"', she said.

'What do you mean, "pantischi"?' I asked her.

'They are "bad"', was her reply.

I began to internally build a logical connection between the various fragments of Anna's verbalisations:

'My eyes are pantischi, bad. I cover and hide them continuously with all that I have to hand. I'm in an eye clinic to have a surgery and change them.'

I tried to enter her world and asked her to show me on a sheet of paper how she would like her eyes to be after the surgery.

Anna drew a pair of eyes (Figure 2.1).

Figure 2.1 (Patient) First drawing of the patient: her eyes are flooded by green.

I symmetrically copied it (Figure 2.2).

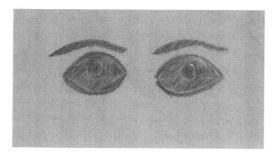

Figure 2.2 (Therapist): Progressive mirror reply.

I asked her if, after the surgery, she wanted her eyes to be just like that. She then drew eyes again without speaking. For months, countless images of eyes followed, all filled completely by a green colour. From the green, a thin black circle emerged which attempted to show a pupil that was actually absent. The result was an expression without a central point of reference, a look lost in the void, lifeless. By looking at the drawing (Figure 2.1) I thought about Anna's inability to define her inner world from the outside. The continuous stereotyped repetition, of the act of covering her eyes with black, could be read as a desperate defence against the feelings of invasive penetration that I evoked as I tried to engage with her. I felt that the act of drawing hundreds of eyes on sheets of paper helped her to accept my presence.

After the time period of one month Anna was able to tolerate my presence for a whole hour session. We met 4 days a week, for an hour each day, drawing in silence. The repeated act of covering her eyes with black decreased notably, until one day she spoke the first entirely comprehensible sentence:

'We need to treat the pantischi (bad) eyes with green sea water because they are no longer virgin.'

The meaning seemed quite clear. Anna associated loss of virginity with wickedness of the eyes, which were to be hidden, and asked me to treat them to make them clear and transparent again.

As often happens in the treatment of psychosis, some of the therapist's interpretations, such as this one, need to take place within the therapist's mind alone. They can be communicated to the patient only when they can be experienced as meaningful and helpful. This process can take years.

A few months later, Anna drew a grey quadrilateral picture, which she called 'the UFO' (Figure 2.3).

Figure 2.3 (Patient): The UFO: the starship whose deafening noise terrified Anna.

Because she could tolerate a few questions, I asked her:
'What is the UFO?'
'The spaceship … that horrible noise …', she answered, showing great agitation.

I read on Anna's face an expression of great terror. It seemed that she had at some time come into contact with something awful, unthinkable and inexpressible. In a subsequent meeting Anna added that she had heard the deafening noise of a spaceship in which there were the "bad UFOs" who wanted to destroy the earth (Figure 2.4).

Figure 2.4 (Patient): The "bad UFOs" who wanted to destroy the earth.

At first I interpreted, in the silence of my inner space, the destruction of the earth, caused by the bad UFOs, as the risk of the destruction of herself, caused by the experience of proximity with me. The duality of relationship with the other, presented by the therapeutic relationship seemed to be experienced by Anna as alien and dangerous. In my progressive mirror response I tried to develop graphical elements of her drawing that would open some glimmer of communication.

Figure 2.5 (Therapist): Progressive mirror reply.

In examining the antennae belonging to the extraterrestrials, I imagined that the extraterrestrials would be able to exchange thoughts telepathically through their antennae without exposing themselves to verbal dialogue, thus avoiding the risk of psychic invasion that words can evoke when the Ego is very fragile. Figure 2.5 is an example of a progressive mirror drawing in which I copied the two figures (the bad UFOs) of Anna's drawing, adding two small details, the contact between the hands and the contact between the antennae by dots. In the therapeutic drawing my intention was to achieve contact by the duplication, the displacement and the overlap (condensation) of the hands and the antennae of the two figures. Looking at a detail of the image of the contact it seems that the aliens exchange thoughts through their antennae (Figure 2.6).

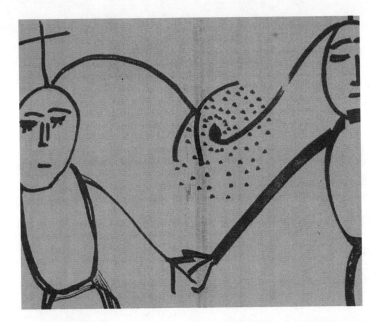

Figure 2.6 (Therapist): (detail of previous figure) The aliens are exchanging thoughts (dots) through the antennae.

The small dots symbolising thoughts result from repeated duplication of the spherical end of the transmitting antenna. These dots spread like a cloud and wrap the terminals of the two antennae (transmitter and receiver). Altogether, they evoke an idea of the kind of pre-verbal, mental, telepathic communication, in which Anna later revealed that she thought she was immersed.

The possibility of receiving this pre-verbal transmission of thoughts, in the silence of the graphic gesture, can be thought of as an image of containing unthinkable emotions, as described by Bion (1962) in his theory of container-contained relations. It seemed to me that containment was developing in the therapeutic encounter. A few years later, the unbearable affects, which made the relationship with the other so threatening and alienating, emerged. At that stage, Anna was able to tell me that disgusting extraterrestrials came out of the spaceship which forced her to join up with her 'bottom part'. It became apparent to me that the delusion of extra-terrestrials distorted Anna's experience of the sexual violence that she had in reality suffered, to defend her against unbearable anxieties. This was confirmed by the patient's mother, with whom I had an interview, when she came to visit her daughter, on one occasion only. After much hesitation, she told me that her daughter had suffered, for years, repeated sexual abuse by a brother-in-law who was much older than her. In the delusion, the rapist or rapists were inhuman beings, aliens who had destroyed her existence, and not a family member.

At this point I became conscious of the tragedy that lay behind Anna's silence; in her mind, every word, every look could evoke violent penetrations. This was why she shut herself up in silence and imprisoned her expression in black, tried to hide her eyes and accordingly, how much she had been forced to see. The intensity of the social taboo of sexual abuse in a family living in a little south Mediterranean island can, in my opinion, be grasped in the psychosomatic reaction of Anna's mother. On the morning after the interview in which she revealed the violence suffered by her daughter to me, she had a sudden stroke that caused her never to speak again.

Anna then drew a pair of plants (Figure 2.7).

Figure 2.7 (Patient): The pair of plants.

The plant in the pot on the left has plenty of greenery, flowers and pollen, in contrast with the plant on the right on which there are three bare leaves without flowers that hang from three stems stuck in the arid soil. It seemed to me that Anna, still unable to depict humans, had represented herself in a proto-identity vegetable state, split between the fruitful plant full of vitality, and the arid, barren, dried-up plant. The triangular shape of the three leaves of the plant on the right, crossed by three stems, suggests the repeated violent penetrations which had emptied her life, leaving her deflowered of her fertility and femininity. By introjecting the abuser's destructiveness, the patient continued to attack and destroy her nature, her eyes, her beauty; she felt dirty and defaced, and hid herself behind the heavy and thick black lines, the bars that walled and erased her existence.

I thought that this image also revealed the transference activated by the encounter with the therapist. What will this new relationship bring? Flowers and pollen, or again the penetration which deflowers and empties?

Figure 2.8 (Therapist): Therapist's progressive mirror drawing: a stem of the left fruitful plant stretches and embraces the leaf of the right stripped plant.

Figure 2.8 is a second example of progressive mirror drawing in which I copied Anna's previous drawing and immersed myself in it, developing and enlivening it with my therapeutic imaging. Using 'dream language', as described previously, I duplicated, moved and condensed a stem of the fruitful plant on the left which extends and embraces the leaf of the stripped plant on the right.

Figure 2.9 (Therapist): Detail of previous figure.

In Figure 2.9, other details of my drawing are highlighted: a cluster transfers its spheres of pollen from the fruitful plant to the sterile plant, thus creating a bridge, a connection between the two plants. One flower of the blooming plant is duplicated, and in my drawing it is moved and transplanted, grafted into the soil of the stripped plant. The duplicated flower becomes part of the stripped plant in a similar way to the condensation dynamic experienced during dreams.

In my description of the images, I intentionally use the impersonal form 'a flower is duplicated, the cluster launches its spheres ... it creates a bridge' to indicate that these images, born in the encounter between our drawings, belong to a transitional area that is relatively independent from the consciousness of patient and therapist. This establishes a distance from consciousness that can help to overcome the resistances of both patient and therapist to getting in touch prematurely with unthinkable emotions whose intensity is capable of disorganising thinking. Only after thirteen years of regular production of images was it possible to talk with Anna about her trauma.

Figure 2.10 (Patient): The good grey cats.

In Figure 2.10 Anna's imagery changes from the vegetable world to the animal world; and seems to me to depict the relationship in its maternal, protective, therapeutic variant. I responded with a progressive mirror drawing where the adult cat approaches the child cat.

Figure 2.11 (Therapist): Write on the paper: the good mother, the child waiting for the milk.

Anna reacted to my image by saying a sentence full of meaning:
'Write on the paper: the good mother, the child waiting for milk' (Figure 2.11)
These words surprised me because they were cognitively and affectively much more evolved than the usual disconnected communications of those times. Then Anna drew the transition from the animal world to the human world (Figure 2.12).

Figure 2.12 (Patient): A pair of rabbits with human faces in which the one kneeling seems to ask for support from the other.

44

This seemed to me to present the therapeutic relationship as a pair of rabbits with a human face in which a kneeling rabbit seems to ask for support from the other. In my progressive mirror reply I move and place the two rabbits closer (Figure 2.13).

Figure 2.13 (Therapist): Progressive mirror reply.

The joined arms create solidarity and a supporting bridge between the two rabbits. The connection between the arms of the two figures reminded me of the pollen bridge (Figure 2.9) that linked the lush plant and the bare plant.

The first human figure drawn by Anna was a child that she called 'Pollino' (Figure 2.14).

Figure 2.14 (Patient): Pollino, a transitional subject made up of parts of the patient and the therapist.

The unconscious choice of the name seems linked to the pollen through which the two plants had entered into a relationship. The pollen was a bridge. It seemed to me that this was a transition between her and me, as well as between her lush, fertile potentialities and her arid and sterile nuclei. The coloured crayons in the image were the means which had structured the intra-psychic and interpersonal communication. This figure is a graphic representation of what I described earlier as a *transitional subject* (Benedetti and Peciccia 1989; Benedetti 1991, 1992), born in the intersubjective field co-created by patient and therapist, and made up of parts of the patient (her eyes covered by black) and parts of the therapist (the coloured crayons introduced by me to communicate).

In the next drawing Anna for the first time portrayed her face (Figure 2.15).

Figure 2.15 (Patient): The first of Anna's self-representations.

The 'sick eyes that needed surgery because they had lost their virginity' are now opened, filled with sea-green liquids. Sea green was the colour that she had used in her early images, that was supposed to treat the 'bad, pantischi' eyes. During that time I dreamed[7] of Anna with two apples corresponding to the breasts, two pears as the hips and two peaches as the ovaries. I connected the dream image to the development of her femininity in the therapeutic relationship: apples, pears, and peaches as symbols of the plant world were placed along the milk lines which in mammals run through the zones of fertility, reproduction and lactation.[8]

Anna then drew what seemed to me to be a presentation of the therapeutic relationship using two human figures: the engaged couple (Figure 2.16).

Figure 2.16 (Patient): The fiancée!.

Maintaining the connection with the plant world, she names the girlfriend Melina (Little Apple) and the boyfriend Pino (Pine). This connection can also be perceived in the flowerpot placed on the table on the right of the boyfriend.

In my response, the boyfriend gives a flower to his girlfriend (Figure 2.17).

Figure 2.17 (Therapist): The gift of the flower.

Even in this case, the movement of the flower from the pot to the hands came from duplicating and moving a flower and uniting it with the hands.

In my thinking, the gift of the flower is 're-flowering', a symbol of a delicate relationship which, in the therapeutic distance, is very different from violent de-flowering. The two lovers in my drawing are crying: the sharing of tears has become the salt water which cleanses Anna's eyes. In her response Anna, who still spoke in fragments, asked me to write the boyfriend's text while she wrote his girlfriend's words in coherent form (Figure 2.18).

Figure 2.18 (Therapist and Patient): T: I brought you these flowers as a gift, Melina P: Thank you for the flowers, Pine.

Looking at a detail of the image (Figure 2.19) we can see that the black petal is in transition between the flower and the eye of the girlfriend, and could be seen as going either way.

Figure 2.19 Detail of the previous drawing: the 'in-florazione'.

The black with which Anna erased her eyes seems to have been absorbed by the flower. In the next drawing (Figure 2.20) Anna wrote this text for the girl-friend: 'My boyfriend says that my eyes are open and clean'.

Figure 2.20 (Patient): My eyes are open and clean.

The reader may wonder why Anna wrote: 'My boyfriend says that my eyes are open and clean', when in fact he has only stated in the text (Figure 2.18):
'I brought you these flowers as a gift'.

In order to give a possible answer, it is necessary to remember that the young woman felt that her eyes were dirty, no longer virgin, and therefore needed to be hidden and changed. It is likely that there was a 'symbolic equivalence' between the vagina and the eyes similar to that described by Hanna Segal (1950), whose musician patient did not want to play cello in public because he feared that every-one could recognise, in this very act, his masturbation. Similarly, by equating the eyes with the genitals, Anna's violated body zone was defensively shifted 'from the bottom toward the top'. Maybe Anna feared that the violent loss of virginity, shifted and condensed in the eyes, could be seen by everyone, so she forced her-self to hide the shame and guilt associated with the violence, hiding herself and her eyes in total social withdrawal.

Communication through images, which is based primarily on processes of du-plication, displacement and condensation, as described in the introductory sec-tion, offered a loving relationship in which Anna received love without being deflowered, indeed by receiving flowers. My interpretation is that this gift, which I previously defined as 're-flowering', is understood by Anna's unconscious as restitution of virginity. This resolves the symbolic equivalence and frees her eyes to see reality. Maybe this is why she writes: "My boyfriend says: my eyes are open and clean". In many languages, the loss of virginity is defined as deflowering whereas the gift of the flower is associated with intimacy, desire, respect, and at the same time with virginity. I am thinking specifically of the many images, painted within the Christian religious tradition, of the Annunciation in which the Angel Gabriel brings flowers, often white lilies, to the Madonna, such as the 'Annunciation' painted by Andrea della Robbia.

Freud (1900) has repeatedly noted that flowers are the sexual organs of plants. In the vegetable world there is no penetration but a sexual relationship at a distance; the plants are fertilised without touching, entrusting their seeds to the wind. The wind with its lightness and its spiritual consistency is the bearer of life among plants. The gift of the flower, the "re-flowering", evokes the restitution of virginity and could be also a symbol of the therapeutic relationship, restoring the intimacy of psychic closeness. In this dimension of spiritual union, the images in the drawings, as well as the flowers, fertilise each other at a distance, even in the absence of contact between the bodies. This virginal intimacy can be seen as making it possible for the patient to get in touch with the split emotions of her violated sexuality; first through the images, and later also through words, which reconstructed and elaborated the traumatic experiences of the abuse.

Here are her drawings in succession: the kiss of the engaged couple (Figure 2.21), their wedding (Figure 2.22), their first night (Figure 2.23), her pregnancy (Figure 2.24).

Figure 2.21 (Patient): The kiss.

Figure 2.22 (Patient): The wedding.

Figure 2.23 (Patient): The first night.

Figure 2.24 (Patient): Pregnancy.

Later Anna drew the birth of the child, a son who needs a name (Figure 2.25).
It seemed to me that Anna, through the son, was renewing her identity.

Figure 2.25 (Patient): Salvatore.

Indeed, she wrote these words on the mother's text: 'My baby, I have to prepare for him a name: Salvatore (Saviour).' At this point the problem of good or bad milk emerged. Anna wrote the following on Figure 2.26:

Figure 2.26 (Patient): Salvatore, is the milk sweet or bitter?

This seemed to me to be saying: 'As a child, did I receive good or toxic milk? Was my mother's womb good or bad? As a result are my breasts and my milk good or bad?', and at the same time, in the transference: 'Is the therapist's milk good or bad? Is he nourishing me or poisoning me?' Salvatore is a transitional subject, the son of the therapeutic relationship, co-constructed by patient and therapist. This child believes in the goodness and beauty of the milk of his mother who instead does not seem sure if her milk is good or bad, i.e. if she is good or bad. Indeed, Anna put the following words into Salvatore's mouth (Figure 2.27):

Figure 2.27 (Patient): Mum give me the milk that comes out of your breast: I'm sure it's
very beautiful.

These words seemed to me to say that her child-self, entrusted to the care of the
therapeutic relationship, can feed on milk that will not be bitter, toxic, destructive, but instead good.

Gradually, the exchange of drawings between patient and therapist created
a series of evolutionary stages of relationship that moved from the mechanical
world of the aliens (Figures 2.3, 2.4, and 2.5), to the vegetable world (Figures 2.7
and 2.8), and the animal world (Figures 2.10 to 2.13), before reaching the human
world (Figure 2.14 et seq.). The human representations of the self and the other,
loving each other and becoming fertile, could be seen as creating a new self, a
transitional subject giving a new healthy identity to Anna.

While she drew, Anna spoke with great difficulty. Her written sentences for
the characters of the drawings were much clearer than her spoken sentences. Her
relationship with reality was severely altered, she did not have a sense of time,
space or other realities such as money. Her relationship with me was dominated
by autism (i.e. an extreme need to be separated from me, not integrated with the
desire to be united with me). I often had the feeling of the uselessness of my presence, and sometimes I felt inclined to act as if she was not there.

The recovery of verbal language and of the relationship with reality proceeded
in parallel with the development of what has been described as a 'progressive psychopathology' (Benedetti 1980)[9], characterised by delusions that, while deforming

reality, gradually opened up communication and reduced the autistic barriers. The first delusional 'progressive' communication was that of the bad 'pantischi' eyes, which needed to be operated on to make them as green as the sea. The neologism 'pantischi' stemmed from combining the name of the island where she was born and the adjective 'disgusting'. I saw Anna's identity as formed in my green eyes watching her, just as the identity of the child is formed in the eyes of the mother. The request to operate on the pantischi bad eyes, to make them become good, green and virginal, is a progressive delusion in the sense that it contains elements which defensively deform reality but at the same time it is the first verbal communication toward the therapist. Anna asked to be looked at, to be loved and not to be preyed upon. By looking at her with respect, I felt I was able to reflect the dignity of her existence, so that she felt that her eyes could be clean and virginal again. 'My boy-friend says my eyes are open and clean', Anna wrote to her Little Apple who had received a gift of flowers from my Pine. It seems to me that the therapeutic communication enabled Anna to open up her view of reality. Her eyes no longer needed to be erased by black, by shame or by guilt; they could be born again in beauty.

Anna then developed a second progressive delusion based on her memory of meetings with the beautiful eyes of the Virgin Mary, who would cry, fearing her death, when she looked at her. At other times the Madonna encouraged her to undergo eye surgery. Maybe Anna, due to the introjection of the violence suffered, projected on to the Virgin Mary's beautiful, idealised eyes her good self that had been split from her bad self (the dirty black eyes that were no longer virgin). Through the therapy, there is a meeting between 'good' and 'bad' selves which could lead to a necessary but also dangerous transformation. The good self (the beautiful eyes) is in danger of being destroyed by the destructiveness of the bad self. In the psychodynamics of the violence, the dirty and bad eyes seem to represent the introjection of the abuser's evil look and Anna is compelled to delete them with the colour black. The danger of being destroyed by the evil can be seen as activating two primitive defence mechanisms: the splitting of the good self from the bad self and the projection of the good outside, into the idealised eyes of the Madonna. The otherworldly vision of the Madonna is then embodied in the reality of the therapeutic relationship.

The tangible exchange of looks with me seemed to put her back in contact with her sense of herself: Anna, through her drawing of the 'Little Apple', generated a son with the therapist, and called him 'Salvatore', Saviour, the name of the Virgin Mary's son. Salvatore, Saviour, is what I have defined earlier as a transitional subject, an analytic third, co-constructed by patient and analyst. As the son of the couple he believes in the goodness and beauty of his mother's milk. The mother does not seem sure if her milk is good or bad, that is, if she is good or bad. But Salvatore is not only the symbol of the child self, entrusted to the care of the relationship, to feeding, to a milk that detoxifies, he is also the son of a loving relationship experienced in the protective distance of the creative space, very different from the traumatic relationship that Anna experienced in the sexual violence. Salvatore is an inter-subjective figure, simultaneously solidly drawn and fantastically imagined, and in my view, was the basis of a new identity, representing the nourishment that strengthens the self and makes intolerable and undigested emotions thinkable.

After thirteen years of therapy, Anna was able to reconstruct and talk about the years of shame, marked by the repeated abuse by her brother-in-law. She remembered having had an abortion, in which she felt the child of the violence had been ripped from her womb in her state of total helplessness. Salvatore was very different from her unnamed unborn child with no identity, and her sense of herself in relation to Salvatore was very different from her previous sense of non-existence, as a woman and a mother.

After Anna had fully reconstructed and communicated the traumas, of the sexual violence and the consequent abortion, her delusions ceased. Benedetti (1980) has described this process, that happens through the development of a series of progressive delusions which tell of a reality that is unbearable and must therefore be deformed. The first time Anna spoke of sexual violence was through the delusional memory of an old man who had raped her and sent a werewolf towards her, wanting to devour her. This idea suggests that the abuse had unleashed conflicts of both genital and pre-genital natures which devoured the patient's self, turning the image of her rapist into a werewolf in her mind. One aspect of the dynamics of abuse is that the abused victim introjects the monstrosity of the abuser (A. Freud 1936), as can be seen in a drawing (Figure 2.28) by Anna at that time in which she takes on the appearance of a monster.

Figure 2.28 (Patient): Deformation of the face caused by the introjection of the monstrous face of the abuser.

In this sense, the violence devours the identity of the victim who is forced to identify herself with and to internalise the destructiveness of, her aggressor who disorganises her thoughts and her relationship with reality. The recovery of verbal language and the development of confidence in me, which in the transference lessened the fear of being abused again, allowed her to tell me her sexual fantasies as she began to elaborate her conflicting experiences related to the trauma. She revealed to me that, within her, eyes and sex were 'connected'. Therefore, certain eye movements corresponded to sexual movements. Anna said to me: "I've done it so many times with you: didn't you ever realise?". With this question she revealed her desire and at the same time she began to doubt the idea that every look corresponds to a sexual penetration, a certainty she had lived with for years.

This is how differentiation between the self and the other emerged, as a natural border which protected her without the need for an autistic barrier which radically separated herself from the world and from others. In the relationship with me, Anna was able to work through a painful conflict. On the one hand, there was her desire to be with me; "to be whole: in terms of feelings, the soul and sex". On the other hand, there was the fear that I too, like the rapist, the old man with the werewolf and the alien, could force her into a sexual union that would destroy her identity.

Anna alternated between moments in which she looked at me intensely and "did it" with me, feeling like: "a child embedded in and embraced by her mother". At other times, out of fear, she defended herself autistically from me. Then, an atmosphere of mutual emotional denial of the presence of the other was created. Both patient and therapist entered into this denial in response to the deep feelings generated by the presence of the other. Consequently, we both behaved as if we were alone and not together during the therapeutic session. The creation of a graphic-affective dimension of the therapeutic encounter allowed us to 'operate' on a double level of differentiation and of union. This mitigated the intensity of the conflict between opposite emotions: those that related to the frustrated longing for symbiotic fusion, and those that related to the need for radical, autistic separation. Also through words, once recovered, we were able to work on the dual plan of union and separation by integrating these deeply split dimensions. On the symbiotic side, there was the possibility of developing fantasies of sentimental and sexual union; on the level of separation, it was possible for Anna to accept the fact that, to her great surprise, no one could read her eyes. She became able to tolerate the frustration of the symbiotic needs she experienced, and she felt protected because I was not aware of the sexual intercourse between our eyes. The internalisation of a deep dimension of emotional union with the therapist enabled her to accept separateness and eliminated the need to protect herself by using delusional and autistic defences.

Developments in progressive mirror drawing and other sensory integration techniques (Simone Donnari)

In the years since Anna's therapy several new technologies have added to the range of media available for image-making in therapy, and I will now discuss some of the developments in progressive mirror drawing that these have made possible in individual therapy and in groups. In my own practice I have sought to incorporate some of these within a particular group framework, where the group consists of several patient-therapist couples sitting together in a circle. During the image-making session, all the couples will make images at the same time, but exchanges of images happen only on a one-to-one basis within each patient-therapist couple.

The main innovation offered by new technologies seems to me to be the opportunity to draw and interact with images simply by using one's own body, without the requirement of learning the skills needed to use keyboard, joystick, or other tools. Simply by moving, the patient can easily play music, draw and by doing so, integrate many sensory pathways. In the last 15 years, many sensory integration media have become available due to the emergence of new technologies and game consoles, and my attention has been focused on using these to develop techniques to create sensory and motor synesthetic experiences[10] that could enhance the therapeutic intervention of progressive mirror drawing. I found that popular game consoles offered a precious and unexpected therapeutic medium, but it was the effects of the application of digital videocameras (video-art therapy) that started an innovative process. I will now discuss four specific applications of new technologies: video-art therapy, progressive mirror drawing animation, motion detection devices and sensory motor integration, and a technique that I have named 'the puzzle of the self'".

Video-art therapy

Since 2001, I have introduced a video camera into the progressive mirror drawing group therapy setting. The operator is one of the therapists. Digital cameras allow the operator to edit and cut the video in real-time. They come with embedded software that offers the possibility of performing cross-fading and mixing of frames during shooting. Thus it became possible to make a video during the therapy session and show it to the patients immediately after. Real-time editing avoids the delays involved in post-production editing and makes it possible to watch the video immediately after the therapy session.

When the group image-making activity ends, the 'distancing phase' described by Rubin (1987) takes place. During this step the maker creates a distance between himself and the image he created. "The powerful emotions contained in the visual product can now be viewed with a certain measure of detachment" (Rubin 1987). During this phase, showing the video of the session reinforces the distancing process and offers the patient's self an opportunity to play the 'observer role'. While distancing from his or her own work, the participant also shares his production with the group, giving it back to the group in which the drawing process happened. This phase can be called 'restitution', and I have described elsewhere (Donnari 2011) the great potential of video as a restitution tool, because by watching the video every participant can see the images of the others, and they can be experienced as the property of the group.

In my experience, the customary use of video cameras as recorders in therapy settings can often be disliked by patients, but when they are used in the way that I describe, I have found that patients often express appreciation for the opportunity to see themselves in the video. In this way of working, the opportunity to watch the video immediately after the therapy session offers the patient the possibility of flowing from the actor-player role (symbiotic self) to the watcher-observer one (separate self). For instance, cross-fading a drawing detail with the picture of the face of its author in the video can strongly convey a message of identity in the distancing phase. Over time, we have found that patients become accustomed to the video camera and perceive it as an art tool, like brushes or colours. The video camera can record images from previous therapy sessions, thus allowing cross-fading effects from bodies to drawings and images, enabling the video to become an actual visual integration between body movements and images, between the act of drawing and the resulting image.

Cross-fading and other editing effects between old and new drawings can create a variation on the theme of merging between old and new which is another of the typical dream dynamics, described by Freud (1900), that we referred to earlier. It seems to me that the medium of video enables experiences of union and separation between the patient's body and the symbols in his drawings to be easily accepted. Through video editing one image can slowly be transformed into another one via "morphing", a visual transformation that creates an animation starting from static drawings. This effect is powerful and eye-catching because it introduces a visual equivalent to dreamlike motion. Morphing of separate images means watching the first one gradually become the second one, which is like a visual translation of the mechanisms of condensation and separation that are experienced in dreams. It seems to me that these dynamics help with the work of healing the break-up between the separate and symbiotic selves by 'training' the patient to oscillate between symbiosis and separation.

In individual therapy, images made by the therapist and the patient are animated through the video and become a sort of 'communal dream' of the therapeutic couple in a similar way to the process described in the clinical example of progressive mirror drawing. The video non-verbally shows emotions not always understood or perceived during the action, and underlines the symbolic meaning of the experience with a moving dream-like language.

Progressive mirror drawing animation

As discussed elsewhere, we have found that tablets and touch-screen devices are also useful media in the field of progressive mirror drawing therapy (Donnari, Peciccia *et al.* 2013). Drawings can be made directly on the tablet or uploaded to it, and then the many digital tools offered by the tablet can contribute to the patient-therapist interaction with the images. Symbols can be isolated from the image and then animated and translated. The patient can operate shifting, condensation and many other dreamlike mechanisms just with his fingers. For example, with his finger on the touch screen the patient can draw the image of a butterfly. Then he can move the butterfly in a different part of the screen (shifting), or he can merge the butterfly with another drawing, e.g. a flower (condensation), and can easily transform the drawing and its symbols. No technical knowledge is required to apply this technique, which is extremely easy and intuitive. Images can be simultaneously projected onto a large screen while being drawn.

In individual therapy, the patient draws freely with his fingers on the touch screen device. By connecting this device to a large screen in the therapy setting, the drawing of the patient is immediately visible and enlarged. The image on the screen becomes the frame of the therapy setting. The patient and therapist are surrounded by the image, and while the image is being drawn they are immersed in visual feedback of the experience. Drawing animation is immediately available on touch-screen tablets. Patient and therapist can actively interact with pieces of the drawing, creating experiences of shifting and condensation by morphing, which, as discussed earlier, seems to us to tap into dreaming mechanisms. We think this is a powerful way to move from symbiosis to separation without raising anxieties for the patient. In these ways, video and digital imaging tools have enhanced the previously described integration effect of progressive mirror drawing.

Motion detection devices and sensory motor integration

More recently, the advent of contemporary video-game consoles has given further opportunities for sensory integration. Game consoles allowed body movements to be translated into drawings which are projected onto a large screen in front of the therapist and patient (Figure 2.29).

Figure 2.29

Body images projected on the screen then become condensed with the drawings initiated by body movements. The relationship between patient and therapist is indirectly realised on the screen. The screen becomes an interpersonal space where the patient can learn to tolerate facing the image of his own body, an experience which is often avoided as it can be a source of anxiety. Both therapist and patient can see themselves on the screen while producing luminous beams and sounds by moving their own bodies. The session can start from an image that carries affective meaning for the patient. For example, the patient can draw a leafless tree which testifies to his feeling of loneliness. The image is reproduced on the screen by the movements of patient's and therapist's bodies. Movement and image are integrated on the screen, and body movements work as a drawing tool. Moreover, the system allows both the drawn image and the reflection of the bodies of the patient and therapist while drawing it to be seen.

On the screen, it is possible to see a merging of one's own body and one's own meaningful images and symbols. The patient can experience himself as the actor because he is the one who makes the drawing, and at the same time as an observer because he can see himself in the 'mirror' of the screen. We have found that this technique seems especially helpful for patients with stereotypical movements, such as patients with autistic features. By watching their own images on the screen and experimenting with the visual effects of their body movements, e.g. watching themselves while rocking or incessantly rotating one hand, the patients can often find a purpose in every movement and this can enable them to overcome stereotypical gestures and use the body movement for a definite purpose, for example, to generate a beam of light that is visible on the screen (Fig. 2.30). Furthermore, patients who feel threatened by new environments seem to react positively when they can watch themselves next to the therapist in the mirror of a screen that seems to contain the entire room.

Figure 2.30

The puzzle of the self

I have also developed a specific technique that I have called 'the puzzle of the self', in which hundreds of images and video frames created in different therapeutic settings are processed by software and then used to create a single 'puzzle' image of the face of the patient. The elaborated image represents the face of the patient made by small pieces. Each piece is a drawing or a video frame made during mirror drawing therapy sessions.

All the different therapeutic techniques described in this chapter aim to create protected spaces, initially external to the patient, where the self's split fragments may be placed in order that they may become available to being 'dreamed' through the techniques that we have described, and to the other forms of healing available within the therapeutic relationship. We can imagine these split fragments as pieces of a blurred puzzle waiting to be put into order and become for the patient a mirror of an integrated and coherent identity. Our digital techniques are able to help the patient to 'solve the puzzle' by starting to 'dream outside himself', integrating both symbiosis and separation experiences. This aims to give the patient an integrated image of the self which can be internalised as a secure and constant symbol.

Sensory motor integration and future developments

As discussed, we think that technology seems capable of amplifying the symbolisation dynamics of drawings and dreaming. Moreover, it can be appealing for patients. Most present day patients are 'digital natives' (Prensky 2001) so they are well accustomed to new technological media, and we have found that it can be valuable to use the same tools that patients often use on their own in the therapeutic frame. The current trend in video games towards enhancing virtual sensations is proceeding in the direction of greater sensory integration, and the authors are confident that this will offer further opportunities for developing therapeutic applications (Donnari and Peciccia 2013). Furthermore, a team of researchers and engineers have developed a customer-designed software capable of fine-tuning the rehabilitation tools according to the rehabilitation needs of patients diagnosed with psychotic or autistic spectrum disorders (paINTeraction technique, Figure 2.31). Body movements can generate drawings, light trails and avatar animation. The software can also record kinetic and autonomic parameters for research studies.[11] By accessing the software, a community of parents and therapists is built around every patient, developing a closer connection between therapy and 'real life' issues.

Figure 2.31

Conclusions

In this chapter we have introduced the therapeutic technique of 'progressive mirror drawing'. Referring to the work of psychoanalysts working with psychotic patients, we introduced ideas about the impact of psychotic fragmentation on dreaming, in the usual sense of the word, and on the use of verbal language. The theoretical basis of progressive mirror drawing is Benedetti and Peciccia's interpretation of psychosis as a result of a split between 'symbiotic self' and 'separate self', one of the consequences of which is that the capacity to dream is hindered. While dreaming, we repeatedly fluctuate between the position of observers, separated-by, and the position of participants, immersed-in the dream (Benedetti and Peciccia 1995). In psychotic patients these fluctuations can generate fears of fragmentation and annihilation that hinder the possibility of dreaming 'internally' and compel the patients to project out split fragments of their self. Racamier (1976) called this process 'dreaming out'. Our clinical approach is aimed at therapist and patient 'dreaming out together'.

We discussed the challenges that working with people in psychotic states present to the therapist, because of the extreme anxieties being suffered by the patient, and suggest that these are minimised by the technique of progressive mirror drawing. The technique, and its evolution over the past 20 years, was described and illustrated by a clinical case study. Our description of the technique of progressive mirror drawing started with a discussion of its similarities with, and differences from Winnicott's 'Squiggle game'. Both are based on the exchange of images between the therapist and the patient, but progressive mirror drawing has significant differences that take account of the patient's vulnerability to feeling invaded by the therapist's image-making.

In progressive mirror drawing images are 'dreamed together' because patient and therapist move, displace and condense them using processes that are equivalent to the dream mechanisms described by Freud (1900). We have introduced the concepts of 'progressive delusions' (Benedetti 1980) and 'transitional subjects' (Peciccia and Benedetti 1989) to describe the images and other experiences that evolve in the intersubjective field established by our approach, and the concepts are linked to a clinical study that shows in detail the way that one patient made use of the approach to emerge from psychotic fragmentation.

We propose that, over time, the multisensory and sensory motor integration techniques of art therapy described in this paper can bring about a shift out of psychotic fragmentation, restore the capacity for thinking, rebuild the representations of self and other and facilitate the development of a differentiated sense of self in psychotic patients. We have discussed these aims with reference to contemporary neurophysiological research, which shows that multisensory integration neural circuits are responsible for self-other distinction and that these circuits are connected with the self-other identification circuits (Mirror Neuron System). Demonstrations of neurophysiological alterations in areas related to the functions of both self-other identification and of self-other differentiation in psychotic states, offer the neural basis for those psychodynamic theories that suggest a lack of integration between symbiosis and separation in psychosis. Furthermore, they open the possibility for empirical research on the efficacy of art therapies and other psychosocial therapies for the recovery of the sense of the self in psychoses.[12]

Notes

1 According to Freud (1924), a 'delusion is found applied like a patch over the place where originally a rent appeared in the ego's relation to the external world'

2 In the world of neurosciences the discovery of mirror neurons in the early 90s in premotor area F5 of the macaque monkey (Di Pellegrino, Fadiga, Fogassi, Gallese and Rizzolatti 1992) and regions of the inferior parietal lobe (Gallese, Fogassi, Fadiga and Rizzolatti 2002), placed the basis for the empirical investigation on the neural correlates of self-other identification. Mirror neurons were active both when the monkey performed particular goal-related motor acts, like hand and mouth grasping, and when the monkey observed someone else performing the same object-related actions. Mirror neuron mechanisms have been interpreted as reflecting one of several mechanisms that allow understanding of others' behaviour, like motor goals and motor intentions. In particular, they could contribute to social understanding from 'the inside' by unifying action perception and action performance within a joint neural substrate (Gallese 2001). Subsequent studies using neuroimaging and neurophysiological techniques suggested the existence of similar neural mechanisms in humans. For instance, they demonstrated that the same, multimodal, neural circuits involved in our own bodily self-experiences are also involved with the pre-reflective understanding of others' actions (Caspers, Zilles, Laird, and Eickhoff 2010; Rizzolatti, Fadiga,

Gallese, and Fogassi 1996) as well as of some other mental states, such as emotions and sensations (Keysers and Gazzola 2009).

3 The term 'boundaries of the self' descends from the concept of 'ego boundaries' defined by Federn (1929). Federn's theory proposed external ego boundaries, between the ego and the external world, and internal boundaries between the ego and the unconscious. According to Federn, psychotic patients had poor cathexis to self boundaries. When the self boundary is weakened or lost, the sense of difference between the self and the other is reduced (Federn 1929). From a neuroscientific point of view Ebisch *et al.* (2013) demonstrated a correlation between damaged self boundaries and sensory integration disturbances and damage to the posterior insula.

4 Freud (1915) writes: 'In schizophrenia words are subjected to the same process as that which makes the dream-images out of latent dream-thoughts—to what we have called the primary psychical process. They undergo condensation, and by means of displacement transfer their cathexes to one another in their entirety. The process may go so far that a single word, if it is especially suitable on account of its numerous connections, takes over the representation of a whole train of thought. The works of Bleuler, Jung and their pupils offer a quantity of material which particularly supports this assertion.'

5 One of the main features of autistic withdrawal is the self-exclusion of the patient from his or her network of social contacts and withdrawal to a private dimension, closed to the interactions and transformations of interpersonal encounters.

6 These are terms in common use in psychiatric settings. Echolalia is a speech disorder in which the subject repeats the words that are said as in the echo phenomenon. Neologisms are words created by the patient which do not have a shared social meaning.

7 Such dreams were defined by Benedetti (1991) as 'therapeutic dreams'. According to Benedetti, therapeutic dreams are not simply an expression of the therapist's countertransference, but also an activity of the transitional subject occurring simultaneously in the patient and the therapist. The therapist, compared with the patient, has more tools to enable him to be aware of this common material. The therapeutic task is to make the patient aware of the presence and activity of the transitional subject. In Anna's case, this is done by the therapist through his drawing with which he shows to the patient the transitional subject's dream.

8 The milk lines are two lines, formed by thickenings of the epidermis (the mammary ridge) along the ventral surface of mammals of both sexes. They extend from the upper limbs (arms) to the lower limbs (legs) and are developed in the embryo. They give rise to the mammary glands and nipples but are otherwise usually not visible in the adult.

9 Benedetti introduced the term of *progressive psychopathology* to describe the positive entrance of the therapist in the delusions of the patient. In this phase the symptoms are still present but they are transformed. The patient accepts the presence of the therapist in his delusions. Thus there is still delusion but it is changed, there is a new openness inside the old symptoms that recalls a dual communication in place of the previous autistic closure (Bernd R. 2000).

10 Synesthesia (from the Ancient Greek syn, 'together', and aisthēsis, 'sensation') is a neurological phenomenon in which stimulation of one sensory or cognitive pathway leads to experiences in a second sensory or cognitive pathway. In our approach we constantly try to stimulate contemporarily different sensory paths (e.g. visual stimuli and sounds) in order to strengthen the integration of different sensory pathways.

11 For some visual examples of the above mentioned techniques: www.atlascentre.eu www.simonedonnari.org www.youtube.com/user/simo4444. Our preliminary tests on paINTeraction technique show that also non psychotic people enjoy this kind of

interaction with images and movements. We are planning to use this tool to create opportunities of social inclusion for people with mental disabilities.

12 We are open to collaborating with other researchers in order to extend the study and to develop new ideas in this area. Everyone who is interested can contact us at the LinkedIn/ISPS Research Network and LinkedIn/Associazione Sementera Onlus— www.sementera.org.

References

Abraham, K. (1908). 'The psycho-sexual differences between hysteria and dementia praecox', *Selected papers on psycho-analysis.* London.

Abraham, K. (1927). 'Die psychosexuellen Differenzen der Hysterie und der Dementia praecox', *Zbl. Nervenheilk. Psychiat.* N.F. 19, 521. (40–1, 65, 70, 76–7) Chap. II.

Auerbach, J.S., and Blatt, S.J. (1996). 'Self-representation in severe psychopathology: The role of reflexive self-awareness', *Psychoanalytic Psychology*, 13(3), 297–341.

Ayres, A.J., Heskett, W.M. (1972). 'Sensory integrative dysfunction in a young schizophrenic girl', *Journal of Autism and Childhood Schizophrenia,* 2(2), 174–81. doi:10.1007/BF01537570.

Benedetti, G. (1980). *Alienazione e personazione nella psicoterapia della malattia mentale*, Torino: Einaudi.

Benedetti G. (1988). *La schizofrenia*, Istituto Italiano per gli studi filosofici, Milano: Guerino.

Benedetti, G. (1991). *Paziente e terapeuta nell'esperienza psicotica*, Torino: Boringhieri.

Benedetti, G. (1992). *Psychotherapie als existentielle Herausforderung* [*Psychotherapy as existential challenge*], Goettingen: Vandenhoeck Ruprecht.

Benedetti, G. and Peciccia, M. (1989). 'Das Katathyme Spiegelbild. Im Bartl G und Pesendorfer F (hrsg.)', *Strukturbildung im therapeutischen Prozess*, 125–39. Literas.

Benedetti, G. and Peciccia, M. (1995). *Sogno, inconscio, psicosi.* [*Dream, unconscious, psychosis*]. Chieti: Metis.

Bernd, R. (2000). *Die Kunst des Hoffens. Begegnung mit Gaetano Benedetti*, Vandenhoeck and Ruprecht, pp. 47–86.

Bion, W.R. (1957). 'Differentiation of the psychotic from the non-psychotic personalities', *International Journal of Psycho-Analysis*, 38, 266–75.

Bion, W.R. (1962). *Learning from experience*, London: Heinemann Medical Books.

Caspers, S., Zilles, K., Laird, A.R., and Eickhoff, S.B. (2010). 'ALE meta-analysis of action observation and imitation in the human brain', *Neuroimage*, 50(3), 1,148–67.

Di Pellegrino, G., Fadiga, L., Fogassi, L., Gallese, V., and Rizzolatti, G. (1992). 'Understanding motor events: A neurophysiological study', *Experimental brain research*, 91(1), 176–80.

Donnari, S. (2011). 'Video-integration in group therapy of psychoses' in 17th ISPS International Congress (2011). *Psychological therapies for psychoses in the 21st century influencing brain, mind and society.* Dubrovnik, 31 May–4 June.

Donnari, S. and Peciccia, M. (2013). 'Therapeutic mirror images in the therapy of schizophrenia: Progressive mirror drawing and video-integration in group therapy' in XII Ecarte Conference (European Consortium for Arts Therapies in Education) (2013). *Through the looking glass: Dimensions of reflection in the arts therapies*, Paris, 11–14 September.

Donnari, S., Peciccia, M., Manco, F. (2013). 'Pietro: The story of a cure. Art therapy, social therapy and sensory-motor integration therapy' in: 18th ISPS International Congress

(2013). *Best practice in the psychological therapies for psychosis: A contemporary and global perspective*, Warsaw, 22–25 August.

Ebisch, S.J. *et al.* (2013). 'Out of touch with reality? Social perception in first-episode schizophrenia', *Social Cognitive and Affective Neuroscience*, 8(4), 394–403.

Federn, P. (1929). 'The ego as subject and object in narcissism' in *Ego psychology and the psychoses,* London: Imago (1953).

Freud, A. (1936). *The ego and the mechanisms of defence,* London: Hogarth Press and Institute of Psycho-analysis. (Revised edition: 1966 (US), 1968 (UK)).

Freud, S. (1900). *The interpretation of dreams* in Strachey, J. (1953). *The Standard Edition of the Complete Psychological Works of Sigmund Freud, Volume 5*, London: The Hogarth Press and the Institute of Psycho-analysis.

Freud, S. (1911). 'Formulations of the two principles of mental functioning' in Strachey, J. (1953). *The Standard Edition of the Complete Psychological Works of Sigmund Freud, Volume 12*, London: The Hogarth Press and the Institute of Psycho-analysis.

Freud, S. (1915). 'The unconscious' in Strachey, J. (1953). *The Standard Edition of the Complete Psychological Works of Sigmund Freud, Volume 14*, London: The Hogarth Press and the Institute of Psycho-analysis.

Freud, S. (1917). 'Introductory lectures on psycho-analysis (part III), Lecture 26: The libido theory and narcissism'. In: Strachey, J. (1953). *The Standard Edition of the Complete Psychological Works of Sigmund Freud, Volume 16*, London: The Hogarth Press and the Institute of Psycho-analysis.

Freud, S. (1924). 'Neurosis and psychosis' in: Strachey, J. (1953). *The Standard Edition of the Complete Psychological Works of Sigmund Freud, Volume 19*, London: The Hogarth Press and the Institute of Psycho-analysis.

Gallese, V. (2001). 'The 'shared manifold' hypothesis. From mirror neurons to empathy', *Journal of Consciousness Studies*, 8(5–7), 33–50.

Gallese, V. (2003). 'The roots of empathy: The shared manifold hypothesis and the neural basis of intersubjectivity', *Psychopathology,* 36(4).

Gallese, V., and Ebisch, S. (2013). 'Embodied simulation and touch: The sense of touch in social cognition', *Phenomenol. Mind*, 4, 269–91.

Gallese, V., and Sinigaglia, C. (2010). 'The bodily self as power for action', *Neuropsychologia*, 48, 746–55.

Gallese, V., Fogassi, L., Fadiga, L., and Rizzolatti, G. (2002). 'Action representation and the inferior parietal lobule', *Common mechanisms in perception and action: Attention and performance*, 19, 247–266.

Hinshelwood, R.D. (1991). *A dictionary of Kleinian thought*, 2nd ed. London: Free Associations.

Keysers, C. and Gazzola, V. (2009). 'Expanding the mirror: Vicarious activity for actions, emotions, and sensations', *Current Opinion in Neurobiology*, 19(6), 666–71.

King, L.J. (1974). 'A sensory-integrative approach to schizophrenia', *American Journal of Occupational Therapy.,* 28(9), 529–36.

Laplanche, J., Pontalis, J.B. (1973). *The language of psychoanalysis*, London: The Hogarth Press and the Institute of Psycho-Analysis.

McCormick, L.M. *et al.* (2012). 'Mirror neuron function, psychosis, and empathy in schizophrenia', *Psychiatry Research: Neuroimaging*, 201, 233–39.

Mehta, U.M., Thirthalli, J., Basavaraju, R., Gangadhar, B.N., and Pascual-Leone, A. (2014). 'Mirror neuron dysfunction in schizophrenia and its functional implications: A systematic review', *Schizophrenia Research*, 160(1–3).

Mentzos, S. (1991). *Psychodynamische Modelle in der Psychiatrie*, Vandenhoeck and Ruprecht.

Ogden, T.H. (1992). 'The dialectically constituted/decentred subject of psychoanalysis. II. The contributions of Klein and Winnicott', *International Journal of Psycho-Analysis*, 73, 613–26.

Ogden, T.H. (1994). 'The analytic third: Working with intersubjective clinical facts', *International Journal of Psycho-Analysis.*, 75, 3–19.

Ogden, T.H. (1997). Letter. *Int. International Journal of Psycho-Analysis*, 78, 160–61.

Ogden, T.H. (2004a). 'The analytic third: Implications for psychoanalytic theory and technique', *Psychoanalytic Quarterly*, 73: 167–95.

Ogden, T.H. (2004b). 'This art of psychoanalysis: Dreaming undreamt dreams and interrupted cries', *International Journal of Psycho-Analysis*, 85, 857–77.

Peciccia, M. and Benedetti, G. (1989). 'Das progressive therapeutische Spiegelbild. Eine neue Methode in der Psychotherapie der Psychosen' in *Neurologie und Psychiatrie* 3, Braun. Karlsruhe.

Peciccia, M. and Benedetti, G. (1992). 'Progressive mirror drawing as a factor fostering the psychotherapy of psychotics with disturbances in verbal communication' in Borri, P. *et al.* (eds.) (1992). *Usa-Europe conference on facilitating climate for the therapeutic relation in mental health services.* Arp. Perugia.

Peciccia, M. and Benedetti, G. (1996). 'The splitting between separate and symbiotic states of the self in the psychodinamic of schizophrenia', *International Forum for Psycho-Analysis* 5, 23–38.

Peciccia, M. and Benedetti, G. (1998). 'The integration of sensorial channels through progressive mirror drawing in the psychotherapy of schizophrenic patients with disturbances in verbal language', *The Journal of the American Academy of Psychoanalysis*, 26(1).

Peciccia, M. and Benedetti, G. (2006). 'Principio del piacere e psicosi', *Riv. Psicol. Anal.* 22,74, 87–118.

Postmes, L. *et al.* (2014). 'Schizophrenia as a self-disorder due to perceptual incoherence', *Schizophr Res.* 2014 Jan;152(1): 41–50. doi:10.1016/j.schres.2013.07.027. Epub 2013 Aug 22.

Prensky, M. 'Digital natives, digital immigrants part 1', *On the Horizon*, 9(5), 1–6.

Racamier, P.C. (1976). 'Rêver et Psychose: Rêver ou Psychose', *Revue Française de Psyco analyse, vol. XL* (1), 173–93.

Reisman, J.E. and Blakeney, A.B. (1991). 'Exploring sensory integrative treatment in chronic schizophrenia', *Occupational Therapy in Mental Health*, 11(1), 25–43. doi:10.1300/J004v11n01_03.

Rizzolatti, G., Fadiga, L., Gallese, V. and Fogassi, L. (1996). 'Premotor cortex and the recognition of motor actions', *Cognitive Brain Research*, 3(2): 131–141.

Rubin, J.A. (1987). *Approaches to art therapy theory and technique*, New York: Brunner and Mazel.

Segal, H. (1950). 'Some aspects of the analysis of a schizophrenic', *International Journal of Psycho-Analysis* 31, 268–78.

Solan, R. (1991). 'Jointness as integration of merging and separateness in object relations and narcisism', *The Psychoanalytic Study of the Child*, 46, 337–52.

Stern, D.N. (1985). *The interpersonal world of the infant*, New York: Basic Books.

Tausk, V. (1919). 'On the origin of the influencing machine in schizophrenia', *Psychoanalytic Quarterly*, 2: 519–56. 1933. Über die Entstehung des "Beeinflussungsapparates" in der Schizophrenie. *Internat. Zeitschr. für ärztl. Psychoan.*, 5, 1–33.

Velasques, B. *et al.* (2011). 'Sensorimotor integration and psychopathology: Motor control abnormalities related to psychiatric disorders', *World Journal of Biological Psychiatry*, 12, 560–73.

Winnicott, D.W. (1953). 'Symptom tolerance in paediatrics' in *Collected papers: through paediatrics to psycho-analysis* (1958), London: Tavistock Publications, pp. 101–117.

Winnicott, D.W. (1971). *Therapeutic consultations in child psychiatry* (The International Psycho-Analytical Library, 87), London: The Hogarth Press and the Institute of Psycho-Analysis.

3

SHAPING CONSCIOUSNESS

Phenomenological art therapy with adults in psychotic states

Hanne Stubbe Teglbjaerg

Maria is painting a landscape in green and blue colours. She normally stays at home in her flat because she feels invaded when she is close to other people and is afraid that she sends 'signals' to others without realising that she is doing so.

Five years earlier, Maria (aged 28) was diagnosed with schizophrenia. For a period of about three years, it was difficult to involve her in any activities. She would not come to appointments with her psychiatrist, and mostly kept her door locked when caregivers visited her at home. Despite her difficulties she agreed to go to art therapy, and has participated in an art therapy group at the local psychiatric centre for one year. She attends most of the weekly sessions and paints eagerly. Although she has no previous art training, she creates intricate, beautiful paintings that seem to be meaningful for her.

After 30 sessions she evaluated the art therapy process in positive terms. She felt that the art therapy had made her "stronger in herself" and enabled her to accept herself 'as a woman'. She also said that the art therapy has diminished her paranoia, and that she felt a sense of belonging in a group for the first time in her life.

Maria participated in an outpatient art therapy group for adults diagnosed with schizophrenia. The particular practice of art therapy used in the group was artwork-focused art therapy inspired by Expressive Arts Therapy.[1] The group was conducted with emphasis on the sensory, artistic process of creating pictures, and the focus was on using art materials, on the aesthetic qualities and poetic meaning of images. I was the group leader and I also followed the group process carefully as part of a research project. There were two men and three women suffering from psychosis in the group. Together with a co-therapist with no training in art therapy I established a therapeutic frame that was intended to provide safety and support for both the individual processes and the group as a

70

whole. The frame involved gathering the group in a circle at the beginning and end of each session. I gave simple warm-up tasks as exercises in order to facilitate a sense of presence and a sensitive awareness within the patients before painting. The patients were given ideas about what to paint, but they always had absolute freedom to shape whatever they wanted (Figure 3.1). At the end of each session, the whole group looked at the pictures and group members could comment on each other's paintings. As the group leader, I took care to ensure that the atmosphere was non-judgemental. Psychological interpretations and explanations were avoided in order to keep artistic curiosity open, to aid in unfolding aesthetic meanings, and thereby to promote the artistic processes. The feedback to the images from the group members was complemented by small exercises encouraging aesthetic and poetic responses, e.g. 'what music comes to your mind when you see this picture?' or 'who do you imagine is living in this landscape?' Attributing meanings in this way was an emergent, playful and spontaneous process.

Figure 3.1 Group member painting in a group session.

Introduction

Maria's art therapy group was one of two groups that I conducted for one year as a part of my Ph.D. project. Alongside Maria's group, which consisted of adults diagnosed with treatment resistant psychosis, I led a comparison group that consisted of five psychiatric patients who were thought not to experience psychosis. At that time, I had been working for ten years as a psychiatrist trained in expressive arts therapy. My experiences of using art in the treatment of psychosis during these years were very encouraging. I found that there was very little research that could explain these experiences. Accordingly, in my Ph.D. I wanted to critically and systematically research if, and how, the art therapy approach that I was using is beneficial for adults with psychosis.

All the participants in the art therapy groups reported that they felt much better after one year of weekly art therapy and directly attributed their improvement to the art therapy. They described themselves, for example, as being less psychotic, less anxious, and more confident. An interesting aspect of the reported positive effects is that in the 'psychosis' group the therapeutic goals seemed to have faded away in the consciousness of the patients during the year of art therapy, whereas the art-making processes seemed to have become their only focus. They had forgotten about their original goals of making changes in their life and relationships and seemed to be more inclined to focus on creating pictures. I was puzzled about this apparent contradiction, that they became better in many ways as they 'forgot' the part of the art therapy that might be considered therapeutic by the standards that I was accustomed to working with.

In this chapter, I present considerations about how we may understand the efficacy of this kind of art therapy that I am naming 'artwork-focused art therapy'. Theoretically, artwork-focused art therapy builds on theories of art and on the philosophy of phenomenology.[2] This theoretical foundation provides an understanding of how art may affect human consciousness and states of psychosis that I find preferable to the explanations offered by concepts from psychology and psychoanalysis. The use of phenomenology as the main theoretical background also has some implications for the practice of art therapy as we will see later in this chapter.

Both art and madness are important issues in several phenomenologists' writings on the subject of human consciousness.[3] To understand the connection between art and psychosis in art therapy I will therefore start by giving a short account of my views on how phenomenology explains psychosis. First I will give a short presentation of the phenomenological view of psychosis as a basic disturbance in the self, and I will also briefly touch on how the self is constituted in the thinking of phenomenologists. These theoretical foundations will form the basis of my considerations regarding the ways in which art-making affects the psychopathology of psychosis.

I will go on to present six prominent factors that emerged as significant in the beneficial effect of the art therapy in my research group: I will (1) pinpoint how art promotes what I define as 'sensory presence' and thereby strengthens the basic sense of self; (2) underline art's potential for creating new forms that contribute to a shaping of consciousness; (3) present the concept of objectivation for the phenomenon of giving form to something that has no form; (4) argue for the importance of playfulness; (5) touch on the role of aesthetics and beauty; and (6) argue for the importance of group coherence in the constitution of the self. These are all suggestions for ways of understanding the efficacy of art therapy when we look at psychosis and art through a phenomenological lens. The concluding section includes an outline of the main differences between a phenomenological and a psychoanalytical approach, and a discussion about the implications for art therapy practice.

Phenomenology and the psychopathology of schizophrenia[4]

In this section, I present an understanding of psychosis that builds on the studies of consciousness made by European phenomenologists. My understanding of phenomenology refers to the philosophical tradition that was founded in the early years of the twentieth century by Edmund Husserl and his followers.[5] The focus of phenomenology is the study of consciousness by a systematic analysis of experience and the way we experience things. By focusing on the interrelatedness between phenomena of the world and our experience of the phenomena the phenomenological understanding of consciousness differs from more commonly used forms of thinking which can be described as dualistic.[6] Many of the early phenomenologists had a keen interest in madness and art as phenomena of human consciousness. Their thinking in these fields gave me a theoretical framework for understanding how and why Maria's painting apparently had beneficial effects on reducing her psychotic symptoms.

During psychosis people may experience significant change in their field of perception, their understanding of the world, their relationships and themselves. From a phenomenological point of view this can be understood as a fundamental change in the consciousness of the patient. The approach to psychopathology that builds on the philosophical tradition of phenomenology highlights this alteration of consciousness and emphasizes how basic changes in the experience of self can give rise to the wide range of symptoms seen in people who are diagnosed with schizophrenia.

An important property of human consciousness is the basic sense of being a person, or comprehending oneself as a person. This sense is part of normal human development and is the foundation of a meaningful perception of our world. In the phenomenological approach, the symptoms of 'schizophrenia' are understood as results of a disturbance in this preverbal or pre-reflective self or what is also called the primary or minimal self (Parnas 2003; Parnas and Handest 2003; Rulf 2003; Saas 2003; Wiggins, Schwartz, and Northoff 1990). This disturbance gives rise to a fundamental insecurity that affects the entire field

of perception, self-demarcation, ownership of one's experiences and the spontaneous experience of meaning, which leads to the development of delusions and
other symptoms.

An interesting empirical study from Norway supports the concept that people diagnosed with schizophrenia have fundamental difficulties in their experience and comprehension of self. The main research question in the study was:
'Which prodromal changes in subjective experience are reported by first episode
DSM-IV schizophrenia patients?' (The term 'prodromal' refers to early, often
vague symptoms that might indicate the start of an illness.) The question was
explored through qualitative open-ended interviews with nineteen persons about
the substantial changes in consciousness that they experienced in the prodromal
phase. The most consistent finding in the pre-psychotic phase was actually an altering of self-perception. This was reported in statements such as: 'painful indif-
ference and distance to myself'; 'something in me had turned inhuman'; 'scaring
feeling of being unreal, changed, and hazy'; 'I totally lost myself; had to remind
myself who I am'; 'lost my feelings, loss of myself, making me another person'
(Moller and Husby 2000).

From the phenomenological point of view the preverbal self is constituted in
perception. We become persons only through our perceptions of the world. According to this, disturbances in the preverbal self, such as those seen in psychosis,
are connected to basic disturbances in the field of perception (Fuchs 2005). It is important to underline that perception in phenomenology means more than just sensing. It is the totality of connectedness with the world that passes through the senses
(seeing, hearing, etc.). In addition to sensing, perception includes the continuous
meaning-making process, or the meanings we attribute to what we see or hear.

Fuchs shows that understanding perception according to the thinking of two
different philosophers; Husserl and Merleau-Ponty, offers an understanding of
the different symptoms seen in 'schizophrenia'. Edmund Husserl, who is considered to be the father of phenomenology, regarded perception as rooted in
intentionality—a central concept in phenomenology regarding the directedness
of consciousness. According to Husserl, consciousness cannot exist without its
intentions: Thinking is nothing without thoughts, hoping relies on something to
hope for, and hearing exists only in the context of sounds. To look at a chair thus
implies an active intention. The looking cannot be separated from the chair we
see. And if we do not suffer from psychosis we immediately see the chair as a
chair, rather than some lines and colours that can be interpreted as a chair. Even
though we only see the three legs of the chair from our perspective, we will
perceive a chair with four legs. This is because we remember how a chair looks
from other perspectives and co-intend how the chair will show itself from other
angles. This is what Husserl called passive synthesis. Due to passive synthesis
we experience an entire chair even though we only see it from one side. The
parts that are invisible from our actual viewpoint effortlessly show up in our
consciousness. This makes it possible for us to perceive chairs and other things
as meaningful objects, rather than just as lines and colours. When psychosis

involves disturbance of passive synthesis, it gives rise to difficulties in organising perception around delimited and connected objects.

Where Husserl attaches great importance to intentionality in his understanding of perception, the French phenomenologist Merleau-Ponty puts more emphasis on how our bodily perceptions are fundamental to all perceiving. He points out that meaningful perception is bound to an experience of the world as an extension of our own flesh and primary body sensations, which imbue our perceptions of the outer world life with vitality. For instance, if I look at the chair, I remember how it would feel like to touch the wooden surface, and my body remembers how it would feel to sit in the chair. As a result the perception is experienced as meaningful. The chair becomes really "chairlike". When psychosis gives rise to a disturbance of the bodily foundation of perception, it will make the perceived objects appear unreal or meaningless.

Using the Husserlian concept of perception (intentionality and passive synthesis), Fuchs (Fuchs 2005) shows how such a disturbance in perception gives rise to a difficulty with the experience of objects as meaningful entities. The resulting distress may eventually compel a person with psychosis to stay passively at home because he cannot differentiate his perceptions and gets overwhelmed by impressions when he goes out. A disturbance, in terms of Merleau-Ponty's concept of perception gives rise to a lack of vitality and the world appears as strange and non-familiar. For instance a person might say that she knows that her house is her own house, but that it doesn't feel like it anymore, and she questions whether somebody has taken the real house, and replaced it with a fake house.

Another important aspect of disturbance of the preverbal self is the weakening of the sense of ownership of one's own perceptions, actions or thoughts, which is called ipseity (Parnas 2003). A person in a psychotic state may lack a stable experience of ownership of her or his own seeing, thinking or doing (Parnas 2003; Parnas and Handest 2003). This gives rise to the phenomenon of experiencing one's own actions or thoughts as being generated from someone or something outside of one's self.

Phenomenological approaches understand 'schizophrenic' states as disturbances in the primary self. These can be fundamental problems in the field of perception, as Fuchs had shown, and/or a weakening of ipseity, creating a partial breakdown in the 'intentional arc' that connects the patient meaningfully with the world (Moran 2002; Saas 2003). Delusions can be understood as the person's creative efforts to bring meaning to their strange experiences. Many other psychiatrists and phenomenological philosophers have contributed to a deeper understanding of 'schizophrenia' as a result of disturbances in the preverbal or primary self. Wolfgang Blankenburg has pointed to the loss of common sense in psychosis. In his seminal article 'The Loss of Natural Self-Evidence'[7] he describes it as a loss of the unproblematic background quality that normally enables a person to take many aspects of the social and practical world for granted. The concept of common sense refers to the basic unity of perception, thinking and will that connects the person to the surrounding social world. This concept has inspired Stanghellini, who argues for a bodily foundation of 'common sense' (Stanghellini 2004).

I also want to mention Louis Sass who has contributed to phenomenological psychopathology with the concept of hyper-reflectivity. The concept concerns the way that persons experiencing disturbances of his or her primary self react by trying to 'think it out'. When a person is challenged by the loss of common sense (such as during psychosis), their thinking is no longer so strongly connected with embodied reality due to the difficulties in perception and break-downs in the intentional arc. Therefore, a person in a psychotic state often ruminates, and seeks answers that can make meaning or sense out of his or her experiences. However, without an intentional connectedness, the rumination gives odd, private answers that may lead to the development of delusions.

The above presentation of phenomenological psychopathology in the understanding of psychosis is obviously brief. My purpose has been to give some basic understanding of this complex theoretical field, on which I build in my art therapy practice. If we accept that symptoms of psychosis are meaningful reactions to disturbances in the primary sense of self, treatment of people in psychotic states may involve a strengthening of their primary or preverbal sense of self. In phenomenology this process is called 'constitution of the self' and is regarded as a continuous process. In the next section I will present some general thoughts about constitution of self that will lead to my discussions of central aspects of artwork-focused art therapy.

Constitution of the phenomenological self

If we understand the symptoms of psychosis as a result of diminished experience of the preverbal self, then treatment must include ways to help the patient constitute a better sense of the preverbal self (Teglbjærg 2011a). And as the minimal self is not a verbal construction but is mainly based on experiences of body and perception, a therapy for psychotic illness must be based on, or at least include, experiences of body and perception.

Seen through the lenses of phenomenology, Maria's experience of painting can be understood as a way for her to sense connections with the outer world. Through painting she becomes engaged in choosing the right colour, looking at the paper, moving her body back and forth, and creating something that holds meanings for her. In other words, she gets into an intentional relation with the world which allows her to let go of hyper-reflectivity for a while. Furthermore, when she sees the image she has made, and the group sees it, she sees the image as a product of her own creativity and feels her self constituted as the authorised painter of this particular image. In this way Maria may be strengthening her minimal self, thus diminishing her anxiety and making it possible for her to connect to the group.

The French phenomenologist Ricoeur argued that we humans do not know ourselves, but find identity in the things we create and in the immediate interpretation of our own creations (Ricoeur 1979). (Ricoeur's concept of interpretation in this context is not the same as the psychoanalytic concept referring to an act of thinking. Rather it refers to interpretation in a way that is similar to Heidegger's formulation: That we are thrown into an interpretation of the world in the very act of perceiving (Heidegger 2007).) The implication is that we do not know ourselves before we dare take part in the creation of our world. When Maria creates her landscape in green and blue, she enters into an act of creation. Through her immediate, spontaneous preverbal interpretations of the image while painting, as well as her verbal reflections with others, she constitutes herself as a person.

We also need other human beings in the process of constitution of a self. Husserl regarded intersubjectivity as a necessary condition, a predisposition, of self-constitution. Standing together looking at the same picture, we experience not only the image. We are also simultaneously becoming aware that the other person sees the same image. This brings about an intersubjective experience in the recognition of 'me', being a person, beside the other person. Additionally, when I am seen by another person, I see both her and myself with her eyes and I thereby experience myself as a person seen by her. Such experiences are natural in the process of the constitution of our self, and normally we pay little attention to them. However, when the primary self is suffering from psychosis, these experiences of intersubjectivity are fundamental to regaining the basic sense of self. Accordingly, being a member of a group with mutual experiences could be an efficient way to foster the intersubjective constitution of self.

After the art therapy ended Maria wrote on the evaluation sheet that the art therapy had made her 'feel stronger in herself', 'less paranoid' and 'more in touch with her feelings'. In the follow-up interview, she likewise reported feeling more present and in tune with her everyday activities, instead of thinking 'big thoughts' (having delusions), and that this had increased her overall life satisfaction. It seems to me that all these positive statements make sense when they are thought of as results of a strengthening of her preverbal self. The art-making can be seen as having strengthened her sense of self, making it possible for her to be a part of a group for the first time in her adult life. And being a part of a group led to further constitution of her primary self. The results can be understood as a strengthened self-experience that diminished her anxiety, hyper-reflectivity and psychotic symptoms.

Outlining my approach to clinical practice

Before returning to the outline of elements that I found contributed to a beneficial outcome in my research group, I will provide a little more background for the empirical material in this chapter.

The focus of my research has been to find out if, and how, art therapy could be helpful for people suffering from psychosis. I had the opportunity to start the research when I was employed as a psychiatrist in an out-patient psychiatric centre in the western part of Denmark (2005–06) and to continue in three-year full-time research at Centre of Psychiatric Research at Aarhus University Hospital (2006–09). I wanted to understand how patients made use of the art in the therapy and if there were differences in how patients suffering from psychosis make use of the art therapy compared to patients without psychosis.

I offered phenomenology-based art therapy, here called 'artwork-focused art therapy' for one year to two groups of patients. One group consisted of five patients diagnosed with schizophrenia with persistent psychotic symptoms despite treatment. They were between 26 and 37 years old and had been suffering from psychosis for between five to nine years. All of them had received antipsychotic medication. The other group had five non-psychotic psychiatric patients who were diagnosed with treatment resistant depression and/or personality disorders. A trained psychiatric nurse took part as an assistant. The patients were all in treatment at the centre and they were offered the art therapy in addition to 'treatment as usual'.[8] The groups met for two-and-a-half hours once a week, for a total of 46 sessions. All the therapy sessions were recorded systematically, and the experience of each patient was examined using interviews and written evaluations before and after therapy and at a one-year follow-up. All the material—session journals, interviews, patients' pictures, ratings, and written evaluations—was collected. The analysis of all this material was performed qualitatively using elements of grounded theory[9] and phenomenology.

Through this research I came to understand several different aspects of art therapy as contributing to the overall positive results (Teglbjærg 2009; Teglbjærg 2011a; Teglbjaerg 2011b). Different patients made use of different elements, but especially for the group with psychosis the strengthened sense of the preverbal self seemed crucial for the outcome. I saw this as better self-confidence, better self-demarcation, better social competences, and increased emotional capacity.

I will now present what I see as six of the central modes of actions in artwork-focused art therapy for people suffering from psychosis. I will illustrate the different elements with examples from my research group.

To be more present as a sensing being

When the process of painting demanded full awareness in terms of selecting colours, light and shapes the patients experienced a shift in focus, from hyper reflective absorption in their own thoughts and feelings to external reality.

Eric was a young man who always slept with a knife under his pillow. He was preoccupied with the fear of being killed by somebody, and if anyone called him, he would interpret it as a threat and refrain from responding. In the art therapy he painted mountains (Figure 3.2) He engaged himself totally in the shapes and colours. Ricoeur might say that he forgot about himself and thereby found himself in front of the created image. Eric got into a state of mind of presence. He changed his focus from a hyper-reflective fixation, trying to control his fear, to an absorption in the actions of his brush strokes. This reduced his anxiety and made further engagement with the painting, as well as with the group, possible.

Standing there in front of his picture with an expression of enthusiasm and joy, it was evident that something important happened. The painting made him feel genuinely present as a sensing being.

Figure 3.2 Mountains.

Eric reported in the interview after the art therapy had ended that the therapy had made him less paranoid. When I asked him why, he simply replied: 'It is because it is so good to paint!' In my understanding of this, he increased his sense of presence, which diminished his anxiety and paranoid thinking as he allowed himself to be absorbed in the process of painting. He strengthened his pre-reflective self in the very process of painting by an intentional and sense-borne interaction with the art material and the motif.

Creating art as shaping of consciousness

From the phenomenological point of view our intentions and emotions stem from perception rather than (verbal) thinking. This means that all our actions and conceptions have their root in body and perception. Accordingly, facilitating changes in patients' preverbal structures of consciousness may be a challenge for psychotherapeutic approaches that rely mainly on verbal language.

Especially when people are psychotic these preverbal structures of consciousness can be hard to express in verbal language because of interpersonal anxiety, the oddness of the psychotic experiences and/or cognitive impairment. Normally we use language to establish shifts in our perspective by listening to other people, but in my experience this can be difficult when, because of psychosis, a person has difficulties in trusting spoken words. The person suffering from psychosis may therefore have difficulties in using verbal language for change. The psychotic experience also often entails a profound experience of 'lacking words' and of going through something that cannot be explained. In many cases it gives rise to a struggle to make meaning in a way that goes beyond normal conceptions, or giving up, altogether, which leads to passivity and isolation.

In these cases, giving form to a piece of art offers a non-verbal way of communicating and creating meaning. In art a new experience can materialise in form without words. The form or the expression holds meaning in itself and doesn't need any further verbal explanation. Here, interpersonal anxiety is not an obstacle to expression. The art work can hold plurality and paradoxes in complex experiences without provoking ambivalence.

An example was Maria who regarded femininity as weakness with which she couldn't identify. She created two pictures with a light pink colour that, for her, connoted femininity and fragility and a dark green colour that she thought of in terms of strength and masculinity. In one of these pictures (Figure 3.3) the two colours are holding each other and creating a mutual expression that made a great deal of sense for her. Her aesthetic dialogues and intersubjective engagement with those paintings seemed to lead her to accept the fact that she is a woman and to help her to be capable of integrating a new perspective on womanhood. She talked about this in the interview after therapy had ended, but in the situation at the time she didn't give any words to the experience and we didn't talk about it. The aesthetic reflection seemed to change her sense of herself as a woman in a way that is beyond language. In this way creating art can be a way of creating or altering preverbal structures of consciousness.

Figure 3.3 Sensuality and strength.

Objectivation or giving shape to mental phenomena

The shaping of feelings in images provides an experience of distance from the feeling, which opens a possibility for aesthetic reflection. A vague feeling or unclear thought gives rise to a form, a shape in lines and colours, which can be seen and reflected on. Inspired by Paul Ricoeur, I call this phenomenon *objectivation*. The objectivations are effective ways of creating a reflective distance from all kinds of mental experiences like feelings, fantasies and emotions.

An example is a patient who said, pointing at her picture: 'That's how it is, it is just like this!' It was a truly powerful expression in the media of paint and collage. Looking at the image I had a felt sense (Gendlin 1981) of the patient's experience. I could not find words for it. I saw the picture, and she saw that I saw it and that seemed to be important. She didn't ask for more, and talking about it might have brought a distance to the experience. We connected in a mutual non-verbal realisation of how it was for her. Even though it was not very pleasant, she felt relieved to face and to share her sensed reality in the image. As her experience took form in the image it seemed to form her own acceptance of her condition and her perception of herself and her reality. This process was entirely non-verbal and direct. This can be understood as an objectivation of her state of mind or experience of the world.

Another example is a patient that came furious to an art therapy session and chose to channel her anger into one picture (Figure 3.4). In the interview after

Figure 3.4 Giving form to anger.

the therapy ended she talked about it. She had felt that the angry picture could hold the anger, so to speak. She could put it upside down, increasing the distance, knowing that it was there without feeling forced to look at it. My understanding of this was that she in that way felt more in control of her anger. She couldn't make the angry emotions disappear but she could create room for the experience in an image instead of keeping it 'inside of herself' and becoming psychotic, which was the usual consequence of strong feelings. There was no verbal reflection on her anger and it was not necessary. The formative activity with the picture itself was a relief for her.

In this way the concrete form of the images enables patients to distance themselves from expressed thoughts or feelings and to cope with them, which produces a change in the original experience. In the interview after therapy one patient expressed it in this way: 'Something magical happens when you take a brush in your hand and get all that stuff that is sitting in here out through the hand. Then you can let go of it.'

The Danish philosopher Knud Løgstrup regarded the creation of form as crucial for our humanity. He stated, 'There are things in our lives that cannot tolerate formlessness—especially what has lots of life. Without form it is ruined; the most vital things demand a bound indirect expression; a medium.'[10] And those experiences that are most alive are in my view often those that are not so easy to put into words. Hanevik *et al.* (2013) have shown that for persons suffering from psychosis it can be especially helpful to express their experience of psychosis in an artistic medium. The creation of a piece of art that reflects the strange and frightening experience of psychosis makes it possible for the patients to reflect on the experience aesthetically and this seems to allow them to get on with their lives.

An interesting but maybe accidental finding was that all the women in both groups made substantial use of objectivations, but it was rarely used by the men and not at all by the men in psychotic states.

The playfulness of art-making

To create art is also to play with possibilities and ideas, and to nourish the curiosity that may be necessary for change. Playing is fun and can bring joy into the often painful life of the patients. The art studio provides a setting within which the play range can be expanded.

The English psychoanalyst Winnicott saw play and creativity as absolutely necessary for developing the inner life and for mental health. 'More than anything else it is the creative approach that makes life worth living' (Winnicott 1990). Many patients with psychosis have not been playing at all for many years. It seems that the stress and insecurity in a life with psychosis narrow the ability to play and restrict creative thinking. A person who cannot play gets stuck. In phenomenological terms the restricted play-range opposes the continuous constitution of the self.

Working with art is also playing with materials, and facilitating playful structures can strengthen this aspect of the work. I used deliberate playful structures
in the group as a tool to loosen up a tense atmosphere of insecurity, anxiety or
silence. We played; for example, we made scribbles to find animals in lines, or
splashed randomly with paint on paper to see what would come up. Or I would
bring two balloons and ask the group to keep them from falling onto the floor until everybody was laughing or smiling. Exercises of this kind brought playfulness
and lightness into the room and brought about a playful attitude to the painting.
Several of the patients in my research assessed playfulness as important for the
positive outcome they had from the art therapy.

Hans-Georg Gadamer is a German philosopher who is concerned with the notion
of play. He sees playing as a form of self-expression that creates a special kind of
lightness and relief by means of expression. According to Gadamer, play does not
need a witness—and this differentiates play from art. In art-making, playing translates into a manifested form, and this manifestation is not necessarily convergent
with the playing person. Playing helps us to enter into art-making and to overcome
the shortcomings that come from the aesthetic idealisation of art[11] (Gadamer 2004).

In his evaluation one patient said that due to the art therapy, he had been able to
participate in the card-playing club in his living quarters. The connection between
the card-playing club and the art therapy relied on the realisation that he didn't have
to be in control all the time and that he might be able to find solutions if something
was difficult. Never before had he dared to go there but now he went with joy, and
was proud that he had succeeded. He had expanded his play range, and that opened
up more playful social interactions with the other men in his living quarters.

Beauty and aesthetic reflections

The search for beauty is regarded as a major motivational force for most artists
(Løgstrup 1983). Beauty, in this sense, is not necessarily what is pretty, but it is
what makes us breathe a little deeper or perhaps let go of a sigh. It can be scary
or even downright ugly but always with a certain experience of something meaningful or true. The German philosopher Hegel regarded the beauty of art as realisation of truth (Jørgensen 2003: 289–99) and Heidegger calls beauty a "becoming
and happening of truth"(Heidegger 1996). According to Gadamer, the experience
of beauty changes the experiencing subject (Gadamer 2004). Dorthe Jørgensen,
a Danish researcher in history of ideas and beauty, states further that beauty
makes us feel connected with a sense of meaning that exceeds social structures
and opens up our perspective (Jørgensen 2008). Beauty expands our thinking and
makes it possible to transcend our normal everyday life (Jørgensen 2008).

> Beauty brings joy because it institutes meaning, and its formation of
> meaning is characterized by not closing, but opening the horizon. It
> institutes meaning, thanks to the feeling of presence that characterizes
> an experience in which one is not oneself (i.e. the goal-oriented subject,

one generally identifies oneself with), but ecstatic and therefore close to the things of the world. And in which the things also step out of themselves (i.e. the objects which the subject usually consider them to be); instead they appear as what they are, namely something in themselves. When this happens, beauty lets us perceive the existence that we and the things share—i.e. the being thanks to which the world is coherent—and this feeling of coherence is meaningful.[12]

Jørgensen (2006: 59)

The sense of beauty manifests in the painter's choice of colours and the sense of a line. An artist knows when beauty arrives (and also when it really doesn't and he or she has to change something in a picture). This is also the case when it comes to untrained painters suffering from psychosis who, for example, can seem to experience an almost bodily felt sense that applying further paint will destroy the emerging image. Here the art therapist's role can be to help the patient to risk spoiling the image in order to let painting continue until beauty unfolds.

The experience of beauty is connected to what Baumgarten[13] called 'aesthetic reflection' (Jørgensen 2003, author's translation). During the process of painting there is an on-going 'aesthetic reflection' in the preverbal experience of shape, colour and form. Aesthetic reflection is a process of applying a sense of meaning at the level of perception. It is not given in word or language and can be impossible to translate into spoken words. It is like sensing the 'meaning' of a piece of music, a sensed experience that is not easily explained to others. Rather than try to explain, you will ask them to listen to the music themselves. This aesthetic reflection is connected to the sense of beauty and 'meaning' in the images. I find this process very important in art therapy as it provides new perspectives beyond spoken language.

The provision of new perspectives and the sense of beauty are further stimulated when a painting is seen by others. That is why mutual reflection on the painted images has a central role in the artwork-focused art therapy group. This aesthetic reflection happens as other group members offer poetic responses to the picture. As an art therapist I frame and facilitate the aesthetic responses to the finished images in the end of a session. For example, I might give the group members a question, like "If this image was the front page of a book, what do you imagine is the story of that book?" Or I might ask them to reflect on each other's images by inviting them to share and apply their fantasies, feelings or stories to the picture. These responses from peers expand the painter's own aesthetic reflection on his/her image, and often the patient starts to really see what he or she has painted. The painter may thereby reach another sense of beauty and aesthetic "meaning" through the other group members' aesthetic responses.

Being part of a group

Painting in a group is a strong way to promote social cohesion. Three of the five patients with psychosis in my research group said that the act of painting made it possible for them to be part of a group. Two of those patients had never before managed to be a member of a group due to social anxiety and psychotic symptoms. The art group was surprisingly different in this aspect. This could partly be explained by the fact that in the art sessions the patients are visible to each other without having to confront each other directly or have eye-contact. One patient expressed it in this way in the interview after ending the art therapy: 'In the art group I felt I was seen without anybody looking at me'. Another patient said: 'Here it is possible to be on my own and still be a part of the group'.

The created images become bridges rather than barriers between the patients through their double function as both 'me' and 'not-me'. The patient is seen as painter when other group members look at her or his images and acknowledge them as paintings. At the same time, the members of the group experience that their reflections about each others' paintings are sources of inspiration for their peers. They give something to one another. Furthermore, the work in the group is concrete. The materials such as the paper and the paint define actions and communications thereby giving the patients something secure to hold on to. The difficulty of having to socialise with others is diminished because the gathering has a purpose that extends beyond them as persons; it is about painting and not about being social. It makes it possible to be there and to have a shared commonality with very little pressure to interact directly. Even in the gathering at the beginning and the end of the session it is possible to refrain from speaking. Only the paintings are always seen and commented on through aesthetic reflections.

All patients in the group with psychosis rated the group experience as one of the most beneficial factors in the art therapy. One explanation could be that it became possible for these patients to be part of the group because the minimal self was strengthened in the process of painting and through the concrete structuring of the group space. According to Husserl, intersubjectivity is one of the most important factors for constitution of the primary self (Zahavi 2003). The sense of belonging to the group seems to strengthen the patients' sense of self further, setting a positive spiral in action.

Art therapy: between phenomenology and psychology

The phenomenological approach to art therapy emphasises the shaping, the beauty and the playfulness in sensing and acting, in order to get to an aesthetically satisfactory expression. It is an approach that puts ART before everything else. I call this kind of art therapy artwork-focused art therapy to differentiate it from analytical art therapy, as it is expressed for example in the American pioneer art therapist Naumburg where psychological interpretations of the images and the relation to the therapist are primary considerations. In the British tradition of art therapy for psychosis, psychological interpretation of images is generally not used as a technique, although the theoretical understanding is based mainly on psychoanalytical theories of psychotherapists such as Winnicott, Jung, Bion, Lacan and others. This form of art therapy is also known as analytical art therapy. Therefore the term "analytical art therapy" is used for a broad range of therapeutic approaches (Killick and Schaverien 1997)

The contrasting approaches referred to here as artwork-focused and analytical have been referred to in different terms by different authors. Most common distinctions are "art as therapy" in opposition to "art in therapy" or "art psychotherapy" (Edwards 2004), and "studio art therapy" in opposition to "clinical art therapy" (Moon 2002). Intermodal "art as therapy" has its own tradition called "expressive arts therapy" (Knill, Levine, and Levine 2005; Levine and Levine 2004). In practice many art therapists make use of both positions.

In artwork-focused art therapy images are seen as guests, as new creations that can talk to all of us in their own language. This view of painting is in contrast to understanding images as expressions of the unconsciousness of the painter. The difference is subtle but I find it important. In contrast to approaches which attempt psychological understanding of the art work, a phenomenological approach focuses on the artistic process, taking a playful attitude. I believe this strongly supports the strengthening of the preverbal sense of self and the preverbal structuring of consciousness.

Furthermore, focusing on the person and psychological interpretations of the images for some patients can stimulate anxiety and hyper-reflection. It can be a big relief for these patients when the focus is held on the images instead of on them as persons. In that way the loss of psychological understanding in the therapeutic process seems to be counterbalanced by more presence as a sensing being, more wordless objectivations and more play.

In my research I have aimed at providing an understanding of the processes in art therapy for psychiatric patients and establishing a theoretical foundation based on the theories of phenomenology and aesthetics. I find that this theoretical foundation has provided a fruitful perspective on my own art therapy practice.

In my view, art is a search for beauty, for meaning, for a differentiated form that has its own life and exists in its own right. Like a visit from a stranger the art work can talk to the artist as well as to other human beings. Artwork-focused art therapy takes place when 'art happens' between the patient and his/her particular artistic creation. I argue that this important artistic process may be provided with more therapeutic power for persons with psychosis when we avoid psychological interpretations. Psychological interpretations inevitably shift the focus of attention from the aesthetics of colours and forms to the person and from the poetic stories and playful fantasies to conceptual understanding. In this shift the very artistic process may suffer.

Artwork-focused art therapy, as I have outlined it here, can be a challenge to the therapist because of the openness towards the artistic process that it demands. It is purely led by a search for beauty and aesthetic meaning. This means that the patient as such is not in focus, but (and for this very reason) capable of finding himself by forgetting himself, sensing his own presence in front of the images that make sense to him. In this situation the therapist is a facilitator who provides the right frames, is supportive of the patient's curiosity and playfulness and helps to overcome whatever obstacles the patient might encounter in the shaping process. But the therapy itself happens between the patient and the images, or between the patients. It takes place, for example, in the search for and selection of the right blue colour.

In this chapter, I have argued for the possibilities that can unfold when we dare to let go of our striving for psychological meaning in favour of trusting the artistic process. I have proposed that the art itself can contribute to a restructuring of consciousness in individuals suffering from psychosis when we offer an appropriate frame and support. I have provided a potential explanation of why the sensing interaction with the art materials makes it possible for fragile minds to create new forms and new meaning. The core of my argument has been that the playful search for beauty in the art work and the active support of aesthetic dialogue with the images strengthens the primary or preverbal self, thereby reducing anxiety and symptoms of psychosis.

Notes

1 Expressive Arts Therapy is an intermodal approach that has the practice of the arts (painting, theatre, music, poetry etc.) as its foundation. It is theoretically inspired by phenomenology and theories of art and aesthetics.

2 'Phenomenology' in this text refers to the tradition in European philosophy which focuses particularly on the nature of consciousness. The tradition is represented by philosophers like Husserl, Heidegger, Merleau-Ponty and many others (Moran 2002).

3 Heidegger, Merleau-Ponty, Ricoeur, and Løgstrup have all written books and articles with art as a main focus (Heidegger 1996, Løgstrup 1983). Several European psychopathologists had their roots in phenomenology; Jaspers, Binswanger, Conrad, Blankenburg and others. Newer phenomenological psychopathology is represented for example by Mishara, Saas, Parnas, Stanghellini and others (Rulf 2003).

4 There is an ongoing controversy as to whether the concept of schizophrenia is a meaningful construct. The research and writings in phenomenological psychopathology however use the term 'schizophrenia' and this is why it is also used in this chapter. Also the term 'psychopathology' is used as it refers to a long tradition of research trying to understand the phenomena of madness, insanity, and also psychosis.

5 'Phenomenology' in many newer writings refers to a descriptive method, and others use the term as naming a subjective stance. This is not the way I use the term.

6 'Dualistic' refers to the separation of mind and matter in western thinking which creates a problem for a deeper understanding of the mutual interconnectedness of "mind" and "world". Dualism is closely associated with the philosophy of René Descartes (1596–1650), which holds that the mind is a nonphysical substance distinguished from the brain.

7 Translated from German: "Der Verlust der Natürlichen Selbstverständlichkeit" Wolfgang Blankenburg 1971.

8 Treatment as usual in this setting includes regularly meeting in the centre with a psychiatrist or psychiatric nurse with focus on medication and coping strategies and social support by social workers that visit the patients and help with daily living, activation etc.

9 Grounded theory is a method of research developed by Glaser and Strauss. Since the first publication in 1967, the method has been developed further as a methodology in the social sciences involving the construction of theory through the systematic analysis of data.

10 Translated by the author from Løgstrup. The Danish text: 'Der er ting i vores liv, som ikke tåler formløshed—især det, der er mest liv i. I formløsheden ødelægges det; det mest levende forlanger et bundet indirekte udtryk: et medie.'(Løgstrup 1983)

11 For Gadamer the separation of art and science gives rise to an aesthetic idealisation of art which means that science is regarded as holding the 'truth' and art is seen as pure aesthetics without potential for realisation of 'truth'. Here play becomes important by exceeding rationality and bringing art back in our lives.

12 In Danish: *'Skønheden er glædesbringende, fordi den virker meningsstiftende, og dens stiftelse af mening er kendetegnet ved ikke at lukke, men derimod at åbne horisonten. Den stifter mening takket være den følelse af nærvær, der kendetegner en erfaring, i hvilken man ikke er sig selv (dvs. det målrettede subjekt, man i almindelighed forstår sig selv som), men derimod ude ved genstanden. Og hvor genstanden også træder ud af sig selv (dvs. det objekt, den af subjektet i almindelighed bliver opfattet som) for i stedet at fremstå som det, den er, nemlig noget i sig selv. Når dette sker, lader skønheden os fornemme den for os og genstandene fælles væren, ved hvilken verden hænger sammen, og denne følelse af sammenhæng virker meningsfuld.'*

13 Alexander Gottlieb Baumgarten (1714–62) is known for the establishment of philosophical aesthetics. In his dissertation from 1750, 'Aestetica', he argues for the sense borne potentials of realisation in aesthetics as equal and complementary to logic realisation.

References

Edwards, D. (2004). *Art therapy*, London: Sage.

Fuchs, T. (2005). 'Delusional mood and delusional perception—A phenomenological analysis', *Psychopathology*, vol. 38, no. 3, pp. 133–39.

Gadamer, H. (2004). *Sandhed og Metode* (translation of *Wahrheit und Methode* [*Truth and Method*], 1960), Copenhagen: Systime Academisk.

Gendlin, E.T. (1981). 'Focusing and the development of creativity', *The Focusing Folio*, vol. 1, no. 1, pp. 13–16. (http://www.focusing.org/gendlin/docs/gol_2062.html)

Hanevik, H., Hestad, K. A., Lien, L., Teglbjærg, H. S. and Danbolt, L. J. (2013). 'Expressive art therapy for psychosis: A multiple case study', *The Arts in Psychotherapy*, vol. 40, pp. 312–21.

Heidegger, M. (1996). *Kunstværkets oprindelse* (translated from *Der Ursprung des Kunstwerke* [*The Origin of the Work of Art*], 1936), Copenhagen: Samlerens Bogklub.

Heidegger, M. (2007). *Væren og tid* (translation of *Sein und Zeit [Being and Time]*, 1926), Aarhus: Klim.

Jørgensen, D. (2003). *Skønhedens metamorfose* (*The metamophosis of beauty*), Syddansk Universitetsforlag / Gyldendals bogklubber.

Jørgensen, D. (2006). *Skønhed, En engel gik forbi* (*Beauty, an angel passed*), Aarhus Universitetsforlag.

Jørgensen, D. (2008). *Agleias dans, på vej mod en æstetisk tænkning* (The dance of Aglia, on the way to an aesthetic thinking), Aarhus: Aarhus Universitetsforlag.

Killick, K. and Schaverien, J. (1997). *Art, psychotherapy and psychosis*, London and New York: Brunner-Routledge.

Knill, P. J., Levine, E. G., and Levine, S. K. (2005). *Principles and practice of expressive arts therapy, towards a therapeutic aesthetics,* London: Jessica Kingsley.

Levine, S. K. and Levine, E. G. (2004). *Foundations of expressive arts therapy, theoretical and clinical perspectives*, London/Philadelphia: Jessica Kingsley.

Løgstrup, K. E. (1961). *Kunst og etik* (*Art and ethics*), Copenhagen: Gyldendal.

Løgstrup, K. E. (1983). *Kunst og erkendelse, metafysik II* (*Art and knowledge, metaphysics II*), published in Danish, only partly translated at Marquette University Press 1995, Copenhagen: Gyldendal.

Merleau-Ponty, M. (2002). 'The primacy of perception and its philosophical consequences' in Moran, D. (ed.) *The Phenomenology Reader*, Albingdon-New York: Routledge, pp. 436–59.

Moller, P. and Husby, R. (2000). 'The initial prodrome in schizophrenia: Searching for naturalistic core dimensions of experience and behavior', *Schizophrenia Bulletin*, vol. 26, no. 1, pp. 217–32.

Moon, C. H. (2002). *Studio art therapy*, London and Philadelphia: Jessica Kingsley.

Moran, D. (2002). *The Phenomenology Reader*, Routledge: New York.

Parnas, J. (2003). 'Self and schizophrenia: A phenomenological perspective' in Kircher, T. and David, A. (eds.) *The Self in Neuroscience and Psychiatry*, Cambridge, pp. 217–41.

Parnas, J. and Handest, P. (2003). 'Phenomenology of anomalous self-experience in early schizophrenia', *Comprehensive Psychiatry*, vol. 44, no. 2, pp. 121–34.

Ricoeur, P. (1979). *Fortolkningsteori* (*Interpretation theory: Discourse and the surplus of meaning*), Copenhagen: Vintens forlag.

Rulf, S. (2003). 'Phenomenological contributions on schizophrenia', *Journal of Phenomenological Psychology*, vol. 34, no. 1.

Saas, L. A. (2003). 'Self-disturbance in schizophrenia: Hyperreflexivity and diminished self-affection' in Kircher, T. and David, A. (eds.) *The Self in Neuroscience and Psychiatry*, Cambridge: Cambridge University Press, pp. 242–71.

Stanghellini, G. (2004). *Disembodied spirits and deanimated bodies. The psychopathology of common sense*, Oxford-New York: Oxford University Press.

Teglbjærg, H. S. (2009). 'Kunstterapi i psykiatrisk behandling med særlig fokus på skizofreni' ('Art therapy in psychiatric treatment with a special focus on schizophrenia'), Ph.D dissertation published in Danish, University Hospital in Aarhus.

Teglbjærg, H. S. (2011a). *Skabende kunstterapi* (*Artwork-focused art therapy*), Aarhus: Aarhus Universitetsforlag.

Teglbjærg, H. S. (2011b). 'Art therapy may reduce psychopathology in schizophrenia by strengthening patients' sense of self', *Psychopathology*, vol. 44, pp. 314–18.

Wiggins, O. P., Schwartz, M. A. and Northoff, G. (1990). 'Toward a Husserlian phenomenology of the initial stages of schizophrenia' in Spitzer and Maher, B. A. (eds.) *Philosophy and Psychopathology*, New York: M. Springer-Verlag, pp. 21–34.

Winnicott, D. W. (1990). *Leg og virkelighed* (*Playing and reality*), Copenhagen: Hans Reitzels forlag.

Zahavi, D. (2003). *Husserl's phenomenology*, Stanford University Press.

4

THE STRUCTURED STUDIO SETTING

An ontological dimension in art psychotherapy
with psychosis using the concept of body
image as structuring function

Jean-Jacques Bonneau

Introduction: on psychosis and its implications for art psychotherapy

This chapter explores a way of working in art therapy, which aims to make engagement possible when individuals' disturbance is characterised by radical defences against external reality (Bell 1995, Bion 1957), with all their ramifications. In particular, I explore difficulties arising in work with severely psychotic patients in relation to disturbances in their capacities for 'embodiment' (Laing 1960) and 'relatedness' (*ibid.*), with reference to the existential concept of body image (Pankow 1961, 1981).

My understanding of psychotic states and their lived dynamics is informed by psychodynamic thinking, with particular reference to the work of Gisela Pankow, and by existential phenomenology (Merleau-Ponty 1964, Laing 1960). In my understanding and experience, significant features in working with psychosis are a disruption of the capacity to symbolise (Segal 1981), a lack of validated sense of identity, of its historical dimension and of reliable self representations (Armstrong-Perlman 1995, Corradi Fuimara 2007), which stem from destructive, fragmentary and dissociative defences against the experience of contact with external reality (Pankow 2004). With reference to clinical vignettes, I will show that these features pose a fundamental problem at the level of the therapeutic alliance. In art therapy, this alliance usually relies on a capacity for working reflectively with images and their contents as representation of an inner life, as well as the capacity for interpersonal relating.

The capacity to use the image as a reflective tool, which is customarily considered to be the primary tool for art therapy (Schaverien 1991), seems initially to fall out of the therapist's reach in my experience of therapeutic interventions with severe psychosis. In my view, the image fails to acquire the meaning of a third object within the therapeutic encounter in the way that Ogden (1994), writing about psychoanalysis, describes as 'the analytic third', because of the deficit in the capacity for symbolic thinking in psychotic states of mind. Failures in symbolic thinking and, therefore, of the capacity to process emotions, result in the image and the setting being experienced concretely, and this can trigger enactments with potentially destructive outcomes. Such behaviour may require holding (Winnicott 1985) and containment (Bion 1977) within the context and physical space of the session. The particularity of such presentations has necessitated a rethinking of the potentials of art therapy beyond the more conventional understandings that are based primarily upon the idea of the image as a receptacle for unconscious content (Killick 1987).

I will describe situations in my vignettes in which potentially destructive phenomena of this kind affect the production of images, their destiny and the therapeutic setting as a whole. Concrete enactments may also occasionally risk actual damage to self and/or others. Consequently, the first task of the therapist at this early stage is to enable the patient to find his or her particular way of tolerating the existence of the artwork within the given space, and my vignettes will give detailed examples of the nature of the work involved.

The nature of psychotic disturbance can be thought of as a particular form of defence against experiencing pain (Winnicott 1985), which has been described by Laing (1960) as 'existential' and by Bion (1977) and Klein (1946) as 'primitive'. This defence radically affects a person's sense of identity and experience of being in the world. Accordingly, severe psychotic states necessitate therapeutic approaches that are quite distinct from approaches which focus on accessing symbolic thinking through interpersonal interactions, in which the existence of fundamental symbolic structures of the mind is in the foreground.

Methods of psychoanalytic counselling, psychotherapy, and art psychotherapy that address patients' difficulties within the conceptual framework of psychic structure proposed by Freud, (1923) in terms of id, ego, superego, conscious and unconscious, are predicated on the assumption that the patient's state of mind includes a capacity to work symbolically. Along with Pankow (2004, 2006) and Balint, in his reflection on psychotic and borderline structures (1989), I believe that these approaches are less relevant to the task faced by the therapist when encountering patients in states of mind characterised by 'symbolic equation' (Segal 1981) and severe trauma in the field of relatedness.

In this chapter, I present my perspective on the psychoses as an escape from the irresolvable dilemma of 'being-in-the-world',[1] with the painful experience of limits that this entails. On that basis, I aim in the initial stage of my therapy practice to provide a setting in which a 'journey into being' can take place; both of the image and implicitly also of its creator.[2] Through sensorial endeavours within a physical space, the creation of a realm of representation may become possible. The function of the therapist at this early stage consists of sustaining and communicating an ontological[3] dimension of the art therapy 'world' by means of verbal reminders of its potentials and of its limitations (its boundaries).

My clinical examples will demonstrate my hypothesis that the spatiality and corporeality of the therapy space is fundamental to the therapeutic intervention and to the establishment of an alliance between therapist and patient, by enabling the potential for interactions to be held in the physical objects and setting, rather than solely in the internal world of the human beings involved. The setting and its objects provide what I think of as a 'membrane' (Merleau-Ponty 1945), or 'skin' (Bick 1968), which is intimately related to the most basic human experience of a body-self coming into being.

My theoretical perspective is primarily influenced by Katherine Killick, who in the 1980s introduced the therapeutic format that I refer to as 'Structured Studio Setting', a model of art therapy adapted to address psychotic dynamics. During that period Killick worked in collaboration with Heiner Schuff, a consultant psychiatrist in psychotherapy, who, to the best of my knowledge, was responsible for introducing the work of Pankow to the world of art therapy theory (1982). Killick described her model in detail in her published work on 'The Art Room as Container' (2000). In my understanding and practice, the Structured Studio is not simply the concrete setting within which art therapy takes place but is in fact the primary tool facilitating therapeutic interventions. I will consider Killick's concept of 'container' (*ibid.*), which corresponds to Bion's 'alpha functions' (1977) in the light of Pankow's concept of the relation between form and content as functions of the 'body image' (1961), which in my view brings further insights in terms of both practice and theory to this specific art-psychotherapeutic approach to psychosis.

Each clinical example that I will give is a reconstruction based upon various situations encountered with patients in art therapy. The manifest contents of these reconstructions have been altered in order to protect patients' confidentiality. In order to be consistent with my references I will be using the word 'patient' throughout this chapter. All translations of Pankow's French texts are my own; as to my knowledge the French revised editions of her work have not been translated into English at the time of writing this chapter.

The concept of body image in Pankow's theory and beyond

Gisela Pankow (1914–98) was a German psychiatrist and psychoanalyst, who practised in Paris from the 1950s onward. She integrated existential phenomenology into her broadly psychodynamic approach, which made use of art as a primary medium for the reconstruction of body image in her work with psychotic patients. She offered a formulation that proposes a radical difference between neurotic and psychotic modes of being, in which the fundamental structures of the mind, conceptualised in psychoanalytical terms as id, ego and super-ego, in both their conscious and unconscious manifestations, are *distorted* in neurosis and *destroyed* in psychosis.

Pankow proposes the notion of the 'body image' to refer to the individual's 'symbolic mode of living in one's body' (Schuff 1982). This concept acts as a focus for understanding individuals' relation to the fundamental structures of being, in other words, how individuals experience their state of being in the world. Pankow refers to Freud's statement that the body is the primary locus of the ego. Freud (1923) proposed that the first stage of ego formation consists of a convergence of self-consciousness and sensory perceptions, which culminates in the development of the 'body-ego' (Freud 1923). The body-ego is the site for our sense of subjectivity and is also the 'social object' (Merleau-Ponty 1945) through which our sense of subjectivity is communicated to others. In this way, embodied existence involves an inherent tension between being simultaneously a subject and an object; a self and an other; a 'felt' body and a 'recognised' body.

It is pertinent here to make a distinction between the body image and the body outline (*schéma corporel*) or 'body as fact'. Françoise Dolto (1984), paediatrician and psychoanalyst, also used the concept of body image in her work with children. She defined the *body image* as the lived synthesis of emotional experiences relating to archaic, yet present, experiences of the body, which are linked to the subject and to the personal history of the subject. In contrast, the *body outline* is more or less identical for everyone and is specific to the human species as a whole, rather than to the subject. This factual dimension of the body takes an interpretive role in relation to the subjective body image and leads towards 'objectivization', as a prerequisite for communication with others, of an 'intersubjectivity' that would otherwise remain a realm of incommunicable fantasies (*ibid.*).[4]

The idea of duality in embodied existence is also central in Laing's theories, in which an embodied self is the condition for being both a separate person and one who is related to others. Relatedness can only happen between individuals experiencing themselves as separate beings. Here lies the paradox, 'the potentially tragic paradox, that our relatedness to others is an essential aspect of our being, as is our separateness' (Laing 1960: 25). This tension can be violently affected by severe trauma in the primary field of relations with confusion and terror arising as a result of subject and object/inside and out/'you' and 'me' becoming entangled and confused.

The idea of the destruction of the body image as a fundamental structuring principle, as outlined earlier, has great relevance to me in my work with people in states of acute psychosis, and offers valuable insights into the difficulty in making sense of a world fraught with disconnections and often driven by persistent delusional beliefs and hallucinations.

Paradoxically the psychotic destruction of these fundamental structures of the self occurs as protection against perceived imminent dangers and intense primitive and/or existential anxiety. The fragmentary and dissociative impulses leading to the destruction of the body/self can be understood in the context of infantile anxieties and defences that come into play when the baby's experience of omnipotence is disturbed in contact with external objects. The as yet unbounded parts of what eventually constitute a body/self come into being for the infant through contacts with the external world. The sensorial quality of these experiences plays an essential role for the infant's capacity to accept, then recognise and own these parts.

As Klein (1946) has shown, both 'good' (gratifying) and 'bad' (frustrating) experiences in early life encounters between the infant and its external world are fundamental to the child's development towards an increasing sense of separateness and to the formation of an ego. In her writing on Klein, Segal (1989) used the concept of 'projective identification' to describe the dynamics of these early encounters in the context of mouth/breast relations. Projective identification, in very simplified terms, employs aggressive impulses in projecting bad experiences into the breast/object. In the absence of sufficiently holding surroundings and of a nurturing agent able to hold and process the infant's distress and aggression, the infant is unable to develop the capacity to recognise and tolerate these experiences. Accordingly projections increase, with increasing fragmentary effects, to eventually dissociate from an object by now perceived as bad and persecutory. The predominating excess of distressing affects threatens the capacity for internalising the body parts that trigger these experiences, as well as desires and longing for sensorial experiences in general, resulting in the destruction of the structuring principle in itself.

The symbolism offered by Kleinian and post-Kleinian thinking concerning the mouth/breast situation provides a vivid scenario for understanding the context of potentially destructive attacks against the formation of an image of the body/self. In my view it is essential to bear in mind that this symbolism epitomises the nature of early dynamics and potentially traumatic situations at the level of early object relations rather than being a literal description of the trauma in itself. Freud (1914) attributed projective mechanisms to a 'death drive', and therefore to a force inherent in human beings, that takes over life enhancing forces as a means of survival. According to his theories about 'repetition compulsion' (1920), early life experiences, such as those of the projective phenomena described above, can reoccur in adulthood when encountering situations associated—or equated—with those of the original trauma. Dissociation from the body and the embodied experience of reality is therefore a phenomenon that is not exclusive to infancy and it is acutely activated in adults affected by psychotic processes.[5]

Pankow (2004) related the origins of psychotic disturbances to the sufferer's immediate family context. She suggested that the psychotic patient hasn't been granted the 'right to be' (*ibid.*), and that consequently he or she cannot live in his or her body as a separate unity. She attributes this to an intergenerational pattern in which a parent (mother or father) cannot separate from her or his own parents and repeats the familiar pattern with his or her offspring. While acquiring organic unity at birth, the infant, in the intergenerational scenario described above, remains an integral part of its parent's inner world. The 'lived-body', according to Pankow (2010), and the sensorial experiences generated by it, is experienced as 'bad', in that it constitutes a threat to the parental established order. The infant in such circumstances is caught in a fundamental contradiction from birth, of being both organically separate and emotionally/psychically required to live

94

in symbiosis with its parent, mother or father. This contradiction in adulthood takes dimension of 'an irresoluble dilemma' (*ibid.*), necessitating dissociative and destructive defences in relation to contact with external reality as a whole, as exemplified in the Kleinian model of the mouth/breast situation in infancy. From Pankow's perspective, psychotic defences are corrosive of the body image as a whole and stem from what Aulagnier (1975) terms 'originary processes', which encompass those processes described as primary in the context of object relation theories as well as secondary processes of the Oedipal phase. Pankow's position in that sense is resonant with Laing's (1960), who saw in psychosis 'an existential death', and Schaverien's (1997) concept of 'lack in being'.

Pankow's dynamic structurisation and its implications for art therapy

Pankow's therapy with psychotic patients consists, in her own words:

> ... of reconstructing their world by at first structurizing an organic rela-
> tion between the part and the whole. It is important to state that a neu-
> rotic patient is able to find the reciprocal relation between the part and
> the whole because for the neurotic the conception of the body as a unity
> is always possible. This cannot be attained by a psychotic patient. The
> dissociated body *(le corps dissocié)* of the psychotic patient takes the
> place of the body in pieces *(le corps morcelé)* of the neurotic patient.
>
> Pankow (1961: 162)

Pankow proposes that in psychosis the body image disintegrates in such a way as to break apart and destroy body boundaries, the experience of relationships between body parts and the whole of the body, and between one's own body and another person's body or the world as a 'structured body' (Schuff 1982), paying particular attention to the issue of dissociation between 'parts' and 'wholes'. Pankow attributes these features, namely the dialectic between parts and wholes and the establishment of form and boundaries in a spatial context, to what she terms 'the first symbolising function' of the body image. This primary structuring function gives rise to the 'second symbolising function' of the body image, which is concerned with meaning and content. Pankow discourages the use of conventional psychoanalytical techniques of working with 'internal conflicts' (Schuff, *ibid.*) with psychotic presentations, because notions of projective mechanisms, mentioned earlier, cannot be experienced meaningfully within a world in which the linking principle of the body image has undergone destruction. This is a world in which 'inside' and 'outside' do not inhabit a stable relation, and in which 'parts' have been split from their correspondence to a potential 'whole', integrated self.

The ideas of 'inside' and 'outside', of 'parts' and 'whole', are evocative of Kleinian theory which, broadly speaking, emphasises the significance of the mother's receiving, holding, and thinking about the infant's projections. This activity is introjected as containing function by the infant and enables the infant to acquire an initial sense of inside and outside. Esther Bick (1968) contributed a concept of 'skin' as a requisite function for this containment and differentiation of inside and outside dimensions to happen. This concept of skin, which is akin to what I have referred to earlier as 'membrane', is central in Killick's approach to boundaries (which I associate to early skin formation and Merleau-Ponty's (1964) concept of 'surface of contact') for the binding, or linkage, of the fragmented parts of the psychotic patient's mind as preconditions for the development of a more integrated self.

Through primary processes of 'splitting' and 'idealization' (Bick 1968), which, in Kleinian thinking, are part of the mouth/breast situation described earlier, the infant eventually achieves introjection of sensorial experiences and a sense of separateness between the self and the breast/object. These developments are possible when experience is processed and made tolerable to the infant by the mother. Bick suggests that 'primal splitting and idealization of self and object... rest on this earlier process of containment of self and object by their respective "skin"' (*ibid.*, p. 484). Pankow's idea, mentioned earlier, that an intergenerational inability to separate affects the psychotic patient, implies that the process of destruction of the body image dismisses all self-enhancing sensorial experiences, including those generated and held by the skin organ as its primary support.

To my knowledge Pankow did not refer directly to Bick, but she recognised the function of the skin as a containing function required for notions of 'inside' and 'outside' to happen. She referred to the psychoanalyst Didier Anzieu's article 'The skin, from pleasure to thought' (1974) where he developed the concept of an 'Ego-skin'. Anzieu proposed that within this 'skin-envelope', not only food, warmth and smell are accumulated, 'the full and the good' (*ibid.*) of breast-feeding, but also that the 'sweet words' (*ibid.*) that the mother speaks as she feeds the infant have entered. I would like to underline here the link that Anzieu is making between sensorial bodily experiences and words as precursor for the acceptance of verbal language as mode of communication. I will illustrate later the difficulties with verbal communication encountered in working with psychotic patients, and I would like to suggest that those difficulties also result from the destruction of the fundamental symbolic structures of the mind mentioned earlier.

In referring to Anzieu's theory of skin Pankow reasserted her initial endeavour in working with psychosis, which was to invite the patient to discover the 'limit' and to access the 'surface' of the body as representation of a 'mental apparatus' (Freud 1923). The earliest ego functions, as we have seen earlier, emanate from physical, bodily sensations for which the binding and tactile capacities of the skin organ guarantee a sense of separateness and relatedness with the world and others.

Pankow describes psychosis as follows: '*Il s'agit de la destruction des processus de symbolisation et où, de ce fait, l'accès au désir n'est pas possible*' (2006: 142). 'In the destruction of symbolisation processes, accessing desire becomes impossible'. I understand 'desire' in this context to refer to Lacan's (1966) exposition of the driving force in human relations, which is central to transference phenomena in the psychotherapies of neurosis. Psychotherapeutic models dealing with neurosis are based on the dynamics existing within 'interhuman relationships' (Pankow 2006: 219). In psychosis these relationships are no longer reliable means of being-with-others due to the destruction (*ibid.*) of the body image that guarantees a sense of separateness between self and others.

Pankow defined the therapist's primary task as the reconstruction of the body image. In her model this is the *sine qua non* condition for restoring ego-functions. A body image with reasonably stable boundaries within which 'conflicts', 'drives' and 'desires' can preside is a fundamental prerequisite for the ability to work constructively (and symbolically) with projective mechanisms and transferential processes (Schuff 1982). Pankow proposed that this reconstruction takes place by engaging its spatial representation, approaching the task of the dynamic building of a body-in-context at the level of concrete, physical experience.

Pankow belonged to a generation of psychoanalysts who believed in giving bodily care to their psychotic patients by means of tactile, bodily sensations, as a preliminary phase of therapy. These techniques included giving massages, baths of various temperatures, and wrapping patients in towels, with the aim of enabling psychotic patients to recognise their body limits in preparation for entering into contact with another being, i.e. the therapist. Pankow (2006) used the idea of encountering the psychotic patient at the level of his or her regression to support these methods. A famous case of such bodily care given to a psychotic patient, which has been discussed by Lacan (1966) and by Pankow herself (1993), is that of Madame Sechehaye (1950) who held her patient in her arms and fed her apples, 'not daring to offer the breast' (Pankow 1993). Following this intervention, the patient improved remarkably.

Pankow clarified that such care giving did not aim to compensate for the lack of it in the patient's infancy in order to bring about changes in the patient's mental state. Rather, a capacity for symbolic linking was triggered by feeding from the apple/breast. Through this physical sensorial experience, the patient could recognise the similarities and differences between the shape and qualities of an apple and those of an expected breast. Pankow introduced a new dimension to this practice of working directly with the body in the form of a dynamic substitute she found in art-making, opening a potential space for play and creativity.

In her re-creation of this '*potential space*', Pankow recognised an alliance with Winnicott. There are also significant differences. Elements differentiating the 'created object', which is central to Pankow's Dynamic Structurisation, from Winnicott's 'transitional object' are, first, that it is 'made' rather than 'found', and second, that the created object is not located in early stages of infant separation from the mothering agent. Winnicott's transitional, found object, is valued for its emotional quality, as a symbol of a union of the mother/infant who are now separated. It is therefore valued for its content rather than for the shape that it takes. Indeed, the object can take forms as varied as those of a blanket or a teddy bear. In contrast, the created object emerges through the process of giving form to something previously non-represented. As I stated earlier, in my view the primary condition for engaging psychotic patients in therapy is the creation of a form that could represent the world that the patient inhabits. This is fundamental to Pankow's practice as well as to the art therapy approach that is presented in this chapter.

Pankow introduced art materials, mainly modelling clay and drawing equipment, into her practice for the making of images whose purposes were to enable structuring of the 'organic' (1961) relation between part and whole, and to facilitate working with structure, limits, borders, and surfaces of contact through their concrete representations. She invited the patient to formulate fantasies about the potential relation between part and whole; these fantasies give form to an unconscious 'phantasm'. The phantasm 'helps the patient to reconstruct the body image primarily in creating its boundaries and thus realizing inside and outside. On this basis, the phantasm also introduces interpersonal relationships because it leads to the interior content of differentiated forms.' (Pankow 1961: 171)

As Schuff (1982) suggested, Pankow's ideas and practice provoke further considerations of the function of image making in art therapy. Within Killick's initial model, Pankow's idea of the reconstruction of form finds a meaningful correlate in art therapy; the artwork is brought into contact with the physical space, introducing and establishing a structural relationship between part and whole, and between 'container' and 'contained'. Using the logic of symbolic equation, the artwork as body 'part' is placed in relation to the 'whole' of the art therapy setting by means of its boundaries and the negotiation of possibilities and limits in relation to the context (Killick 1987, 1991).

As I will go on to show through clinical examples, within the Structured Studio model the transferential relationship is relocated by proxy into the interactions between objects and the setting, and accordingly usefully distanced from the 'you and me'. This relocation aims to open up a space for meaning to arise through a process of forming linkages between parts and whole, in such a way as to restore an 'as if' dimension and eventually to re-enter the order of symbolisation.

The therapeutic setting

Une philosophie de l'espace est condition sans laquelle la psychothérapie analytique des psychoses reste nosographie. (A philosophy of space is the condition without which the analytical psychotherapy of psychoses would remain nosography (i.e. an assessment tool).)[6]

Pankow (2004: 13)

In the statement above, Pankow underlines the vital significance of attention to issues of space in psychotherapeutic work with psychosis. In my view, the most basic and essential form of therapeutic work relies upon the corporeality of the spatial field, and particularly upon interactions between the setting and the objects produced within it. Within the model of the Structured Studio Setting, considerations of space are fundamental to therapeutic interventions. Killick (2000, 1995a, 1995b) has written in detail about the concreteness of the setting as well as the transactions that take place within it as potentially absorbing 'the impact of primitive affective states' (*ibid.*), and paving the way for 'the evolution of symbolisation' (*ibid.*). Killick attributes to these potentials the ability to enable 'those ego functions which are weakened by psychotic processes, to strengthen, in particular fostering the emergence of a sense of self' (2000: 99).

The practice that developed within my own clinical setting retains the essential concepts of Killick's model, namely those of working with concreteness and physicality, and bearing in mind notions of structure and structurisation as a means of rebuilding a rather disintegrated universe. At the same time, this model has developed into a responsive framework that can be sensitive to changing dynamics and to the impact of the spatial field.

NHS organisations have changed considerably since Killick launched her model. These changes have resulted in adaptations to the contemporary use of the approach. One significant example is that the move from 'asylum-type' institutions to 'community' settings has meant changes to the nature of the physical space available to art therapy. The spaces available are usually greatly reduced in scale from those that were common in the 1980s, and this has led to a more limited range of possibilities for the positioning of the therapist within the space. Therapists now take up a more visible and constant presence. The increased intensity of the experience of the presence of the therapist brought about by increased proximity can stimulate anxieties of a psychotic nature in patients for whom contacts can be experienced as intrusions, and consequently can trigger psychotic means of coping with these anxieties. This has necessitated a rethinking of the positioning of therapist and participants in the space available and the negotiation of seating arrangements has become a more common feature of contemporary practice than it was within the art therapy setting described in Killick's work.

The service that I developed is based in a psychiatric hospital that has retained a dedicated art therapy studio where patients admitted to the ward and those living in various community settings can attend. The studio may accommodate up to five patients at a time, attending usually on a weekly basis, with intermittent individual appointments to review their work. It is furnished with a sink, and tables that are placed as to give participants some sense of privacy, with cupboards, shelves and plants that screen each individual space. A large table is set with art materials, shelf space provided for the storage of paper and of folders containing participants' two-dimensional artwork, and clay figures and art objects are stored on additional shelves and windowsills. Art books and illustrated magazines are on display for people to look at, as well as magazines, which can also be directly used for art-making. There is a table with tea and coffee making facilities, where participants may help themselves to hot drinks during sessions.

One requirement of the setting is that artwork is kept within the art therapy space for the duration of the therapy with the aim of maintaining links to contextual reality that are so frequently undermined by psychotic processes. Although the therapist firmly maintains this requirement, he or she is flexible in enabling people to find individual ways of meeting it. People may negotiate to store their work in alternative places to those that I have mentioned, and give different names to their different storage spaces and different folders, as greater differentiation takes place and the artwork coming into existence is endowed with various qualities.

Weekly assessment sessions are run on each of the acute admission wards. These take place in multipurpose activity rooms, which are reorganised prior to each session in a Structured Studio format so as to give participants the experience of inhabiting individual personal spaces. These sessions provide an opportunity for patients to make informed choices about whether to attend art therapy, with the possibility of continuing in the dedicated studio when transferred to the community.

Speaking, which is generally a core condition of psychotherapeutic practice, is in many cases very difficult, and verbal interactions frequently lead to confusion and to painful mental reactions in both patient and therapist. '*Une seule parole peut provoquer l'effondrement d'un schizophrène*': 'A single word can trigger the breakdown in a schizophrenic person.' (Pankow 2006: 224). In psychosis, language seemingly loses its conventional contextual (symbolic) and mediating function, with confusing and powerful effects.

An example that illustrates this concerns a meeting between the therapist and patient in the ward corridor. Pacing the floor in an apparent state of distress, the patient announced that he would not be attending his session on Friday. Caught by surprise, the therapist responded 'Perhaps you will see on Friday'. Confronted with this patient's immediate and visible reaction of horrified shock, the therapist realised the mistake of using such a common, so metaphorically charged, expression as 'seeing' with someone likely to understand the statement literally. Indeed, as understood later on by the therapist, the patient was thought to experience visual hallucinations that he perceived to be messages from God personally addressed to him.

Yet speaking is inevitable. The therapist needs to introduce the service and the art therapy setting to patients. Indeed, these interactions are the conditions for the potential to form therapeutic alliances. Hence specific attention is given to initial verbal interventions, particularly those involved in introducing patients to the art therapy setting. The therapist will attempt to use language and bodily attitude as a whole in such a way as to dilute the symbolic and interpersonal elements inherent in language. Interventions that redirect attention to the setting, the art materials within it, and the physical space, are necessitated by the potential confusion that another presence, in this context the therapist, may trigger. The boundaries relating to time and place, and to the most basic purposes of the therapy, constitute an ontological dimension of art therapy, with its immutable givens, and these are frequently undermined by psychotic defences.

I have introduced the Structured Studio Setting as a format acting as a primary tool for therapeutic interventions. It becomes a space for rechanneling potentially destructive enactments into contextually acceptable expressions, while providing basic sensorial experiences through art-making. The focus of the therapist's interactions on the physicality of the setting and the objects within it enables the holding and containment of psychotic dynamics, such as fragmentation and dissociation from embodied experiences of the setting, and invites interactions and negotiations between patient and therapist.

I will now illustrate these claims through some clinical vignettes.

1. 'The lost body'

My discussion of the psychotic condition may well leave us wondering, 'how does the psychotic patient live in his/her body?'. Pankow (1961: 166) discussed the phenomenon of dissociation and of the 'lost body'; that is the capacity to *leave* the body and take refuge in other manners of being:

> *Par le terme de dissociation, je définis donc une destruction de l'image du corps telle que ses parties perdent leur lien avec le tout pour réapparaître dans le monde extérieur.* (By using the term dissociation, I define a destruction of the body image such that its parts lose their link with the whole in order to re-appear in the external world.)
> Pankow (2004: 119)

An initial contact with the setting

Betty had been attending art therapy sessions for approximately three months. On arriving for her weekly appointment, she told me that two pictures were missing from her folder. I responded by saying that her folder had been kept safe and confidential within this setting and that it was here and available for her to check on whether pictures were missing or not. Betty declined this invitation saying that she did not need to check as she has seen these two pictures exhibited in a prestigious gallery under a famous person's name. Her dismissal of the physical evidence that the content of her folder was untouched reiterated a pattern that had been consistent in her presentation for approximately the first six months of her therapy. During that initial period, Betty avoided looking at her images, which when completed went straight into her folder.

In this therapeutic context the folder and the artwork within it are symbolically equated with a body with its content. This understanding is associated with Killick's use of the concept of container/contained and with Pankow's concept of a body image. Although Betty never attempted to physically destroy these objects, she nevertheless discarded their physical existence by ignoring their reality as well as that of the context within which they were produced and within which they would eventually acquire purposes and meanings. I thought that

Betty was taking refuge in a delusional mode of escape from reality in which parts of this 'body of artwork' were dissociated from the whole to reappear, in her mind, in the enviable public world of wealth and fame. Betty escaped the contextual and embodied world of art therapy into a dimension where her fantasies merged with reality.

In contrast with Betty's initial avoidance of recognising her immediate surroundings, the next example demonstrates a patient's initial interest in the art therapy space and specific objects within it.

Adam was admitted to an open ward in a psychotic state and, at a later stage, was diagnosed with 'early onset of schizophrenia'. He made his first entrance to the art therapy studio unexpectedly, the door having been left open in between sessions. Two members of staff from the ward followed him, visibly concerned by the young man's state of agitation. Adam appeared to be lost, rolling his eyes and mumbling to himself without any apparent point of focus, very probably experiencing auditory and possibly visual hallucinations. The therapist described the setting and its purpose so as to give the patient a sense of direction. Adam appeared curious and pleasantly interested by the space and it was agreed between the therapist and nurses that Adam could spend the remaining twenty minutes prior to his lunch in the art therapy room. Adam wandered around the room still talking to himself and ignoring the therapist's presence. The therapist gave further explanations about art therapy and an introduction to the setting. Adam directed himself enthusiastically towards the art materials, expressing interest in the paints and crayons, whilst simultaneously stating loudly, as if responding to the therapist's speech, 'I cannot do art therapy, I am nothing, nobody … might as well be dead.'

Nevertheless, Adam spent twenty minutes engrossed in using a variety of art materials to make a picture, which he then described as 'a complete mess'.

Moving towards the development of an interactive space

The therapist responded to Adam's reluctance to leave the space at the end of the twenty minutes by giving him a written memo with dates and times for a series of twice-weekly art therapy sessions. Following this, Adam left without difficulty.

Adam attended these sessions without fail, initially accompanied by a nurse who sat in the corridor at the entrance of the art therapy room. He presented with an imminent risk of absconding, which required close monitoring by ward staff. Liaison with the clinical team suggested that Adam claimed not to have any intention to run away from the hospital but believed himself to be 'just an inch' floating in thin air with no anchorage, drifting from one opening to the next without sense of direction. Adam's stay in art therapy was an exception. In order to attend art therapy independently Adam made an agreement with nursing staff that he wouldn't get lost, drift away, or escape while he was there because he felt safe.

Adam discovered two major points of attraction within the setting; the art materials table, where he seemed to thrive on a feast of textures and colours, and the tea and coffee table. Adam claimed to be '*magnetised*' by the coffee table. He repeatedly stopped there on his way to collect art materials, helping himself to three cups, one filled with tea, the other with a large amount of coffee grounds, the last filled with milk. He commented to the therapist that one cup also contained sugar whereas the others did not. These actions seemed to be resolving a difficulty that he was having with making choices and decisions. Mumbling to himself in a slurred and uncoordinated manner, the contents of the cups pouring onto the floor, Adam journeyed from the coffee table to the art materials and back to his working location, using the landscape of the room to enact '*a complete mess*'.

These rather scattered interactions with the art therapy surroundings, frequent during his earlier stages of engagement, began to be increasingly focused. In response to the therapist's frequent reminding of the purpose and boundaries of the setting, Adam's use of the substances and the materials in the room became progressively more contained within his allocated space and eventually focused within the making of images and, later on in his therapy, upon the concrete contents of his pictures. Negotiation about Adam's coffee consumption resulted in an agreement that one cup of coffee per session was sufficient, and that a single cup could contain ingredients for the cup of coffee required. Although interventions of this kind may appear to be purely practical in nature, they hold symbolic significance, initially for the therapist and, in time, for the patient. The negotiation concerning the body of the cup and its content can be perceived as an enactment of a shift from a fragmented body image towards integration of the fragments, in this instance taking the shape of coffee grounds, milk and sugar.

Differentiation and the coming into being of an image

Le schizophrène a besoin en effet de se retrouver, d'abord dans l'espace, où il ne peut plus se situer comme corps, et où il devra refaire l'image de ce corps morcelé, puis accepter de se sentir un être limité (. .) ensuite seulement, il retrouvera le temps de son histoire et le pouvoir de vivre.
(In effect the schizophrenic patient needs to find himself again, initially in the inhabited space, where he can no longer locate himself bodily, and where he will have to recreate the image of his fragmented body, then accept his limits. Only then will he recover his sense of historicity and the power of living.)

Favez-Boutonier (1956, in introduction
to Pankow 2006: 11)

In the process of making artwork, Adam kept losing the initial pencil outlines he drew under a profusion of paints and pastels. At first colourful, these pictures ended as muddy, shapeless surfaces. After a month of twice-weekly art therapy, Adam called the therapist to his table. He presented the therapist with an image outlining a labyrinth-like structure leading to a square space that he described as the art therapy space, and as a safe space for the 'Inch'. The therapist enquired where the 'Inch' could be in this picture. Adam designated a corner in the square representing the art therapy room, adding that the 'Inch' was so small that it was invisible. The therapist replied that if one could imagine this 'Inch' to be developing, how might it appear in a drawing? Adam responded by scribbling a matchstick-like shadowy figure in the corner of the square. From that moment, a shift within the patient/therapist interactions became apparent. Allocating time during sessions to talk about Adam's pictures, which had been irregular and *ad hoc* in nature, became both regular and more mutually negotiable.

At this precarious stage the pictures were spoken of in terms of their possible imaginary contents, which avoided direct references to the patient/therapist relationship. With reference to Pankow, Foster (1997) emphasises the need to place and deal with the artwork as a 'body' that is not directly connected with either the person of the therapist or the patient, but rather to treat the object as separate, as a concrete entity, which has no relation with the individuals involved. This method allows for the object itself to be understood to hold imaginary potential for the recreation of a world of object relations. By facilitating a practice which aims at the concrete reconstruction of the body image via an external object, the therapist enables the art object, which holds externalised and unidentified pieces of the self, to become 'more differentiated and … more identified with' (*ibid.*).

In the case of Adam, his first task was to re-establish for himself the most basic, structuring function of the body image—a sense of skin, boundaries and the potential for containment. By allowing for experimentations with journeys around the room, with the use of materials, and with subsequent negotiations about limits with the therapist, the setting facilitated an experience of boundaries, limits and holding space. Through the allocation of a personal space within the shared area of the room, Adam was enabled to discover a sense of separateness. In transporting containers to different areas of the room, Adam explored a process of bringing parts into contact with the whole, represented by the space. Through a journey which evolved from sensory experiences to a recognition of self, the image eventually came to function as a shared object with the therapist, and Adam was able to locate himself within the picture and in this way to re-find a way of representing and thinking about himself within a context.

2. Physical space and the mapping of the patient's world

An initial contact with the setting

Le concret du sensorial paraît bien plus primitif que le concret du monde des objets ou des faits, ainsi que des fonctions psychologiques qui s'édifient sur eux. C'est un concret vécu et non pensé. (The concrete of the sensorial appears far more primitive than the concrete of the world of objects or facts, or of psychological functions stemming from them. It is a concrete that is lived and not thought about.)

Pankow (2006: 157)

In this vignette of a patient I will call George, I attempt to illustrate how spatial representation may support a shift towards thinking and away from persecutory experiencing of the concrete sensorial domain.

George believed that hidden cameras were planted everywhere he went, that his thoughts were being recorded in order to be broadcasted in the media. His beliefs of a persecutory nature pervaded his art therapy sessions in the early days of our weekly meetings.

He welcomed the therapist in a gentlemanly manner at first contact and reiterated his interest in meeting weekly for art therapy. In contrast with this first impression George was very distressed when he came for his first session, talking incessantly in a thundery voice while pacing up and down the room. His irrational disjointed speech was hard to follow; however, the therapist could identify elements of his persecutory beliefs in what he said.

The therapist remained empathically silent, trying to understand George's distress in terms of possibly offering respite. However, this mere intention to reach out to the patient to alleviate his pain appeared to have the effect of increasing his distress. George's speech became louder and more pressured at the very moment when the therapist experienced this intent. Instead of relieving the patient's distress the therapist's emotions and humanity aggravated the situation. When the therapist became conscious that they were in a situation that excluded interpersonal modes of relating and that accordingly his emotional response exerted pressure on the patient, he resorted to a more 'matter of fact' professional role.

Speaking over George's speech, he said: 'It's time for art therapy ... a place where people may find means of taking care of themselves and benefit from while using mental health services ... There are art materials available to experiment with at one's own allocated place ...' During this brief interaction, refocusing concerns for the patient from an abstract inter-human relating onto more concrete matters, the therapist walked towards a table at the opposite end of the room from were he was sitting, taking a lump of clay on his way that he put on the table, saying 'Here is a piece of clay to do something with to talk about with the therapist'. The therapist's physical intervention set limits to the impingement of his empathic reactions on the patient, which were impossibly demanding. This seems to have provided the respite from emotional involvement that was needed to facilitate the patient's engagement. During the therapist's movement across the room George followed him to the table, where he sat and began to shape the clay. An arrangement was made to meet prior to the end of the session to talk about George's experiences in making his object. Recognising that his presence was potentially distressing for the patient, the therapist left to sit at an acceptable distance from George so as not to be experienced as intrusive.

Some twenty minutes later, George called the therapist. He presented his clay work with an apparent expression of satisfaction on his face. He made three different little objects with almost geometrical shapes, indefinable, smoothed and well polished.

George became agitated again when the therapist tried to engage in a dialogue about his experience of forming these shapes. His speech, already difficult to follow, escalated into greater confusion. The therapist then tried to change the focus of his interaction, from the objects themselves and the experiences of the patient in making them, to the setting itself, enquiring where would he think of storing his work within the art therapy space. George threw an inquisitive glance at the space around him, stood up, holding his clay pieces in his hand and walked around the space visibly hesitating about where to store his work. He resorted to hiding different pieces in different places scattered around the room: cardboard boxes lying under a table, under a pile of wrapping paper in a cabinet and so on. His anxious mumbling as he scattered his objects around the space clarified his intention to confuse inquisitive and invasive spies.

Moving towards the development of an interactive space

For the next three sessions George appeared calmer and continued making clay pieces and scattering them in hidden places at the end of the session as before. As the work and storage places multiplied he became concerned that he might forget where the artwork had been placed. The therapist invited him to think about a solution to help him to remember where the artwork was placed, and this increased George's agitation. The therapist understood that asking an open question, and accordingly, engaging George in thinking about a solution for himself, had failed. He then told a story about a situation in which 'a patient' wrote down the exact positions and places where his artwork was kept every week. George appeared to find relief in this impersonal story and drew a map of the room, with the various locations in which his work was kept. He chose to place the map in a sealed envelope in order to ensure that no one would look at it in his absence. He then placed the envelope in a drawer close to the therapist's sitting place, leaving him in charge of its safety.

From then on the situation in art therapy changed. George negotiated to sit at a table closer to where the therapist sat, near the drawer containing the map in its envelope. Soon all the clay pieces were gathered in one place near his table in a cupboard and eventually were glued together in a shape that he, later on, described as 'an airplane'.

Differentiation and the coming into being of an image

George continued working on his clay figure, adding elements, painting the various parts in different colours for approximately two further months. During that period speaking about his object remained difficult. The therapist's attempts to engage him in talking about the artwork continue to trigger confusion.

George eventually appeared more detached from his work and announced that it would soon be finished. As he completed his clay piece he became more amenable to talking about it. In response to the therapist's enquiries George explained that this airplane could only have space for two people, the pilot and the co-pilot. The plane, according to George, was still too basic and fragile to go further than Poland in order to ensure a safe return to its place of departure. The story about the plane was resonant with the situation in art therapy. The fragility of his engagement at this point, which made it impossible to venture on too great a journey, as well as the collaborative relation between the two inhabitants of the vessel, could symbolically be associated to his newly established relationship with art therapy. However the 'fragility' was also understood by the therapist as a warning that an attempt at interpreting this metaphorical link could have been precarious. Accordingly, the therapist maintained his method of engaging the patient in creating more stories, encouraging a pattern to emerge from these stories, before attempting to link the patient's imaginary realm with his embodied reality. George's anxiety decreased in this setting and he left his clay model on display on a windowsill near his allocated place.

The therapist's technique of focussing interactions upon the physical space appeared to help George to tolerate his surroundings in art therapy sufficiently to engage in a sensorial experience in the making of clay models, and later on in paintings, that eventually could be thought about as separate objects that were able to hold content. His initial concrete enactment, of a fragmented state of mind at risk of annihilation by what he perceived to be external forces, led George to perform the mapping and linkage of his world with the effect of greater sense of integration of a self represented in an art object.

3. Towards restoration of the body image

Initial contact with the setting

... le malade vit dans un corps sans limites. Lorsque la dissociation dans le monde de l'espace est réparée, le malade peut entrer dans son histoire, car la dissociation de l'image du corps s'accompagne simultanément d'une perte de la dimension historique de la vie du schizophrène. (... the patient lives in a body without limits. When the dissociation in the spatial world is repaired, the patient can enter into his history, because the dissociation of the body image entails simultaneously a loss of the historical dimension of the schizophrenic life.)

Pankow (2006: 144)

Carlo had a first contact appointment after receipt of a referral from the clinical team, to discuss conditions for a weekly art therapy individual session and make arrangements to meet. Carlo was a young person diagnosed with paranoid schizophrenia, refusing to engage with any support or therapy services, who lived in a state of isolation from social and human contacts. Until then he had been under the exclusive responsibility of the medical team for his treatment. The referral to art therapy was the ultimate attempt of the team to engage him with a psychological therapy. A major factor in this decision was that he often spent his time drawing on his own.

Carlo came on time the following week for his first session, and loudly demanded assistance for reproducing his artwork on an industrial scale, to the therapist's dismay. Ignoring the therapist's attempts to remind him about the therapeutic nature of the session as an integral part of his mental health treatment, Carlo proceeded to search around the room for the equipment he needed to achieve his grand ambition. Carlo maintained this position for at least the first four months of therapy, making further demands, such as requiring to be taught a foreign language in order to settle abroad, after his fame and fortune were achieved. It appeared that Carlo had a very grandiose and concrete understanding of the prospect of recovery and the move towards greater independence as promoted by the mental health team around him; he seemingly believed that attending art therapy was a means of fulfilling a grand project that would enable him to live his life as far as possible from the catchment area where he was treated.

During that initial period, Carlo engaged with the art materials with gestures that appeared automatic and devoid of conscious intention or reflective thoughts. He took the materials most readily available without apparent discrimination to produce drawings in which previously drawn outlines were blurred by careless colouring, overstepping the boundaries of the former pencil drawing to a shapeless outcome.

The therapist's interactions led to further confusion. Carlo's descriptions of his pictures muddled historical, fictional and mythological stories. He asserted that these were 'all the same'; for instance, equating inter-galactic wars from science fiction literature with historical conflicts. A consistent theme of an endless battle emerged, which bore significance for the therapist in relation to the present situation in art therapy. However, the process of making his pictures and his comments about their heroic contents, clearly signalled Carlo's destructive attacks on shapes and contents. These were possibly a protective defence against the intrusion of external reality, represented in this circumstance by the therapist's presence. When the therapist reapplied his attention to more concrete considerations and encouraged choosing an appropriate space to store his artwork in art therapy, Carlo dismissed his images, saying that it was 'all in his head'. Carlo discarded the physicality of his images in the same way that he discarded the experience of his own contextual reality.

Eventually Carlo came to his session and cleared his table of his pictures, which had been left there piling up, and threw them on the floor. Facing the therapist with a suspicious frown, Carlo warned him about a catastrophic world event to come due to a conspiracy against his artistic activity, which put his project in jeopardy. Carlo left his session fifty minutes early that day saying that he would return the following week to observe the therapist, believing that he was psychoanalysing him and had mysterious powers.

Moving towards the development of an interactive space

> The principal difficulty is to make the patient touch the modelling clay. One patient told me recently: "Each acceptance of form in the sense of an external outline is a menace for me. [Pause.] The moment I accept a definite form, I shall be lost."
>
> Pankow (1961: 162)

There was no apparent respite from the ordeal of this encounter between two incompatible worlds. Carlo expressed strong desires for 'help', but did so in such a way that the therapist felt unable to respond to these within the terms of his role. The therapist stood increasingly rigidly within his role and functions with a client battling to fulfil an impossible dream arising from a state of oblivion in relation to the reality of time and space, dis-allowing the existence of shapes and outline, as we have seen, in his art-making.

The therapist then attempted to set up the conditions through which the patient's demands could be responded to within the acceptable bounds of the art therapy setting. He decided to wait for Carlo with a lump of modelling clay situated in front of him. When Carlo arrived for his session he asked immediately 'What are you doing?' To which the therapist responded, 'I don't know. Any ideas about what could be done with that clay?'

The interaction that followed led Carlo to direct the therapist in the making of a clay figure. Carlo wanted the figure to represent a mythical beast and, step-by-step, instructed the therapist about its realisation. Carlo expressed his pleasure about the outcome and wanted the object for himself. The therapist suggested that he make his own version, with his own hands, and Carlo agreed. He struggled with the clay and worked clumsily, losing parts of the figure while sticking new ones on. Yet he achieved the production of a figure that apparently gave him great pride. The figure, he commented with an expression of surprise, was different from the one that he had instructed the therapist to make. His was of another mythical beast, more appealing to him than the original.

For the first time in this setting Carlo could experience an interaction in which his demands and his requirement for control over the therapist could be met in the making of an object. This object that he could name and that he could invest with particular qualities was no longer for him 'all in his head' but could exist within the art therapy space in relation to another, similar to, yet different from, his own. Carlo was able to create an object with an outline, with an inside and an outside, and to give content to this object in relation to another that early on would have represented a threat to his world. I understand the outcomes of this intervention from a transferential perspective in that through establishing a situation in which the patient's demands, and desires, could be answered positively, the patient could regain his 'right to be' (Pankow 1961: 155), with the effect of decreasing the constant threat that the other and the external world represented for him.

The two clay models were placed on different shelves facing each other so that, still according to Carlo, they could observe one another. They seemed to me to be expressing in their representation a dreaded scenario that had so far been enacted in the setting rather than reflected upon. Various ways of being together could then be explored between client and therapist through these figures whose positions in space could be altered accordingly.

Differentiation and the coming into being of an image

This intervention marked the beginning of a change in the patient/therapist interactions. From then on patient and therapist could work more collaboratively in making imaginary stories about Carlo's pictures. A theme clearly emerged out of these many stories in that they were exploring ideas of togetherness, exchanges and separation between different figures represented in his artwork. Also Carlo took care of his artwork within this space, that he learned to trust more, by placing it in various folders that acquired for him various significances; a folder of spoiled images, one of mythological images and eventually one of autobiographical pictures. Carlo soon recognised that these activities had significance for him and wondered whether the stories made out of the pictures could be a reflection of the dynamics in art therapy. A process of differentiation of the object produced in the session took place enabling the image to stand as a separate object capable of holding imaginary contents, which acquired metaphorical dimensions after approximately two years in therapy.

Discussion

The clinical examples given above reveal the considerable difference and individuality of patients' presentations, and of their means of engagement with the setting and the therapist. In my opinion, although Adam and George were immediately responsive to the physical aspects of the setting brought to their attention by the therapist's interventions, Betty and Carlo, in contrast, appeared to avoid this physical dimension. Rather, Betty and Carlo both persistently escaped the here and now of the art therapy session into a delusional world.

For Carlo the therapist's presence in itself constituted a threat to his world and he defended himself accordingly. By redirecting the focus of attention to the concrete-physical objects of art and the joint making of clay figures the structuring of the patient's world could begin and more reflective processes could take place. His initial failure in achieving communication through verbal language, as a consensual mode of communication, led the therapist to resort to concretely enacting a situation in which Carlo could make choices and formulate demands that could be met. I suggest that this is an example of an intervention that has the effect of re-opening the possibilities for a realm driven by desire and for interpersonal relating in the patient.

Further investigations of these vignettes would reveal the complexity of each clinical situation and of the therapeutic methods applied. In this chapter, however, my focus is primarily on core elements in psychotic patients' presentation and the introduction of the ontological therapeutic method.

Conclusion

The approach that I have described in this chapter was launched by Killick in the 1980s. I was introduced to this therapeutic format by Fiona Foster, when I started working as an art therapist in an 'asylum-type' institution in 1989, before transferring my service to 'community settings' in the mid-1990s. The approach has evolved and adapted to the changing context of NHS services and remains in practice to this day. I have tried to demonstrate the adaptability of this practice through establishing theoretical parallels between the work of Killick and that of Pankow, retaining the most essential elements in Killick's theories and practice of structuring the world of psychotic patients by implementing boundaries as a prerequisite condition for the restoration of ego function, in the light of Pankow's concept of a re-construction of the body image. I have introduced Pankow's concept of body image as a useful means of understanding psychotic dynamics and of devising adapted therapeutic methods involving the physicality of the art therapy space and images primarily at the level of their 'first symbolising function', conceptualised as form. I hope through this chapter, and through my references, to draw attention to well established approaches in art therapy that are based upon aspects, which I refer to as 'ontological'. I would like to close this chapter with an open question as to whether this approach, focusing upon the physicality of space and art material, and primarily upon issues of form in the making of images from which eventually emerge content and meaning, could constitute an art therapy ontology as a whole, beyond the field of the human experiences described in this chapter.

Notes

1 'Being-in-the-World' or 'Being-here' are translations of Heidegger's concept of 'Dasein' (1962). Hyphens in the spelling refer to Sartrian existentialism (1943) emphasising the indelible link between the being and the world, which exist in 'an embrace' (Merleau-Ponty 1945) and in correlation to one another.

2 My comment about an implicit becoming of the image, and thus of its creator, applies a principle developed by Merleau-Ponty (1945) who described in his 'phenomenology of perception' an interrelatedness between our body and the world brought to our awareness through sensorial perceptions, and reciprocally, contacts with the world give rise to our sense of being. The image becoming for its creator a separate object would entail that its creator in the process would become a more separate person.

3 The word 'ontology' is etymologically rooted in ancient Greek, meaning sciences of the being. It is commonly used in existential philosophy to address general, immutable given in human existence (in contrast with aspects which are specific to each

individual), such as those of 'being-in-the-world' and of our embodiment. In the context of this chapter I apply this concept to the immutability of a specifically furbished space, including art materials, for art therapy to take place and through which participants may experience their most fundamental therapeutic contacts.

4 This factual dimension of the body that takes an interpretive role of the intersubjective body image is evocative of the specular image of Lacan's mirror stage (1966). Although Lacan described as 'jubilation' the discovery in the mirror of a unity of a body previously experienced in pieces, he also emphasised the confusing effect of such a discovery, particularly when the infant's fragmentary experiences of the body have been too intense, as in the case of the patients described in this chapter. I suggest that Pankow's therapeutic methods with severely psychotic patients could be perceived and summarised as a forerunner of recognition and greater acceptance of a specular image of the body and of its outline.

5 I would like to acknowledge here other areas of human experiences where such dissociations occur, although momentarily. Pankow (1981) referred to the testimony of victims of torture having momentarily dissociated from their body under severe beating. Also, further remote from our immediate interest in this chapter, mystical trances and initiation rituals in tribal cultures are known to be means of inducing dissociation from an earthly body in order to rejoin the divine or spirit worlds.

6 Here Pankow re-asserts her belief that conventional psychoanalytical methods fail to provide efficient therapeutic means in the treatment of most severely psychotic disorders. She found her theoretical complement in 'ontological philosophy' (2004), including Merleau-Ponty's phenomenology that emphasises the role of the body in the construction of a spatiotemporal world and of its centrality in the becoming of the subject.

References

Anzieu, D. (1974). *'La peau, du plaisir à la pensée'*. In *L'attachement,* Neuchatel: Delachaux et Niestle.

Armstrong-Perlman, E.M. (1995). 'Psychosis: The sacrifice that fails?' in Elwood, J. (ed.) *Psychosis: Understanding and Treatment.* London: Jessica Kingsley.

Aulagnier, P., Castoriadis (1975). *La violence de l'interpretation*, Paris: Presses Universitaires de France.

Balint, M. (1989). *The basic fault*, London: Tavistock/Routledge.

Bell, D.L. (1995). 'Knowledge and its pretenders: Bion's contribution to knowledge and thought' in Elwood, J. (ed.) *Psychosis: Understanding and Treatment*, London: Jessica Kingsley.

Bion, W.R. (1957). 'Differentiation of the psychotic from the non-psychotic personalities'. *International Journal of Psycho-Analysis*, 38.

Bion, W.R. (1977). 'Learning from experience' in Bion, W.R., *Laing Servants*, New York: Jason Aronson.

Bick, E. (1968). 'The experience of the skin in early object-relations.' *International Journal of Psycho-Analysis*, 49, 484.

Corradi Fuimara, G. (2007). 'Self formation, symbolic capacity, and spontaneity' in Ambrosio, G., Arigentieri, S. and Canestri, J. (eds.), *Language, Symbolisation, and Psychosis*, London: Karnac.

Dolto, F. (1984). *'L'image inconsciente du corps'*, Paris: Seuil.

Foster, F. (1997). 'Fear of three dimensionality: Clay and plasticine as experimental bodies' in Killick, K. and Schaverien, J. (eds.) *Art, Psychotherapy and Psychosis*, London: Routledge, pp. 52–71.

Freud, S. (1914). 'On narcissism: An introduction', in *Metapsychology and Theory of Psychoanalysis*, Standard Edition II, Middlesex, UK: Penguin Books.

Freud, S. (1920). 'Repetition compulsion' in *Beyond the Pleasure Principle*, Standard Edition 18, Middlesex, UK: Penguin Books.

Freud, S. (1923). *The ego and the id*. Eastford, USA: Martino Fine Books (reprinted in 2011).

Heidegger, M. (1962). *Being and time* (translated by J.Macquarrie and E.S. Robinson). London: Harper and Row, 1962.

Killick, K. (1987). 'Art therapy and schizophrenia: A new approach' (unpublished MA thesis), Hertfordshire College of Art and Design.

Killick, K. (1991). 'The practice of art therapy with patients in acute psychotic states', London: *Inscape*, Winter 1991.

Killick, K. (1995a). 'Working with psychotic processes in the art therapy' in Elwood, J. (ed.) *Psychosis: Understanding and Treatment*, London: Jessica Kingsley.

Killick, K (1995b). 'The evolution of the symbolic in art therapy with patients in psychotic states of mind', paper given at a conference on 2 September 1995, *Theoretical Advances in Art Therapy*, at Warwick University.

Killick, K (2000). 'The art room as container in analytical art psychotherapy with patients in psychotic states', in Gilroy, A and McNeilly, G. (eds.) *The Changing Shape of Art Therapy: New Developments in Theory and Practice*, London and Philadelphia: Jessica Kingsley.

Klein, M. (1946). 'Notes on some schizoid mechanisms', *International Journal of Psycho-Analysis*, 27.

Lacan, J. (1966). *Ecrits*, Paris: Seuil.

Laing, R.D. (1960). *The divided self*, London: Tavistock Publications (1959) Limited.

Merleau-Ponty, M. (1945). *Phénoménologie de la perception*, Paris: Gallimard.

Merleau-Ponty, M. (1964). *Le visible et l'invisible*, Paris: Gallimard.

Ogden, T.H. (1994). 'The analytical third: working with intersubjective clinical facts', *International Journal of Psycho-Analysis*, 75:1.

Pankow, G. (1961). 'Dynamic structurization in schizophrenia', in *Psychotherapy of the Psychoses*, in Burton, A. (ed), New York: Basic Books, Inc.

Pankow, G, (1981). 'Psychotherapy: A psychoanalytic approach. An analytic approach employing the concept of the "body image"', in M. Dongier and E. Wittkower (eds.) *Divergent Views in Psychiatry*, New York: Harper and Row.

Pankow, G. (1993). *L'homme et sa psychose*, Paris: Flammarion, coll. 'Champs'.

Pankow, G. (2004). *Structure familiale et psychose*, Paris: Flammarion, coll. 'Champs'.

Pankow, G. (2006). *L'être-là du schizophrène*, with an introduction by Dr. Juliette Favez-Boutonier (1956), Paris: Flammarion, coll. 'Champs'.

Pankow, G. (2010). *Structuration dynamique dans la psychose. Contribution à la psychothérapie analytique*, Paris: Campagne Première.

Sartre, J-P. (1943). *Being and nothingness: An essay on phenomenological ontology* (translated by Hazel E. Barnes), New York: Philosophical Library, 1956.

Schaverien, J. (1991). *The revealing image: Analytical art psychotherapy in theory and practice,* London and New York: Routledge.

Schaverien, J. (1997). 'Transference and transactional objects in the treatment of psychosis' in Killick, K. and Schaverien, J. (eds.) *Art, Psychotherapy and Psychosis,* London and New York: Routledge, Taylor and Francis Group, pp. 13–38.

Schuff, H. (1982). 'Dynamic body building', in unpublished papers presented in a two day conference, *Art and Drama Therapy*, at University of Hertfordshire School of Art and Design.

Sechehaye, M.A. (1950). *Journal d'une schizophrénie,* Paris: P.U.F.

Segal, H. (1981). *The work of Hanna Segal*, New York: Aronson.

Segal, H. (1989). *Klein.* The Institute of Psycho-Analysis, London: Karnac Books.

Winnicott, D.W. (1985). *Playing and reality*, London: Pelican Books.

5

A LACANIAN PERSPECTIVE ON ART THERAPY WITH PSYCHOTIC PATIENTS

Rafael Cohen

This chapter aims to share insights and understandings that have developed during the author's work as an art therapist in a psychiatric setting that can be considered typical of those available to people experiencing psychosis in the USA. The author has found that the work of French psychoanalyst Jacques Lacan (1901–81) provides many useful footholds in approaching the question of art therapy with psychotic patients, although his work did not explicitly address art therapy.

The author intends to show that Lacanian psychoanalysis has much to contribute to understanding the value of art therapy as an approach to psychosis. It will begin with a discussion of general considerations concerning psychosis, including differences between the psychiatric and the psychoanalytic perspective, symbolic functioning in psychosis in general, and the relation to language in particular. These issues will then be examined from a Lacanian perspective, and various formulations specific to the Lacanian tradition, both theoretical and clinical, will be introduced, followed by an exploration of how the practice of art therapy with psychotic patients can be informed and influenced by this model of psychoanalysis.

In conclusion, it will be proposed that art therapy, understood and practised using a Lacanian model, offers a unique approach to working with psychotic patients that places a high priority on the unique subjectivity of their experience, and it will be argued that this constitutes an ethical way of working with the complexities of the clinical picture.

Other writers have also worked towards integrating Lacan's ideas with art therapy. Joy Schaverien (1997) used Lacan to elaborate some of the ways in which the relationship with the art object can help the therapist to understand the transference. Fiona Seth-Smith (1997) speculatively applied Lacanian linguistic theory to her work with images in an effort to expand the concept of the image within art therapy. Mavis Himes (2013) worked on moving beyond the dichotomy between art-based and verbal approaches to therapy and discussed how art therapy can address that which cannot be symbolised. The French group 'Insistance' has also been working with a range of questions about art and creativity in relation to Lacanian psychoanalysis. To my knowledge, however, the Lacanian perspective on psychosis has not previously been brought together with art therapy.

Terminology

The term 'psychosis' can be used very differently depending on the context. Most often it indicates a break with a certain understanding of consensual reality, for example psychosis might imply an experience of delusions or hallucinations. However, mental illness is an area of study that sustains widespread debate across a variety of overlapping professional and lay contexts. This can lead to difficulties in specifying the usage of the relevant terms. For example, from the perspective of Lacanian psychoanalysis the term 'psychosis' is a diagnosis, in that it describes the psychic structure of a patient. Within the medical discourse used by psychiatry, 'psychosis' is often used not as a diagnosis but as a symptom or a sign linked to a wide range of possible diagnoses, as well as a diagnosis in itself. Using the most popular diagnostic texts, the 'DSM' and the 'ICD',[1] psychosis may play a role in a number of diagnoses, for example: Major Depressive Disorder, Bipolar Disorder, and Schizophrenia. Psychosis might even be seen as secondary to a medical condition such as a traumatic brain injury or an endocrine condition like hypothyroidism. The medical discourse addresses psychosis primarily in terms of descriptions of subjective experience and observable behaviours, whereas a more psychoanalytic perspective on psychosis emphasises psychic structure, and dynamic internal processes.

There is another issue present within the questions of terminology, and that is whether the underpinnings of psychosis are understood in biological terms, or in social and psychological terms. As indicated by Yrjo Alanen, this controversy has a 'long history' (2009: 3) and his writing describes important milestones in that history. Despite much research, there appear to be no definite answers in this area, and it seems impossible to deny that both perspectives have some validity. With the understanding that the term psychosis can be used in such different ways, it is important to make clear that for the purposes of this chapter, the term will be used in a way that is closely aligned with the psychoanalytic perspective. Like Alanen, I believe that: 'successful therapeutic work with such patients requires intimate examination and knowledge of their personality development, family environment, and current problems' (2009: 8).

Treatment approaches and their relation to subjectivity

These different theoretical perspectives also lead to different treatment approaches. There is a way of practising psychiatry that is sometimes called 'biological psychiatry' (Vanheule 2012: 135), which is predicated on the assumption that mental disorders are primarily brain diseases. Within this model, psychosis is assumed to be an outcome of physical processes that are (or someday will be) measurable, and this leads accordingly to the perspective that chemical and biological treatments are the most valuable and the most appropriate.

If mental disorder is seen as brain disease, pure and simple, then the patient's history, words and ideas become accordingly less relevant. Psychoanalysis, on the other hand, has long focused on environmental factors, both past and present, as well as acknowledging 'the profound significance of the content of [psychotic] symptoms' (cited in Silver 2002: 49), whereas biological psychiatry is not concerned with meaning in individual delusions. The images and words generated by a patient during an art therapy session provide an opportunity to explore exactly that area of human subjectivity and personal meaning, which, according to Vanheule, is excluded by a biological reductionist model. If these areas are taken into account in treating a psychotic patient, then a space remains open for the possibility of radically different ways of being in the world. The psychotherapist who is able to tolerate and respect these differences can appreciate and work with the truly individual nature of those who pass through his or her practice.

All psychiatrists are individual subjects with different priorities and many of course engage in a deep and attentive listening to the subjectivity of their patients. Furthermore, psychotropic medications can be extremely helpful and even essential, and in many circumstances can allow for the possibility of beginning psychotherapeutic forms of treatment, including art therapy. In practice these clinical perspectives, along with other variations and combinations, frequently work well together in many treatment settings.

There are also important differences between treatment approaches that are focused on psychotherapeutic techniques. One of the issues in question is the role of the therapist, especially with regard to providing verbal interpretations to the patient. When working with a patient diagnosed with schizophrenia, Hanna Segal wrote of her intention 'not to step out of the role of the analyst who interprets, into that of an ally or an educator' (1950: 268). Segal also wrote of her work: 'It will be seen that the analytical technique I used was different in many important respects from the technique used and described by the American analysts ... that the analyst must not give interpretations that would introduce into consciousness any new unconscious material' (1950: 277). This comment illustrates the diversity of treatment approaches even within an area as specific as psychoanalysis.

Harold Searles also wrote in detail about the verbal interpretations that were the therapist's 'task' (1963: 253), but it is clear from his writing that this is indicated only conditionally, at a later point in the process of therapy and after other factors have been established. Likewise for art therapy, Katherine Killick described a transitional moment in her work with a psychotic patient: 'Until this point it was unnecessary for me to explore the content and meaning of his images in order to be of service to a therapeutic process, and I think that an attempt to do so would have been experienced as extremely persecuting' (1997: 49). After the moment in question the patient is able to use an image to communicate with her. The possibility that certain types of interventions might be damaging or problematic for psychotic patients is shared by a variety of clinical approaches and will be addressed to a greater degree below.

Pamela Fuller described two modes of intervention: 'fortifying' and 'uncovering' (2013: 15). Fortifying is an intervention with the goal of making a patient feel safer and uncovering is seen as approaching unconscious material and encouraging the expression of affect. She describes the importance of finding a balance between these modes of intervention when working with psychotic patients. With regard to determining the right moment, she wrote of 'the importance of carefully dosing the intensity and nature of ... interventions based on the individual's ... status' (2013: 10).

Another important distinction between treatment approaches is the relation to the symptom. Fuller has written: 'Often, treatment professionals assume that reduction of hallucinations and delusions is a goal of intervention that is shared by the client. However, it should not be automatically assumed that the person wishes to eliminate voices or change a delusional belief' (2013: 17). One person might hear voices which are persecutory and frightening, but another might find the voices they hear to be comforting. Fuller's approach here clearly takes the subjectivity of the patient into account.

Symbolic functioning in psychosis

There is an area of consensus in understanding, regardless of theoretical perspective, which is that one significant feature of psychosis is a certain impairment in symbolic functioning. In order to examine the implications of this idea, I will now look in more detail at symbols. Most basically, a symbol can be defined as a thing which stands in for, or represents, a different thing. The thing being represented is not present, and in fact Susan Deri described the essence of a symbol as the 'presence of an absence' (1984: 48). This definition evokes the etymology of the word *symbol*, from the Greek *symbolon*, referring to a type of token of identity made from one of two halves, which was then verified by comparison with its other half. Thus the theme of absence and lack is associated with the essential nature of symbols.

Segal's work extends this concept of absence and evokes the experience of loss in connection with the use of symbols. When describing the concept of Symbolic Equation, a primitive version of symbol formation which is associated generally, although not exclusively, with psychosis, Segal wrote that in Symbolic Equation 'the symbol is equated with the thing symbolised. The symbol does not represent the object, but is treated as though it was the object ... The symbol is used to overcome an accepted loss' (1978: 316). In order to truly use symbols, and to approach our full potential in this regard, one must in some sense acknowledge or mourn the loss of the thing being represented. Wilfred Bion (1970), perhaps similarly to Segal, delineated a kind of overactive but diluted symbol formation process in psychotic patients—increased in quantity but decreased in quality. Searles wrote that in schizophrenia there was a 'lack of differentiation' (1962: 23) between concrete and symbolic, and thus both genuinely symbolic thinking and genuinely concrete thinking were to some degree inaccessible for those patients.

Within the medical discourse psychosis is often associated with an overemphasis on concrete thinking, and complementary deficits in abstract thinking. One who is limited to concrete thinking is understood to have difficulties generalising and using abstract concepts. In assessments used by psychologists and psychiatrists, patients may be asked to give the meaning of proverbs in an attempt to determine their ability to engage in metaphorical thinking. A patient might be asked to explain what is meant by the statement 'the grass is always greener on the other side of the fence' and if the patient is unable to move beyond concrete thinking, their answer might involve fences, or the colour green, as opposed to an abstract understanding of the concept of idealisation. Although concrete thinking is not precisely the opposite of symbolic thinking, this aspect of psychiatric assessment indicates a link between all the disciplines in question.

The unquantifiable

The very wide variety of mental health disciplines are all in some form or another descendants of the discourse of science, but some are closer to this lineage than others. Art therapy and psychoanalysis can be brought together in a way that allows for a significant departure from the specific limitations of the medical discourse and its roots in the discourse of science. This chapter describes a clinical practice in which a space can be maintained for the mysterious and unpredictable truth being presented by the patient. By avoiding the pitfalls associated with quantification and generalisation, it is possible to sustain a certain respect for the profound individuality of the subjectivity of each patient.

The contribution of art therapy is significant for many reasons, not least of which is its relation to symbolic phenomena. Art therapy is a form of psychotherapy that makes use of the process and product of art-making activities and the verbal communications around those activities, as well as the relationship with the practitioner. These phenomena and interventions inherently have the capacity to move beyond the concrete and call into play a relation with the symbolic. All clinical disciplines have the potential to intervene towards psychotic patients in a way that respects their subjective experience but art therapy is specifically situated to address the vital concern of symbolic functioning, for which there is no unit of measure.

In the context of work with psychotic patients, art therapy proposes to provide 'practice in symbolizing, by making visual images' and can help patients 'develop the ability to symbolize' in situations where this ability is impaired, especially 'when using language is too difficult—or too frightening' (Wilson 2001: 47). The function of art-making and, more specifically, the relationship between verbal productions and art productions is a complex and important issue which will be addressed in more detail in this chapter. Killick provided a valuable perspective on precisely this question: 'The pre-verbal thinking functions involved in the creative use of visual image-making can contain and transform the raw material of experience within the therapeutic relationship, paving the way for symbolisation' (1993: 30). Referring to the work of post-Kleinian psychoanalyst Wilfred Bion, Killick also implied one of the features inherent to art therapy and psychoanalysis, which is the capacity to work with phenomena that are not directly knowable, observable or measurable. In my opinion the therapist must be able to acknowledge a lack in their own ability to completely understand a patient if there is to be space for psychosis as a complex human experience.

Lacan and language

The issues discussed above will now be revisited with specific reference to the work of Jacques Lacan. In doing so, this chapter will attempt to offer a model of Lacanian psychoanalysis that is relatively accessible. The material included here is necessarily simplified to some degree for reasons of clarity and succinctness, despite the complexity of the theory in question. Lacan's work evolved continuously and significantly during his career, with work being presented throughout a period of almost 50 years, and during that time his theories developed to such a degree that later work can be interpreted as contradicting earlier work. This chapter will certainly not attempt to integrate all of Lacanian theory. This writing will instead provide an introduction to several aspects of Lacan's work that readers can continue to examine in more detail if they find value there.

The human relationship to language is prioritised within the work of Lacan. In fact, it is prioritised to such a degree that linguistic phenomena are perceived in many aspects of psychic life that might not be seen as language-based in any obvious way for other theorists. He believed, for example, that the most central of the phenomena proposed by the psychoanalytic discourse, the unconscious, was 'structured like a language' (Lacan 1955–56: 167). Lacan's prioritisation of language might be seen as an obstacle to an effort at integration with art therapy, wherein language and image must share the spotlight. Although psychoanalysis, particularly Lacanian psychoanalysis, is first and foremost the 'talking cure', in my view there are clear paths towards bridging these two areas. Darian Leader has applied Lacanian theory not to art therapy but to art theory and criticism, and using his work an important link can be made. He wrote that 'our immersion in the visual world is guided by language' (2002: 111). Thus the sheer ubiquity of linguistic phenomena within Lacanian theory allows for the possibility that art therapy can take part in the therapeutic transformations he described.

There is a set of linguistic concepts called the 'signifier' and the 'signified' used within Lacanian theory. These are seen as the basic units of language and meaning and are closely linked with Lacan's ideas about the Symbolic. The signifier is the 'acoustic image' of a sound (Evans 1996: 186) and the signified is the corresponding psychological image linked to that signifier. Simplistically stated, it could be said that the signifier is the word and the signified is the meaning, however there are many different ways of describing the signifier within Lacan's work and the signifier is not only a spoken word. Leader wrote that an artwork is 'like speech' (2002: 120) insofar as it represents us to others, and that 'viewing it as a work of art makes it a signifier' (2002: 121). This perspective allows further advances towards an integration of Lacan's linguistic work with art therapy. For Lacan the signified is somewhat inaccessible and the signifier is prioritised and is what leads us in our work.

Lacanian theory holds that there is an impairment in symbolic functioning which is inherent to psychosis. Although there are important differences, this is a link with the work of Segal, Bion, and Searles, mentioned above. Lacan specifically recognized language difficulties as the primary manifestation of this symbolic impairment: 'If the neurotic inhabits language, the psychotic is inhabited, possessed, by language' (1955–56: 250). This evocative aphorism is a way of addressing an aspect of the radical difference that marks the psychotic subject's relation to the world.

There is a further commonality between the general psychoanalytic perspective on symbols and Lacan's work, which is the idea that symbolic functioning comes only at the cost of a certain experience of loss. In linguistic terms this means that in order to more fully use language we must all lose something of the immediacy of our experience. By using language to symbolise experience, one is submitting to a socially constructed system and accepting a lack of control over others' understanding of one's words. For Lacan, the loss associated with the symbolic is seen as particularly unassimilable for the psychotic subject. The degree to which this loss is not assimilated by the psychotic subject correlates with the appearance of neologisms, highly idiosyncratic speech, and other language difficulties that are sometimes seen in psychosis.

The symbolic order

In order to develop the Lacanian understanding of the impairment in symbolic functioning that is present in psychosis, it is necessary to explore the concept of the Symbolic Order. Lacan divided the field of psychic reality into three registers or orders of experience: the Imaginary, the Symbolic and the Real. The Symbolic Order is associated with the law, social structure, signifiers, language, and the unconscious. It has many aspects, as it must, being one of only three categories designed to encompass all of psychic life. Only the Symbolic Order will be addressed in this chapter and the focus will be further limited to only the few aspects of the Symbolic Order as they are relevant to the present discussion.[2]

Although there is some overlap, Lacan's concept of the Symbolic Order is not synonymous with what is commonly referred to as symbolism. Frederic Jameson has written: '...we would be tempted to suggest that the Lacanian Symbolic Order be considered as having nothing to do with symbols or with symbolism whatsoever in the conventional sense' (2003: 12). Lacan's Symbolic Order is distinct from attempts at universalisation that manifest in such forms as dictionaries of symbolism. Instead the Symbolic Order concerns the specificities of the individual patient's relationship with language and society. Vanheule wrote that whereas certain psychoanalytic perspectives maintain that 'symbols, as they appear in dreams for example, have standard meanings that can be decoded, Lacan stresses the contextual determination of meaning' (2011: 40).

Sigmund Freud describes the interpretation of dreams as the 'royal road to a knowledge of the unconscious activities of the mind' (1900: 608), and dreams are, for Lacanians, an important manifestation of Symbolic Order phenomena. In order to further clarify the distinction between conventional symbolism and Lacan's Symbolic Order, one can look to Freud's distinction between the manifest and the latent content of dreams. In The Interpretation of Dreams Freud described the manifest content of the dream as requiring a particular kind of interpretation in order to be properly understood. 'If we attempted to read these characters according to their pictorial value ... we should clearly be led into error' (1900: 277). I believe Freud is using the phrase 'pictorial value' to indicate a kind of universal that is linked with what Jameson refers to as symbolism 'in the conventional sense' (a bee as a symbol of a worker, or a queen bee as a symbol of royalty). Freud also gives the example of a rebus (1900: 278), in which a dream image of a bee might not represent a bee at all, but in fact a word (be) or even a syllable of a larger word (for example: be-neath, or be-gin, or be-tray). What is essential about these signifiers is that they are representatives of unconscious processes that leave traces which may become accessible by listening to the words of the patient.

In the context of art therapy, one could imagine that a patient created an image of a suit of armour during a session. Symbolism in the conventional sense might indicate to the therapist that the patient feels a need for some form of protection, or that there is an experience of aggression, or a kind of battle brewing. However, according to the logic of the Symbolic Order, the patient's associations are the most important thing, and they will undoubtedly lead in unexpected directions. The word 'armour' might refer to a book about knights that belonged to the patient's grandfather and thereby indicate concerns about lineage or other family-related issues, or the patient's associations might point to the fact that the word *armour* contains the word *arm*, which in its turn leads to the idea of a tattoo that the patient is contemplating having inscribed on her/his arm, and the proposed meaning of that tattoo. This also provides an example of how signifiers refer to other signifiers along a signifying chain (armour > arm > tattoo). This chain lays out before us the path of Lacan's Symbolic Order via the odd, linguistic elements of unconscious communication that emerge in the patient's unique associations.

It is precisely this kind of functioning that falls into question in psychosis. Danielle Bergeron wrote that, for the psychotic subject, 'signifiers ... will not fully chain' (Apollon, W., Bergeron, D. and Cantin, L. 2002: 78). Symbolic functioning is deeply linked with signifiers, and according to Lacan, those diagnosed as psychotic are essentially excluded from the Symbolic Order of experience (Evans 1996: 156).

Diagnosis

The Lacanian tradition uses a system of diagnosis which calls into question certain ideas about classification and labelling. Leader wrote that using labels in certain ways 'eclipses the creative, positive aspect of psychotic phenomena' (2011: 8), and the model proposed here attempts to preserve those positive qualities.

Whereas psychiatry produces a vast number of diagnoses, Lacan developed a system that contained only three main diagnoses: Psychosis, Neurosis, and Perversion.[3] Although normality is a concept whose value was ardently questioned and even undermined by Lacan, Neurosis is not distinguished from normality within the Lacanian diagnostic system (Evans 1996: 123). In other words, it is the most common psychic structure. Lacan's way of thinking may seem simple because of the smaller number of diagnoses when compared to the DSM or the ICD, but it is not simple in practice, and in fact it offers something unique.[4] The small number of diagnoses sharply defines the extent to which diagnosis is actually useful. Lacanian diagnosis is not meant to encapsulate everything important about the patient or their symptoms, and the process of diagnosis is de-prioritised by the smaller number of classificatory options. By its inherent structure the Lacanian model confronts the clinician with the irreducible singularity of the patient and directs the clinician's resources towards working with and respecting this uniqueness. By encouraging the clinician to wrestle with the impossibility of fully knowing the other, this system avoids an overemphasis on categorisation which could undermine respect for the patient. By drawing the focus away from similarities between patients the way is opened for a focus on difference, and for the consideration of the patient's individuality.

My experience of the culture of Lacanian analysis is that analysts frequently disagree about the diagnosis of particular patients in clinical case presentations, which mitigates against becoming fossilised in a position of 'knowledge'. If a fellow psychoanalyst calls into question the diagnosis proposed for a patient, and puts up a very good argument, then it is that much more likely the presenting analyst will listen to the patient even more carefully next time. Although some of these qualities may also be present in the work of other clinical cultures, whether psychiatric or psychodynamic, the Lacanian tradition offers explicit mandates against taking on a position of rigid expertise in order to more firmly establish a position of respect for the patient through a practice of listening.

The current perspective of Lacanian diagnostics also includes the concept of 'ordinary psychosis' in which a person may have what is essentially a psychotic structure that has never been triggered and thus has never developed into an observable psychotic episode. These people may never require psychiatric hospitalisation because they do not exhibit obvious, explicit symptoms and they might have the ability to get along very well in society, despite any odd beliefs they harbour. Likewise, there are patients who exhibit significant and disruptive symptoms, including those requiring hospitalisation, yet who may not fall into the Lacanian diagnostic category of psychosis, despite a DSM diagnosis of schizophrenia.

Psychosis

Lacan's early work indicated less ambiguously that psychotic patients simply had no access to the Symbolic Order, and thus created a more rigid distinction between psychotic and non-psychotic. This clear demarcation, while convenient for describing and discussing psychosis, is problematic. It is perhaps more accurate in practice to allow for variations in capacity along a continuum as opposed to a simple threshold between access to the Symbolic Order and no access to the Symbolic Order. After all, we each carry our own idiosyncratic relationship to language and social structure, although for neurotic subjects the idiosyncrasies are relegated to the background.

The clarity of the dividing line between neurosis and psychosis is an open question, still debated in Lacanian circles. Bruce Fink wrote:

> ... in [Lacan's] later work (from approximately 1973 to 1981), ... Rather than say that there is no genuinely symbolic dimension ... in psychosis, he postulated that while all three dimensions—imaginary, symbolic, and real—are generally present in psychosis they are not tied together as they are in neurosis and do not operate together in the way that they do in neurosis.
>
> Fink (2007: 262)

In neurosis, for example, a person who has an unusual bodily experience, such as urinary incontinence, might feel ashamed. The body is typically associated with the Imaginary Order, and for the purposes of this example, the experience of shame is tied to the Symbolic Order in the sense that incontinence represents loss of control. In psychosis the same urinary incontinence might be experienced as completely unembarrassing and easily forgotten because there is little or no integration between the areas of Imaginary and Symbolic, and there is no link from incontinence to the experience of loss of control. Thus, according to later Lacanian theory, the lack of coordination between the three Orders does not mean that there is no aspect of psychic experience that remains within the Symbolic Order for psychotic patients. In fact, there is, but it is experienced differently, and there are difficulties in integrating it with its counterparts. Although there are limitations to the ability of psychotic patients to use one thing to represent another, the ability to use symbols is not completely absent either in the conventional sense or within Lacan's terminology.

For a person with a neurotic structure, there is a flexibility in the relationship between words and their meanings. Certain identical sounds can mean different things in different contexts, and familiar words can develop new meanings. This flexibility is limited by certain points of stability that are lacking, however, within the psychotic structure. This is a part of what Lacan was describing when he wrote that 'in psychotic experience ... the signifier and the signified present themselves in a completely divided form' (1955–56: 268). The Symbolic Order is thus inaccessible for the psychotic patient in the specific sense that there is 'an inability ... to see several different meanings in one and the same portion of speech' (Fink 2007: 240). Similar observations are to be found in the work of Harold Searles. His extensive psychoanalytic work with patients diagnosed with schizophrenia led him to describe a patient who is able, only after years of work, to communicate in metaphorical as well as literal terms and to see 'both levels of meanings in his own comments' (1962: 31).

The inflexibility of the relationship between the signifier and the signified is relevant to the work of art therapy. Whereas in neurosis the patient might speak or create artwork and then discover other meanings within their production (signifier and signified are linked in an ambiguous and shifting way, with points of stability), the psychotic patient knows exactly what s/he means and can be limited by the certainty of her/his experience.[5] Taking into account Leader's idea (cited above) that viewing an image as a work of art makes it a signifier, one can begin to describe a space that exists between the creation of a work of art and its reception. This space is threatened by certainty but sustained by the ambiguity which is essential to symbolic functioning in the Lacanian sense.

For the acutely psychotic patient, the existence of this space is in doubt because in psychosis there is nothing absent, there are no limits, and there can be no question about the reception of meaning: 'There is no room for error or misinterpretation: the meaning of experience is self-evident' (Fink 1997: 84). In acute psychosis idiosyncratic functioning becomes prioritised over consensual reality and shared social functioning which would allow the space for questioning and reinterpretation. As an art therapist, when working with neurotic patients, one naturally sustains an area of unknown associated with the signifier a patient produces; for example, a tree. There is a space set aside for whatever meaning that tree has for that particular patient at that particular time. But for the psychotic patient the tree may be 'just a tree' or may very specifically, idiosyncratically, and unalterably represent something else, for example, evil spirits, as was the case with a patient I worked with. This young man was driven to tear the branches from the trees in his surroundings, reporting the presence of demons he felt compelled to remove. He came into conflict with his neighbours and with the law repeatedly due to these actions. Part of his work in art therapy was to create new ways to represent the forces he was wrestling with.

Art-work

Although it is not synonymous with art therapy, there is a concept within Lacanian theory that covers some common ground, called the 'sinthome'. This is a phenomenon by which a patient can use creative efforts in order to construct a stabilising force in their life that prevents or mitigates more acute psychotic episodes. Fink described the sinthome by saying that an 'artistic endeavour ... or otherwise creative activity' (2007: 263) can be retroactively hypothesised to have prevented a psychotic episode in a patient with a psychotic structure. The sinthome can be the very thing that holds together the orders of the Imaginary, Symbolic, and Real in situations where they threaten to come apart.[6] In fact, the classic example of the sinthome given by Lacan in his 1975 seminar about the work of James Joyce specifically takes the form of an artistic expression.

The concept of the sinthome can also be linked with a certain stereotype of the artist as a 'mad genius' whose creativity is awe-inspiring and whose desperate commitment to their project knows no bounds. Informal examples are easy to summon, such as Vincent Van Gogh, Salvador Dali, Andy Warhol, and Jackson Pollock. In fact, it may be more accurate to say that in the case of artists whose work constitutes a sinthome, the underlying statement or construction is not even addressed to the audience of the wider world, but is instead a statement that the artist is compelled to create, and one which stabilises their own experience of the world. The stereotype fits prolific artists who were in some way disengaged with the priorities of the society around them in order to dedicate their energies to projects that sustained them on another level.

It should be stated that the project of the sinthome is not one that every psychotic patient will be able to undertake or carry through. Not every patient has the creative powers of James Joyce, nor a specific set of circumstances and motivations comparable to his. However Lacan clearly describes the potential stabilising effects of creative efforts for the psychotic subject. Although the sinthome is not something one can expect from all patients, it may be one outcome of the patient's involvement in art therapy. The theoretical concept offers us a path in terms of directing an art therapy treatment for psychotic patients and a place to continue working on the theoretical integration of Lacanian psychoanalysis and art therapy.

Séraphine

The 2008 film *Séraphine* provides an excellent example of the sinthome, as well as of some of the other concepts presented in this chapter. This film is the dramatisation of the real life of a woman named Séraphine Louis who was born in France in 1864. She worked for most of her life as a housekeeper but spent her last years in a mental institution suffering from hallucinations and paranoia. Beyond her work as a housekeeper, she was a committed painter, who apparently worked largely in secret and in isolation. In the film, she reports that she was commanded to paint by the Virgin Mary, and in these efforts her hand was guided by a guardian angel. Although the actual dates for the beginning of her creative efforts are difficult to accurately specify, it would appear that she painted actively for approximately twenty-five years, and in a style that was uniquely her own. Her work was eventually recognised and appreciated by a German art collector, named Wilhelm Uhde, who became her patron. He was also a collector of works by, and patron to, Picasso, Braque and Rousseau and organised exhibitions of their work as well as hers. She became known as Séraphine de Senlis.

Although it is quite impossible to verify a Lacanian diagnosis of psychotic structure in the case of this woman, for the purposes of this chapter, it will be assumed that she was psychotic based on her representation in the film. The possibility of a psychotic structure is strongly indicated by the degree to which she decompensates, in combination with the circumstances surrounding her illness. Her painting is an example of a sinthome because of the purpose it served for her.

The creative efforts in which she engaged appear to have contributed significantly to extending the period of her life during which she was not seen as requiring institutionalisation. Other elements of her experience were certainly at play as they would be in any life, and these may also have contributed to her stabilisation, but her artistic work can be seen as a practice which channelled and embodied important psychic experiences for her. Clearly it was an important aspect of her identity based on the fervour with which she pursued it, and it contained a relation with an ideal, an image with which she apparently wanted to be identified. She selectively pursued public venues for her work and appeared pleased when her patron told her that her paintings were comparable to those of the 'grandes artistes'.

Her particular sinthome was perhaps not strong enough to hold her world together when faced with certain challenges, but for a time it appears to have sustained her and provided her with a central project that was in no way antithetical to society. There were almost certainly other protective factors beyond her painting, possibly including her frequent isolation and her long hours at work as a housekeeper, which can be deduced based on the timing of her decline; when these were no longer present in her life she became increasingly unstable. Another element contributing to her decline appears to be her encounter with phenomena of the Symbolic Order. It can be extremely destabilising for a patient who has no access to the Symbolic Order to be confronted with experiences that unequivocally refer to it.

Mr. Uhde took a position with respect to Séraphine that was unmistakably enmeshed with the Symbolic Order. He gave her money and told her he would cause her work to be seen by others based on an intangible value he perceived in her paintings. When the European economy began to decline, he told her he could no longer support her in the way that he previously had. His claims invoke complex social structures and changes therein. He saw a kind of value in her artwork that cannot but involve the Symbolic Order, and his exchange with her was Symbolic. The exchange of money concerns more than just the Symbolic Order, but because it was based on the abstract assessment of her artwork as opposed to the concrete work of cleaning houses, the Symbolic element was emphasised. Séraphine's confrontation with these elements of her experience appears to be one of the factors which contributed to her destabilisation. Her behaviour became increasingly bizarre and disturbing to those around her. She responded to voices no one else could hear, and at a certain critical moment she donned a wedding dress and wandered through the streets giving away many of her most treasured belongings. Her relationship with her patron, as well as the changes it brought about, put her in contact with experiences she may have been unable to integrate. These factors challenged the stabilisation provided by her sinthome and the other protective factors described above. This interaction with Mr. Uhde will serve as an illustration in the discussion of clinical work that follows.

Clinical work

The Lacanian construction of psychosis has been an extremely valuable tool in my work as an art therapist on inpatient psychiatric units. When a clinician has begun to approach a stable understanding of a patient's structural diagnosis within the Lacanian framework, it is possible to extrapolate basic guidelines for working with that patient. According to a Lacanian view, when working with psychotic patients it is essential not to emphasise the underlying content of the material presented. Fink described the psychotic subject's confrontation with the Symbolic as 'trying to have a chess piece land on a certain square on a chess board when that square has simply been cut out of the board' (2007: 249). Taking a position with respect to the patient that would require them to accept the existence of hidden or unconscious layers of meaning in their words, acts, or creations would be tantamount to highlighting the 'hole in the symbolic' (Fink 1997: 101), a position the therapist should avoid. Fink translates Lacan's name for this position as the 'One-father' and says that by taking this position, it is possible to trigger a psychotic break, or worsen a psychotic episode.[7]

The relationship that is introduced by such an intervention can be seen as an attempt to 'triangulate' (Fink 1997: 104) a previously dyadic experience of the world, something which the structure of the psychotic patient cannot tolerate.[8] Lacan invites us to seek 'dramatic encounters with such a One-father at the origin of every psychotic break' (Fink 1997: 106) highlighting again the centrality of the link between symbolic phenomena and psychotic phenomena. For a clinician who is used to only working with neurotic patients, or is not trained to work with psychotic patients, it is easy to find oneself in such a position. It could be something as simple as providing a verbal interpretation of a dream or art product that places the therapist in the position of the One-father.

Unfortunately, many clinicians do something very close to what Lacan advises against, and often with patients who do not have the option of leaving treatment. A clinician may tell a patient that their delusional beliefs are incorrect, or they might say: 'you are hearing voices which are not real, which means that you are schizophrenic, and therefore you should take a certain antipsychotic medication, or undergo a certain kind of psychotherapy.' This is an act which, intentionally or not, explicitly invalidates the experience of the patient and risks confronting the patient with an experience of the Symbolic that destabilises them further. For a variety of reasons, a therapist may wish for the beliefs of the patient to change and indeed to become more in line with the therapist's experience of reality, but this is a position strongly criticised by Lacan when he described the 'infatuation with normalizing analysis' (1966: 328). Lucie Cantin asserted that 'the analyst cannot contest the truth of the psychotic's delusional certainty for the sake of common sense or commonplace reality any more than the analyst may question the psychic reality underlying a neurotic's fantasy' (Apollon, W., Bergeron, D. and Cantin, L. 2002: 95).

Any clinician, of any theoretical orientation, may fall into the trap of imposing their 'knowledge' on a psychotic patient. However, from a Lacanian perspective: '... the clinician must adopt a very different position, intervening not from a place of knowledge and meaning, but, on the contrary, from a point of not knowing: more like a student than a teacher' (Leader 2011: 307). An interpretation from an authoritative position may invoke the Symbolic Order and imply new meaning, and may suddenly outline a role that has no precedent in the history of the psychotic patient whose capacity to metabolise such experiences is poor. Fink has written that: 'The goal with psychotics is to reconstruct meaning, not deconstruct it' (2007: 53), as it might be with a neurotic patient. When working with psychotic patients, the position advised by Lacan, and others who have followed in his tradition, is that of the 'witness' or the 'secretary' to the patient (Nobus 2000: 88).

The therapeutic position described here will help locate Lacanian psychoanalysis in relation to other treatment approaches mentioned above, specifically with regard to the question of interpretation. The position of the 'secretary' is in certain ways significantly more passive than the position of a psychoanalyst or psychotherapist working with neurotic patients, and does not align with Segal's position of providing interpretations (1950). A secretary or a student defers and transcribes; a witness does not contribute to or undermine the narrative they are witnessing. Beyond simply listening and asking explanatory questions, Leader's writing indicates the importance of interventions which aim deeper: 'The therapist has to encourage a process of questioning, acknowledging a point of non-understanding yet avoiding too great a sense of enigma or mystery' (2011: 314).

Although Lacanians do not advocate providing direct interpretations of unconscious material to psychotic patients, we find an indication of the value of more active interventions that are conditional upon previous factors having been established, in the same vein as Searles and Killick, cited above. Fink states that when there is trust between the analyst and patient, and when the analyst has a relatively solid understanding of the patient's life and circumstances, it may be helpful to 'encourage the pursuits of the psychotic analysand that seem to foster stabilization and to discourage those that have often led to considerable conflict' (2007: 250). The Lacanian art therapist can encourage creative work, and in fact, there is a precedent for this in the Lacanian tradition: 'As regards the encouragement of specific outlets … Lacanians have valued the analyst's role as a clinical [patron] for the artistic projects in which patients may indulge' (Nobus 2000: 143).

This alternative position is curious and supportive in the face of psychosis, and Freud very clearly formulated an important reason to listen in this way: 'The delusional formation, which we take to be the pathological product, is in reality an attempt at recovery, a process of reconstruction' (Freud 1911: 71). With this perspective, a clinician's attempt to provide a 'reality check' may in fact be undermining the patient's own attempts at self-cure. Leader wrote that 'delusion is less a problem than a solution' (2011: 70). There is a creative quality to delusional constructions as seen from the Lacanian perspective and they are conceived of as potentially stabilising for the psychotic patient. The potential for the therapeutic action of a treatment is greatly increased if it can be oriented in such a way as to acknowledge the creative value of the work the patient is already doing. Therapeutic treatments that ignore this aspect of the patient's efforts are likely to further alienate the patient.

In order to engage with the subjectivity of the patient it seems most appropriate to create a space in which patients can elaborate their beliefs and their experience, whether through words or images; according to Leader: 'educative and rehabilitative endeavours are set aside in favour of projects of "self-elaboration", in which patients often construct roles for themselves … each psychotic subject's project of restructuring their world must be taken seriously' (2011: 301).

Stabilisation

Darian Leader, using a Lacanian perspective, has outlined a number of specific factors which can be stabilising for the psychotic patient. The notion of adherence to an image is given as an example of a stabilising factor by Leader, and this comes together with the 'construction of an ideal', which is seen as a '… form of restitution, … a particular image gives the person a compass point, an orientation around which to build their life' (2011: 197). The position in question need not be one that is traditionally or widely seen as ideal, and the image of the solitary artist is an example that may be useful for the art therapist to keep in mind. Although solitude may be stabilising for one patient, the ideal image of celebrated and commercially successful artist may be more stabilising for another patient. Neither the solitary nor the celebrated artist is a role that an art therapist should arbitrarily advocate or propose to a patient, but either could be delicately supported or encouraged in cases where such an identity was taking shape and appeared to be a stabilising factor in the patient's experience.

The ideal that stabilises the psychotic patient need not be one that is obviously reachable. In fact, the status of an ideal as unreachable may contribute to its power to stabilise. Leader highlighted the danger of following a normalising path in regard to this type of intervention:

> … the social imperatives to 'achieve' and to 'act' may lead the therapist to encourage the subject to undertake some activity when in fact it is essential to them that it remain forever unrealised, always situated in the future … non-triggered psychoses may remain stable due to an interest in ideals that remain unrealised.
>
> Leader (2011: 297)

As long as the ideal does not fade, and as long as the patient is not required to either take the place of this ideal or have a direct encounter with someone who embodies it, the stabilising effect can be sustained, albeit in a potentially fragile form.

In the context of art therapy and art-related identities specifically, the model described here may indicate the therapeutic value of an intervention such as helping the patient to take steps towards having work exhibited, helping them to research or prepare for increasingly monumental artistic endeavours, or finding or creating venues in which to sell their artwork. The Living Museum, in New

York City, USA, shows work produced by patients at the Creedmoor Psychiatric Centre, and is a compelling example of an intervention which may help patients with this form of stabilisation. Generally, when a certain step has been achieved, it may be in the interest of the therapeutic work to help the patient formulate a new goal in order to preserve the stabilising power of the project by offering a path for a continuation of the patient's efforts and energies.

Leader describes the 'establishment of a logic of exception' (2011: 302) as a stabilising factor. Psychotic subjects often instinctively pursue or identify with a singular role independently of therapeutic intervention.

> Why the ubiquity of this motif of being the exception in psychosis? Whether it's as hero or scapegoat, the subject occupies a special unique place ... They are not so much interested in inflating their ego as they are in simply surviving. And to survive entails creating a singular, indi- vidual space, which is not part of some pre-existing set or group.
>
> Leader (2011: 92)

What better path towards establishing a singular and exceptional position than the creation of artwork? No two artists ever create work in exactly the same way, and it is possible to offer the patient a healthy and productive model into which they can channel their belief that they have something unique to offer the world.

Conclusion

The model of treatment proposed in this chapter may be different from many other kinds of treatment. Current cultural trends champion efficiency in treat- ment, but neither art therapy nor psychoanalysis is a 'quick fix' and a longer treatment may offer more profound results.

Lacanian art therapy aims to avoid a preconceived relation to the symptom. Because certain delusions are seen as stabilising, it is the intention of Lacanian treatments to allow the patient to articulate their symptoms, rather than to sim- ply change or remove delusions. Via this interaction the patient can construct a new relation to their world. 'Therapy can do no more and no less than to help the psychotic subject do what they have been trying to do all their lives: create a safe space in which to live' (Leader 2011: 330).

Lacanians disagree about whether Lacan can be interpreted as indicating that a psychotic structure cannot ever be modified or changed into a neurotic struc- ture (Fink 1997: 82). Some assert that appropriate psychoanalytic intervention can have a significant effect on a psychotic subject at the level of structure. All would agree, however, that significant positive changes can be seen in psychotic patients as a result of modified analytic treatment. According to Laurie Wilson, the result of art therapy treatment in the case of schizophrenic patients can be described as an increase in the capacity for symbolisation (2001: 44). Many of the other writers mentioned above (Bion, Killick, Searles) have written explicitly of an evolution in the symbolising capacities of psychotic patients during treatment. Using Lacanian terms, it is possible to understand these changes in terms of the level of coordination and integration between the three orders (Imaginary, Symbolic and Real) instead of solely as a change in symbolic functioning.

There are many practicing psychoanalysts who use Lacanian theory to support their work with psychotic patients. There is a clinic in Quebec City, colloquially known as the 388, whose treatment goals are described as follows:

> ... treatment at the '388' aims to restore a sphere of subjective psychic activities to patients ... and [enable them to] recapture sufficient control of their personal and social lives that they can take a certain satisfaction from coexistence. The treatment aims to stabilize the delusion and to control the disorganizing effects of the psychosis.
>
> Apollon *et al.* (2002: 17)

Although art therapy is more or less accepted within psychiatric facilities to be an appropriate form of treatment for psychotic patients, its value as a treatment remains to be fully established. This chapter describes a model of art therapy that incorporates theoretical and clinical guidelines extrapolated from Lacanian psychoanalysis, and intends to further clarify the value of such a mode of treatment. Lacanian Psychoanalysis is a method that offers a strong theoretical framework from which to conceptualise the therapeutic action of art therapy. The value of Lacanian art therapy is that it 'creates a space for the expression of the truth of that psychotic [patient]' (Apollon *et al.* 2002: 17). In my opinion this form of expression is essential and has great potential for positive therapeutic change. By constructing meaningful communications, patients working in this way can develop creative projects that engage their attention and energy and bring increasing cohesion and satisfaction. Lacanian art therapy offers the opportunity to respectfully engage with all that is unique and vital about an individual human subject.

Notes

1 The Diagnostic and Statistical Manual of Mental Disorders (DSM) is the authoritative text on psychiatric diagnosis in the United States, and it is also influential elsewhere in the world. The International Statistical Classification of Diseases (ICD) is another diagnostic tool, more wide-ranging than the DSM, but also including psychiatric diagnoses.
2 The other orders in brief: The Imaginary is the realm of images, body-image, mirror-like equivalencies of perfect understanding, and of idealisation that develops into rivalry. The Real is distinct from reality, and is linked with trauma and anxiety, and is characterised by that which is impossible to symbolise.
3 There are also sub-categories within the diagnoses he defined, such as obsessional neurosis and hysterical neurosis, melancholic psychosis and paranoid psychosis. Because this chapter is not designed to provide an in-depth exploration of Lacanian diagnostic structures, going forward the focus will be limited specifically to the

Lacanian conception of psychosis, and only insofar as it is relevant here, leaving aside the sub-categories, and some of the more theoretical vicissitudes of the concept.

4 The Lacanian tradition is not the only psychoanalytic tradition to oppose itself to the medical discourse in terms of diagnosis. One can also look to the Psychodynamic Diagnostic Manual (PDM), and the manual for Operationalized Psychodynamic Diagnosis (OPD).

5 According to a Lacanian perspective "certainty is characteristic of psychosis, whereas ... doubt is the very hallmark of neurosis" (Fink 1997: 84).

6 The three orders are sometimes represented as three overlapping rings, in which each of the three rings requires the presence of the others in order to remain stabilized. These are sometimes called Borromean rings using mathematical concepts from the field of topology. The sinthome is sometimes described as the fourth ring in this knot, necessary to hold things together in cases where the initial knot has been insufficiently linked, as in psychosis.

7 Lacan's original name for this position is the *"Un-père"* which sounds, in spoken French, identical to the root of the word for the imperative tense. It would seem that Lacan intended a certain connotation of imperativity: the one-father commands.

8 The dyadic relationship is characteristic of the Imaginary, and the triangular is characteristic of the Symbolic. Psychotic subjects may have difficulties expanding their sphere to include the Symbolic third, and their relationships often function through the lens of the binary, either/or.

References

Alanen, Y. (2009). 'Can we approach schizophrenic patients form a psychological basis?', in Y. Alanen, M. Chavez, A. Silver, and B. Martindale (eds.) *Psychotherapeutic Approaches to Schizophrenic Psychoses*, London: Routledge.

Apollon, W., Bergeron, D., and Cantin, L. (2002). *After Lacan: Clinical practice and the subject of the unconscious*, Albany, NY: State University of New York.

Bion, W.R. (1970). *Attention and interpretation*, London: Tavistock Publications.

Deri, S. (1984). *Symbolization and creativity*, New York, NY: International Universities Press.

Evans, D. (1996). *An introductory dictionary of Lacanian psychoanalysis*, New York, NY: Routledge.

Fink, B. (1997). *A clinical introduction to Lacanian psychoanalysis: Theory and technique*, Cambridge, MA: Harvard University Press.

Fink, B. (2007). *Fundamentals of psychoanalytic technique: A Lacanian approach for practitioners*, New York: Norton.

Freud, S. (1900). *The interpretation of dreams*, translated by J. Strachey, in *The Standard Edition of the Complete Psychological Works of Sigmund Freud (Vol. 4)*, (1953), London: Hogarth Press. Available online at http://pep-web.org/document.php?id=se.004.r0009a (accessed 1 January 2014).

Freud, S. (1911). 'Psycho-analytic notes on an autobiographical account of a case of paranoia', translated by J. Strachey, in *The Standard Edition of the Complete Psychological Works of Sigmund Freud (Vol. 12)*, (1953), London: Hogarth Press. Available online at http://pep-web.org/document.php?id=se.012.0001a (accessed 1 January 2014).

Freud, S. (1917). 'Introductory lectures on psycho-analysis', translated by J. Strachey, in *The Standard Edition of the Complete Psychological Works of Sigmund Freud (Vol. 16)*, (1963), London: Hogarth Press. Available online at http://pep-web.org/document.php?id=se.016.0241a (accessed 1 January 2014).

Fuller, P. (2013). *Surviving, existing, or living*, New York, NY: Routledge.

Himes, M. (2013). 'Verbal to the second power: An encounter between Lacan and expressive arts therapy', *Canadian Art Therapy Association Journal*, 26: 26–33.

Jameson, F. (2003). 'Imaginary and symbolic in Lacan', in S. Zizek (ed.) *Jacques Lacan Critical Evaluations in Cultural Theory*, New York, NY: Routledge.

Killick, K. (1993). 'Working with psychotic processes in art therapy', *Psychoanalytic Psychotherapy*, 7: 25–38.

Killick, K. and Schaverien J. (1997). *Art, psychotherapy and psychosis*, New York, NY: Routledge.

Lacan, J. (1955–56). '*Le seminaire, livre III, les psychoses*', seminar presented at Societe Francaise de Psychanalyse; translated by R. Grigg, in *The Seminar, Book III, The Psychoses*, (1993), New York, NY: Norton.

Lacan, J. (1966). *Ecrits*; translated by Bruce Fink, in *Ecrits* (2006), New York, NY: Norton.

Leader, D. (2002). *Stealing the Mona Lisa: What art stops us from seeing*, New York, NY: Counterpoint.

Leader, D. (2011). *What is madness?* London: Penguin.

Nobus, D. (2000). *Jacques Lacan and the Freudian practice of psychoanalysis*, London: Routledge.

Schaverien, J. (1997). 'Transference and transactional objects in the treatment of psychosis', in Killick, K. and Schaverien, J. (eds.) *Art, Psychotherapy and Psychosis*, London: Routledge.

Searles, H. (1962). 'The differentiation between concrete and metaphorical thinking in the recovering schizophrenic patient', *Journal of the American Psychoanalytic Association*, 10: 22–49.

Searles, H. (1963). 'Transference psychosis in the psychotherapy of chronic schizophrenia', *International Journal of Psycho-Analysis*, 44: 249–81.

Segal, H. (1950). 'Some aspects of the analysis of a schizophrenic', *International Journal of Psycho-Analysis*, 31: 268–78.

Segal, H. (1978). 'On symbolism', *International Journal of Psycho-Analysis*, 59: 315–19.

Seth-Smith, F. (1997). 'Four views of the image', in Killick, K. and Schaverien, J. (eds.) *Art, Psychotherapy and Psychosis*, London: Routledge.

Silver, A. (2002). 'Psychoanalysis and psychosis: Players and history in the United States', *Psychoanalysis and History*, 4: 45–66.

Vanheule, S. (2011). *The subject of psychosis: A Lacanian perspective*, New York, NY: Palgrave Macmillan.

Vanheule, S. (2012). 'Diagnosis in the field of psychotherapy: A plea for an alternative to the DSM-5.x', *Psychology and Psychotherapy: Theory, Research and Practice*, 85: 128–42.

Verhaeghe, P. (2004). *On being normal and other disorders*, New York, NY: Other Press.

Wilson, L. (2001). 'Symbolism and art therapy', in J. Rubin (ed.) *Approaches to Art Therapy* (2nd ed.), New York, NY: Routledge.

6

THE SIDE-BY-SIDE APPROACH IN ART THERAPY FOR PSYCHOSIS

Deflation and empowerment within the
therapeutic relationship

Helen Greenwood

Throughout this chapter, with the exception of one previously published example, case illustrations are fictional.

This chapter considers art therapy in a context of psychodynamic approaches for people who experience psychosis or psychotic thought processes. Summers and Rosenbaum (2013: 337) define these psychodynamic interventions, 'as those where unconscious factors are taken to be important and where patient-therapist relationships and interactions are regarded as crucial sources of information'. They note modifications of classical psychoanalysis that place emphasis on supportive elements in the therapist's approach to the patient. Within the field of art therapy I have called this a 'side-by-side' approach (Greenwood and Layton 1987). The intensity of transference phenomena is intentionally minimised and the employment of interpretation and confrontation avoided; the balance is shifted from an interpretive and explorative mode to a supportive approach where the therapist is more active.

In psychosis, the boundary between self and other, and thus between client and therapist, may be confused. This chapter will explore this issue in terms of the way that power is experienced in the therapeutic relationship. The Kleinian psychoanalyst Hannah Segal (1975) describes how patients may feel that they are losing identity within the therapeutic relationship. She makes the important point that the transference and the therapist's interpretations may be experienced as concrete in nature and thus taken literally. This chapter proposes that for those who experience psychosis, this perceived power differential between self and other can be intensified by experiences of stigma, poverty and racism. I think that the power of a biomedical model that aims to diagnose and treat can further intensify this experience so that respect by mental health professionals for the individual person is undermined. Internalised stigma may also result from abusive and bullying relationships where there is an overall disregard of the victim's point of view and thus a sense of self will be impoverished. Consideration of all these factors, both internal and external, has led me to believe that a shift in the balance of power in the therapeutic relationship is necessary. This shift moves towards empowerment of the service user and what I describe as 'deflation' (Greenwood and Layton 1988) of the therapist's power.

Discrimination, stigma, disempowerment and the tranquillising effects of medication are all major barriers to recovery for people with psychosis. Read, Mosher and Bentall (2013) have shown that the biomedical model of schizophrenia is responsible for unwarranted pessimism with regards to recovery; the individual becomes de-contextualised with scant interest in what has happened to them or what they might want. Morrison, Hutton, Shiers and Turkington (2012) question the assumption of medication as the first line of treatment for people with psychosis. This is in the light of the effectiveness of antipsychotic medications being overestimated and an underestimation of their toxicity (Morrison *et al.* 2012). Read *et al.* (2013: 5) present evidence that 'human misery is largely inflicted by other people and that the solutions are best based on human—rather than chemical or electrical—interventions'. The maxim, that bad things happen and can drive you crazy, is repeated in this literature. These bad things include poverty, ethnicity, inequality, deprivation, sexual abuse and other childhood traumas. The tide is beginning to turn and research has been produced to support the hypothesis that abuse in childhood has a causal role in the development of psychosis. The results of research by Bebbington *et al.* (2011) suggest that there is a stronger link between childhood sexual abuse and psychotic disorder or symptoms when the abuse has been more severe. Evidence summarised by Read (2013) demonstrates a dose-response relationship between the degree of childhood adversity and the probability of psychosis; a combination of different forms of abuse, neglect, bullying or parental death and with greater frequency result in a higher risk of psychosis. In the light of developing research and evidence, Read (2013) expresses the hope that mental health services will offer support and therapy that will address life histories.

Within this chapter I will describe relevant theoretical concepts and give a picture of what this 'side-by-side' approach involves. First, I will describe the origins of the side-by-side approach in group art therapy. Second, I will explore the appropriateness of this approach in individual art therapy with people who have experienced psychosis and suffered abuse or significant losses.

Historical background

The naming and development of what has commonly become known as the 'side-by-side' approach arose from my work in an outpatient art therapy group for people recovering from long-term psychotic illnesses more than three decades ago in the 1980s (Greenwood and Layton 1987, 1988; Greenwood 2012). This work was undertaken in a context of the UK National Health Service (NHS) when care and treatment were shifting from hospitals to community settings.

In the 1980s, I was employed as an art therapist within a setting that provided a daily programme of group psychotherapy. This was for people with relationship and emotional problems and psychosis would have been an exclusion criterion for the programme. A small, terraced house provided the setting in an inner city location, many miles from the parent psychiatric hospital. Therapy groups took place in the upstairs rooms. The downstairs kitchen and bathroom housed a depot injection clinic to administer medication for the treatment of people with a diagnosis of schizophrenia and also a lithium clinic for people with a diagnosis of manic depressive psychosis. These service users queued quietly and their presence made little impact in the building but left a sense of discomfort in the therapeutic milieu with regards to what was perceived as the dehumanising process of queuing for injections or blood tests. For some, their social withdrawal and lack of motivation might now be described as negative effects of schizophrenia. The idea of a weekly outpatient art therapy group for these service users emerged in the minds of an art therapist, community psychiatric nurses and a medical psychiatrist and became a reality. Referrals were made from the clinics and from psychiatric caseloads of nurses and doctors.

Over time, the group became warm and cohesive and members' admissions to psychiatric hospital greatly reduced. The lifespan of this group was eight years, and I was involved for the first four years. Members had mixed diagnoses, a broad age span, were unemployed and were mostly male, white, and single. It was facilitated by myself and one co-therapist; new members joined until we had a core of eight and there was no fixed ending. My co-therapists were male, with professional training in psychiatric nursing or psychiatry. We all had additional training in psychodynamic group therapy. At the time staff morale in the service was high with a strong pioneering attitude. Structures and support were in place to provide containment of anxieties generated in the group. The group's primary function was art therapy and that was how it was presented and viewed by its members. The art therapist had ownership of the group. At the time, this represented a radical shift in the balance of power held by professionals in treatment settings, in that the art therapist assumed the leadership role customarily held by the psychiatrist.

As the group became more cohesive, members began to arrive early and congregate in the kitchen downstairs. By socialising with each other they gradually separated themselves from the queue for the injection clinic and then moved upstairs prior to the session. Here they had some interaction with the psychotherapy group who appeared to feel themselves to be the most important group in the building as they were in therapy every day. The art therapy group cleared, tidied the room and erected tables ready for their session. We discovered that they had made an arrangement to go off for an early evening drink at the local pub after the session. Such an activity would have been given scant value within the ethos of the daily programme of psychotherapy but for us it illustrated improved social skills and pleasure in each other's company. We thought that it contributed to, rather than threatened, group cohesiveness.

In a period of art therapy history, from the early 1980s to mid 1990s, Wood (1997) identifies Katherine Killick and myself as promoting particular approaches for people who experience psychosis. Killick and I co-wrote a chapter (Killick and Greenwood 1995) that defined common features in our thinking and approaches, and identified significant differences. Killick's work (1991, 1993, 1997, 2000) focused on clients in the midst of acute psychosis in hospital settings, whereas my work was in community settings with people who had a history of psychosis. Together with one of my co-therapists, Geoff Layton, who was a psychiatrist, we used a descriptive method of process research to generate hypotheses and to consider the meaning of changes within the outpatient art therapy group. This has been previously published (Greenwood and Layton 1987, 1988) and further developed (Greenwood 1994, Killick and Greenwood 1995, Greenwood 1997, 2012). We did not consciously set out with an adapted model of therapy for this group but it evolved, and through our reflective thinking and research, we were able to name and describe it. The side-by-side approach is one aspect of this model.

The 2014 National Institute of Clinical Excellence guidelines for psychosis and schizophrenia in adults (NICE 2014) made recommendations for psychological and psychosocial interventions. These are based on the previous guidelines from 2009. According to the NICE guidelines, cognitive behavioural therapy should be offered to everyone, then family interventions for all families and, third, a consideration of arts therapies is recommended, specifically for the alleviation of negative symptoms. According to NICE guidelines these arts therapy interventions (which would include music, drama and dance movement therapies) should be provided in groups by qualified professionals with experience of working with people with psychosis and schizophrenia. Interestingly, the provision of counselling and supportive psychotherapy is not recommended.

The latest randomised control trial in the UK, called MATISSE (Multicentre evaluation of Art Therapy in Schizophrenia) (Crawford *et al.* 2010), appears to have shown that art therapy is no more clinically and cost effective than the control treatments of the usual activity groups and treatment. Critical reviews of the MATISSE project (Wood 2013, Holttum and Huet 2014) have challenged the trial's conclusion that art therapy is of no value for most people given the diagnosis of schizophrenia. One of the issues they raised in these reviews was that the method of conducting the art therapy groups was largely based on Waller's group interactive model (Waller 1993) which did not include reference to working with psychosis. The question of whether condition-specific treatments are more effective than generic approaches is raised by Springham who states, 'The MATISSE results suggest that generic art therapy approaches to schizophrenia do not appear to be effective' (Springham 2012). In her review, Wood outlines the elements of an adapted art therapy approach for people who experience psychosis which she draws from art therapy literature. These include clear communication with other colleagues involved in a care package, meeting with clients and preparation work before they join an art therapy group. Wood highlights the value of being directive and encouraging with regards to art-making. She advocates reducing levels of anxiety in the group by a supportive approach, which is collaborative and has less intensity of transference (Wood 2013).

Theoretical background

Psychoanalytical ideas that informed my thinking about art therapy and psychosis are primarily rooted in theory developed by Segal, Bion and Rosenfeld, who were all analysands of Melanie Klein. I have also been influenced by American ego psychologists such as Kohut. Segal (1975) proposed that analysts treat people with psychosis by focusing on the healthier part of the ego, within a positive transference, believing that no one was completely psychotic. Like Segal, Bion distinguished the psychotic personality from the neurotic personality and it was Bion's concept of containment (Bion 1962) that enabled us to conceptualise what was happening in the art therapy group (Greenwood and Layton 1987).

A useful discussion of Bion's theories, with regards to the process of thinking and acquisition of self knowledge, is provided by Bell (1995). It is understood that in the process of containment, originating in the infant/mother interaction, unthinkable thoughts are projected into the mother, and are then transformed by her reverie to become thinkable. In time the infant internalises this function and it is by means of this function or apparatus that Bion believed we come to know ourselves through experience. In psychosis, Bell emphasises that there is not simply a negation of reality but a negation of the apparatus concerned with awareness of internal and external reality (Bell 1995). This thread is picked up by Holmes (2010) when he explores mentalising in the context of attachment theory. 'Exploration, including thinking itself, is inhibited until attachment needs are assuaged. Secure-base provision is the "real" power that the therapist has to offer her patient' (Holmes 2010: 71). The capacity to mentalise emerges in the context of secure attachment with primary care givers and the essence of this capacity is the ability to see ourselves from the outside and others from the inside. Mentalising is related to the ability to put ourselves in the shoes of others, social intelligence, empathy, reflective thinking, and learning to mediate between stimulus and action. A supportive therapeutic relationship, of the kind I have outlined, is considered to have the potential to develop mentalising capacity, for growth of sense of self, and knowledge of others. This can be actively facilitated and in the case of mentalisation based therapy (MBT) has been put into a training manual.

Shifting to the psychoanalytical perspective of ego mechanisms of defence, I have been interested for many years in how mature defences can occur within the context of psychotic illness and in how they can appear alongside psychotic defences (Greenwood 1997). Humour may emerge as an adaptive mechanism of defence at both social and psychological levels in therapy with people diagnosed with psychosis. I believe this should be noted and admired by mental health professionals. The diagnostic and statistical manual of mental disorders (DSM III-R) first included a diagnostic axis of defences in 1987 (American Psychiatric

Association 1987). The classification was largely based on Vaillant's hierarchy of psychotic, immature, neurotic and mature defences. At one end of this scale, psychotic defences can profoundly alter perception of external reality, for example: delusional projection or denial, whereas, at the other extreme, mature defences are more adaptive than pathological and can look like voluntary coping strategies to an onlooker. When mature defences—such as sublimation or humour—are deployed, components of conflict are allowed more consciousness.

The psychoanalytic concept of ego mechanisms of defence refers to processes that occur unconsciously rather than to conscious problem solving strategies. However, through extensive longitudinal research in the USA, Vaillant showed that patterns of defence evolve throughout adult life. He contributes a hopeful attitude towards increased health where defence may 'transmute irritating grains of sand into pearls' (Vaillant 1993: 3). I was inspired by Vaillant to understand that in an environment of empathy, understanding and mirroring, defences can become less pathological and more adaptive. In order to facilitate this, the social milieu needs to be predictable and supportive. Vaillant maintained that we are likely to feel safe enough to deploy mature defences in an atmosphere of warmth and support. From a perspective of ego mechanisms of defence, insight orientated, dynamic psychotherapy is offered to people employing neurotic defences and where interpretation is a useful tool. Where defences are immature then supportive psychotherapy is useful with an emphasis on understanding and management rather than interpretation. For people who experience psychosis it becomes important to reinforce their adaptive defences rather than risk challenging defences against insight (Koehler, Silver and Karon 2013).

I think all the arts therapies facilitate the occurrence of humour and sublimation, as creativity and play are central and this is one of their values. The Clinical Practice Guideline (for people prone to psychotic states) (Brooker *et al.* 2007), advocates humour as enhancing development of playful, inventive and imaginative processes in art-making and social interaction. This was also the focus of my paper written with Geoff Layton called 'Taking the Piss' (1988) and then developed in my chapter 'Maturation of the Ego' (Greenwood 1997).

When there is a shift of perceived power in the therapeutic relationship this may be indicated by the emergence of humour and other forms of sublimation and, in my view, developments of this kind should be understood and accordingly respected by therapists as indications of recovery. Sublimated activities, such as art, music or sport, are socially valued and can leave the participant with feelings of well-being. They too can be indications of health and recovery.

The side-by-side approach in group art therapy

Someone who has lost interest in daily life, avoids social contact, has poor concentration and appears emotionally flat will find engagement in therapy a challenge. These characteristics might result from negative symptoms of schizophrenia but may also result from the effects of anti-psychotic medication reducing motivation and energy, and social stigma and the experience of marginalisation. As proposed earlier, the perceived power differential between self and other can be addressed in the therapeutic relationship in order to achieve engagement and the side-by-side approach offers one way of doing this.

In our paper describing the side-by-side approach (Greenwood and Layton 1987) we took the view, 'that exposure to the therapist's good objects, their ability to think, paint, experience, indeed to their personality in general, was a major therapeutic agent' (Greenwood and Layton 1987: 14). This is one way in which the intensity of transference can be intentionally minimised. We described how sharing the experience of making pictures gives opportunity for strengthening boundaries and feeling relationships between individuals, thus providing opportunity for development of self in relation to others and sharing and modifying anxieties (Greenwood and Layton 1987). Revisiting these ideas in the context of contemporary thinking I now understand that this approach is one that facilitates a mentalising attitude. Furthermore, the therapists' participation in art work models their continuous reflection on what goes on in their mind.

In the approach that we developed, therapists participate in the art process, produce art which is observed visually by the group, and are prepared to say something about themselves through their art. However, they do not use the group for their own therapy and it is important they can let go of their art work immediately (Marshall-Tierney 2014). Self disclosures are authentic and serve a didactic purpose to the group, for example in modelling the expression of thoughts and feeling through transformation into art form. Therapists' art work may often contain anxieties that belong to the group, in the counter transference, and these can be usefully named and explored. Art therapists Franks and Whitaker (2007) describe how a mentalising process is made visible in groups and individuals are encouraged to look into the minds of others through their art.

In this process therapists have to be prepared to lose face. Their artistic ability is exposed and can be ridiculed. For example, doctors might be at the top of a medical hierarchy but their artistic skills might be found to be deficient in the group. The value of this stance is confirmed by Bateman and Fonagy (2006) in their work with people with borderline personality disorder, 'A detached, aloof, refined, defended therapist is unlikely to form a relationship with a patient which helps the patient find himself in the mind of the therapist in an accessible and meaningful way' (p. 99). To aid the development of mentalisation they advocate therapists to be open minded, safe in their own failures and appropriately doubtful about their viewpoint (Bateman and Fonagy 2006). Therapists demonstrate that they are participants and not observers of the group: 'the therapist's stance is inquisitive, active, empathic and at times challenging but most importantly the therapist should refrain from becoming an expert who knows' (Bateman and Fonagy 2006: 101).

In 1987, we found support for therapist participation in art from the work of Lachman-Chapin (1979), an American art therapist, who followed the theories of Kohut (1966), a self psychologist who used empathy as a keystone of treatment.

Lachman-Chapin stressed the need for the art therapist not to be neutral but to present themselves with more freedom. She described the value of producing art work alongside the patient, stressing the importance of providing an empathic and nurturing experience. This was considered important in addressing early narcissism, rooted in the pre-verbal period of infancy. The practice for art therapists to make artwork alongside service users is becoming more common, yet it remains marginalised in UK literature (Marshall-Tierney 2014).

Satire and the idea of deflation

Through studying aspects of satire and the art of the Dada artists Marcel Duchamp and Francois Picabia, we came to understand a particular form of humour we called 'taking the piss' (Greenwood and Layton 1988). The phrase is derived from 'deflation of a bladder of conceit' (Beale and Partridge 1984). In groups for people with psychosis, we found that humour and particularly satire can usefully be employed. 'It is as if the subject which feels most taboo at that moment can be addressed and confronted in a playful and entertaining way, deflating tension and preventing social disintegration. Cohesiveness was actually strengthened in the group by frequent use of TTP' (Greenwood and Layton 1988). Satire transforms difficult feelings into humour and play. The satirist is not cut off from the world but comments on aspects that might be impossible to talk about because of taboo or censorship.

Thus, a group member who was uncommunicative and withdrawn from interpersonal interactions produced art work imbued with satire (Greenwood and Layton 1988, Greenwood 2012). His art was presented with a stony face and no one knew how to react until his face was lit up by a sparkling wit, and the humour was shared. He deflated the people and things most precious to the group, ridiculing the importance attached to them. I was depicted in black leather with a whip, as an authoritarian school teacher or on another occasion blowing dandelion clocks; the psychiatrist was drawn dancing. Pictures of up to the minute news items and recent disasters illustrated his involvement in the world. His image of God overseeing men who operate pumps to fill leaking buckets created an ironic comment on the world. Similarly, Arman (1985) described how the Dada artists ridiculed man's tendency to attach undue importance to any ideal or institution. In their art they adopted a machine style which attacked the role of the artist. Duchamp was concerned by the absence of meaningful human bonds and the futility of man's systems. I think that this experience was shared by this group member who had been hospitalised for many years and treated for schizophrenia.

Within therapy groups for people with psychosis the use of humour, and particularly satirical humour, can have an enlivening, creative and empowering function. Bateman and Fonagy (2006) state, 'Humour and playfulness are necessary in our view to enhancing mentalisation, partly to demonstrate that mental states are inherently modifiable and malleable. This approach to subjectivity produces a creative stance to the world' (p. 8). In MBT the active therapist stance is described as, 'able to withstand being dismissed, ridiculed or made to feel use-less' (Bateman and Fonagy 2006: 156). O'Connell (1976) describes a jesting yet serious approach with an absence of a hierarchical doctor-patient relationship in which roles are reversed and the doctor is sometimes the patient.

Deflation, cutting down to size or belittling, are devices common to satire and our experience of 'taking the piss' in the art therapy group. Politics, because of its overt use of power is the most common subject of satire. In the context of this chapter, I share the view that the damaging supremacy of a bio-genetic ideology (Read *et al.* 2013) requires challenge, and as I perceive 'deflation', in favour of humanistic and social approaches.

Psychotherapy that addresses adversity in childhood

Read (2013) has laid down the challenge of offering people who experience psy-chosis and who have suffered abuse, neglect or significant losses, the kind of support and psychotherapy that addresses their life histories. Herman (1992) describes the disguised presentation of survivors of child abuse who present a bewildering array of symptoms, accumulating different diagnoses and receiv-ing fragmented and incomplete treatment. The link between childhood trauma and presenting problems can become severed and mental health services can inadvertently replicate the dynamics of abuse. A hierarchical doctor-patient re-lationship can maintain defences for all parties involved in that any underlying trauma can remain safely locked away protecting the service user, their fami-lies and others from painful unspeakable truths. Many people with early trauma stay within the NHS psychiatric system and are treated for illness in a model where contextual factors such as trauma, racism and poverty play no role in causation (Read *et al.* 2013). Hearing voices can be taken as a positive symptom of schizophrenia, and as a result any interest in the meaning of symptoms is currently at risk of being lost within the prevailing biomedical ethos. The global Hearing Voices Movement has developed over nearly three decades and has, amongst others, challenged the dominant, potentially disempowering biomed-ical model. Romme and Morris (2013: 267) believe they 'provide evidence that voice-hearing can be understood as an integral part of the emotional and think-ing life of a whole person, not as a fragment of a wider disease process.'[1] They recognise the background of traumatic experience and like Read (2013) they make a plea for therapists with expertise in treating trauma to also help people with distressing voices.

The side-by-side approach in individual art therapy

When I was employed, later on in my career, as an art therapist in an NHS com-munity based psychotherapy team my role afforded considerable clinical auton-omy. Whilst my individual art therapy work primarily addressed early trauma, abuse and deprivation this was only occasionally in the context of psychosis.

I have met people who want therapy to address earlier trauma and abuse in their lives who may have a medical diagnosis of schizophrenia or manic depressive psychosis, who may hear voices, and who may be prescribed anti-psychotic medication. It is these people I will now discuss with regard to individual art therapy. In the NHS in the UK, at the time of writing, there can be an overt exclusion criterion of psychosis for referral to psychological therapy services; accordingly, structures and management may not facilitate access.

The empathic and nurturing nature of the side-by-side approach, together with reinforcement of adaptive defences, can improve mental health and strengthen the ego. These aspects lend themselves to the cultivation of positive transference feelings. I believe that if the transference remains too positive, the underlying trauma will not emerge. There may come a time when the service user is able to tolerate more negative transference feelings, and when this is possible, it is important to allow these to emerge in order that trauma can be responded to and related to. The side-by-side approach in individual therapy is very different from the approach that I described in group art therapy. This individual therapy feels deadly serious, and I think it would be grossly inappropriate for the therapist to initiate any humour to deflate this tension. Similarly, I have never produced art work alongside adult clients in a context of individual therapy. I think the art therapist should be cautious regarding his or her active involvement in the therapeutic relationship and in art-making because past abusive relationships may all too easily be re-enacted in the transference.

In my place of work, I was fortunate enough to have a large dedicated art therapy room. There were numerous tables and chairs as well as a wide choice of art materials. Sessions always started and finished on time and although I had a standard structure I was prepared to make modifications through negotiation. For example, if the standard session duration of 75 minutes was experienced as intolerable I was willing to cut it to 60 minutes. For those service users with no experience of art, the therapist can facilitate an exploration of the art materials to help them find the materials they feel most comfortable to use. Similarly, therapist and service user can try sitting in different chairs as a way of regulating the therapeutic relationship. Many service users struggled with the intensity of relationship if I sat next to them while they engaged in art work. Some liked to keep their art work out of my sight.

In my 'ideal' structure, we start the session sitting at the corner of a large table, neither directly facing each other, nor alongside. I prefer to keep this time as short as possible; there might be some feedback from the week and notice of holidays, but this is a preliminary chat before moving onto art work. I remain seated in my original chair and the service user is invited to collect art materials and encouraged to use these in the area nearest the sink and furthest from me. Unless I deem it necessary to help with any problems experienced in the use of art materials, I do not move and I do not initiate any conversation. As I see it, I offer the space for engagement in an art process that might involve self-absorption and reflection. In the last part of the session, we come together again and both sit observing the art work and conversation arises from this. I take an interest in the developmental stages of the art work and I can shift attention to either concrete or symbolic aspects (Killick and Greenwood 1995). The therapeutic relationship can be maintained by a suspension of reference to meaning and a shift to the concrete aspects of art-making, and then returning to symbolic ways of thinking when appropriate. For service users with avoidant relationship patterns this offers the opportunity for them to stay connected by shifting attention from interpersonal issues to the activity of art-making.

Managing the balance of power

I am now going to consider ways in which the balance of power can be altered in the therapeutic relationship to make the process of therapy manageable, first by looking at the therapeutic alliance. I propose that to engage in therapy and develop a therapeutic alliance, opportunities for empowerment must be maximised for the service user and that negotiation is the central focus in the process of establishing a therapeutic alliance and creating a collaborative bond. I understand the concept of therapeutic alliance as a relationship with the part of a client that knows he or she is in therapy and can distinguish between the therapeutic environment and the rest of his or her life in the real world. It involves those factors that keep a client in therapy and enable them to remain there when therapy gets difficult, in periods of resistance and hostile transference. It is a treatment contract that involves both conscious and unconscious aspects of the persons involved. Sandler, Dare and Holder (1992) give the example of a patient who might appear hostile to treatment with a strong resistance to analytic work but have an underlying conscious wish to cooperate. In the case of outpatient treatment of psychotic patients, it may sometimes be helpful to have an extended alliance where the cooperation of other professionals and family might facilitate attendance (Sandler et al. 1992).

Examples of the ways I believe the balance of power can be addressed in the therapeutic relationship include attention to confidentiality and to negotiating the goals of therapy. Elements of confidentiality can be negotiated, for example whether or not I attend Care Programme Meetings, and discussion about the content of written communications. I found that it suited service users that their Community Mental Health Teams, who co-ordinated their care, were not in the same part of the organisation (physically or managerially) as the psychotherapy team. Sometimes they were happy to travel considerable distances by public transport to attend therapy. Negotiating the goals of therapy is a sensitive task of listening to and helping to articulate the service user's wishes whilst assessing whether the goals are achievable and appropriate. Similarly, Morrison et al. (2012) advocate a more collaborative approach when it comes to decisions about antipsychotic medication, taking account of the service users' goals and values.

If someone cannot express an opinion as to whether they want to engage in a process of art therapy, I sometimes offer a short trial after which we can both discuss and weigh up whether or not we think art therapy could be helpful. If somebody constructed a narrative, for example, where I bore witness to an account of childhood sexual abuse and violent rape or assaults as an adult, then through the short trial of therapy their difficulties might be described as making sense in terms of their life experiences. If they declined to continue art therapy with me or pursue other therapy options, then this could show a preference to maintain allegiance to the expert figure of a psychiatrist. Through provision of appropriate medication and other care, psychiatrists demonstrate attention to their patients. For someone with experience of repeated breakdown and admission to psychiatric hospital, risks might outweigh benefits when deciding whether to engage in therapy. This is also a consideration for families and carers. Maintaining a 'sick role' might be an important dynamic that either the patient or their carer would not want to relinquish. If the service user can be facilitated to say 'no' to treatment such as art therapy, and to have the experience of this being respected and accepted, then this can be a positive treatment outcome in itself. This illustrates an important aspect of the side-by-side approach which is the opportunity that it offers to deflate the authority of the therapist. Offering choices is a simple means of facilitating empowerment and this has to include the choice of engaging in therapy.

Vignette

A service user who describes himself as having schizophrenia is referred for art therapy. He expresses a wish to develop his sense of who he is and to be able to move on from the past. He has experienced abandonment and loss in the context of a bullying relationship. He wants to regain a position of some respect in his family and to become more independent without risk of losing his connections to them. In making negotiations he likes the idea that he does not have to tell me everything about his imagery. He values the art-making process as a time when thoughts and images can emerge. This helps him get hold of what he really wants to talk about at a deeper level. His more usual experience is sharing his worries and seeking advice. During the assessment he warms to the idea of art therapy; he already attends an art class and is aware that art brings out emotions in him, but he struggles with the strain of getting things right; he welcomes the space to become more creative. He wants the art process to be on his terms and tells me the only way he can tolerate it is if I sit at my desk with my back to him, getting on with some work that is not about him. I duly conform and go through these motions, but remain receptive and thoughtful about him. In therapy it is a delicate balance to both facilitate empowerment yet not get caught in a re-enactment of the bullying transference.

A therapeutic alliance is negotiated and a period of two years' individual art therapy on a weekly basis is agreed. I hold in mind issues of abandonment, dependency and isolation and think about these in the context of the ending of therapy. Steady progress occurs in the first year but this recovery seems to increase panic and he withdraws requests to reduce medication and reduce professional involvement. At times his insecurity seems worse and he fears becoming psychotic again and needing hospital admission. He fears I will abandon him by getting sick from the attacks of his 'bad thoughts'. A narrative of his childhood experiences emerges through his art work and we are able to make links to the therapeutic relationship and the forthcoming ending of therapy.

Ideally, therapy takes place at a time when the service user feels ready, and professionals involved in his or her care consider there is sufficient stability: everyone is working towards the goal of recovery with minimum dependence on services. It is helpful if both the service user and their carers (both professional and family) understand that therapy may be disturbing and that they need to be respectful of the courage involved in the therapeutic process.

Prolonged and repeated childhood abuse

When childhood adversity consists of different types of abuse, and these are prolonged and repeated, this is linked to greater severity of adult mental health problems (Read 2013). I think a much longer duration of therapy is then indicated. At this point I will attempt to describe some of the complexities of this longer term therapy. It is the task of the therapist to balance supportive and disturbing elements of therapy in order to avoid unhelpfully increasing anxiety and making the person's difficulties worse.

A service user might arrive for art therapy where childhood abuse has been designated the focus of the work, either by themselves or their referrer. A context of psychosis or psychotic thought processes will exist. There will usually be an idea that the inclusion of art might aid communication and make the therapeutic relationship manageable. Hopes and expectations may be high. I think it is important that the therapist is comfortable with, and has some confidence in, working with both childhood abuse and psychosis. From the provision of a secure base, I think the task of therapy is to bear witness to the service user's experiences and individual story, in a supportive, side-by-side approach. Given the complex context of victimisation and of psychosis this task can be very difficult. There is a risk of the therapist becoming identified with the traumatised victim or being inadvertently dragged into the role of perpetrator within the abuse dynamics. The therapist has to be able to endure this and remain able to think both for him or her self and with the service user. Support systems, including clinical supervision, should be in place for the therapist as well as support systems for the service user.

A narrative of what has happened in the person's life will hopefully emerge. Words may be hard to come by and transference and counter transference become crucial sources of information. The emotions of an experience, such as terror and humiliation, may be felt in the counter transference, before the therapist knows what happened. The intensity of the feeling, projected into the therapist, is a good indication of the severity of the abuse. Art work is also an important source of information and plays an important part in speaking the unspeakable. It concretely exists and can be seen; then when the therapeutic relationship feels safe enough, the imagery can disclose its meaning. However, as I have discussed elsewhere (Greenwood 2000), instead of making the therapeutic relationship manageable, artwork can sometimes heighten anxiety to intolerable levels.

Vignette

Mrs A, a 40-year-old woman, is referred for art therapy within a psychological therapy service. My assessment of her becomes delayed as she is admitted to psychiatric hospital and prescribed anti-psychotic medication, and then referred to a community mental health team. Her symptoms include hearing voices, self-harm and threats of suicide. During the assessment I gain a picture of her current circumstances and family, as well as a narrative of her life as a child. She completes a psychotherapy questionnaire which offers insights into her thoughts and feelings and details of her childhood background, work experience and key relationships. I offer a period of weekly long term individual art therapy in consultation with professionals involved in her care and with her husband. It becomes apparent to me that Mrs A can only respond to my questions but cannot initiate conversation. This had gone unnoticed in the more directive nature of the assessment. She welcomes the space for art-making but then finds she cannot develop a conversation from her imagery. There is an unbearable silence and I struggle to make comments based primarily on my counter transference experience. Her imagery contains two figures distinguished by height, which give the impression of being engaged in hide and seek activity. I wonder if she is illustrating her voices, or actual or invented experiences; my counter transference informs me that this is not a pleasurable or playful activity. I have no context from which to develop a dialogue so I wonder if the images represent traumatic memory lacking in verbal narrative and context. Mrs A says nothing.

Therapy is difficult but it does not feel as if I am up against something impenetrably negative that is beyond both of us, as described by Garland (1998). In trying to establish a therapeutic alliance, Mrs A reassures me she wants to attend art therapy and wants to be able to tell me what has happened to her, but agrees she would prefer me to know without her saying. She smiles warmly when I express how stupid and clumsy I feel when it seems I am getting things wrong. My attempts to become empathic involve putting more of myself into the therapeutic relationship and being very much more active, especially faced with Mrs A's silence. This does not involve disclosing any personal information, for example either my family situation or aspects of my own childhood. I think Mrs A will pick up an impression of my personality and perhaps some of my beliefs and attitudes. She learns I am dependable and reliable, and she observes some of my interactions with the environment and other colleagues. My responses to unexpected disruptions and intrusions into the therapy space are assessed. Am I trustworthy, can I take in the experiences of violent and sexual abuse without being knocked off-balance and still remain open to hear her viewpoint? Based on these observations, I think it takes time for trust to develop in a realistic way. In the transference relationship I think Mrs A slowly begins to feel less threatened by me and the power dynamics eventually become manageable and she is able to steer me in the right direction to witness the true horror of what has happened to her. It is only towards the end of therapy that Mrs A begins to enjoy the art process and the therapeutic relationship. Becoming creative and empowered she produces some impressive abstract paintings. By this time, she has turned her life around, returns to work and abandons the role of being a psychiatric patient. We both enjoy the flow of conversation between us.

People like Mrs A are not only disempowered by the stigma of mental illness but also by degradation and humiliation from abusers who have terrorised them. They are not surprisingly silenced. These dynamics will be experienced in the transference and counter transference. The therapist will need to tread carefully and require great patience to endure long periods, often of several years, seeing no progress and feeling useless but at the same time being aware how imperative it is for therapy to be maintained.

Duration of therapy

In the NHS it is currently difficult to offer long enough therapy to address life histories of people who experience psychosis and who have suffered childhood abuse. In my experience, where abuse has been repeated over a prolonged period of time, the duration may need to be weekly for 5 years or more. When childhood adversity is more limited and a therapeutic alliance can be developed, I have found that two years' weekly art therapy is helpful. Moving in the direction of recovery will cut the costs of hospital admissions and prescription of medication, and needs for community support will be reduced or disappear. Although this is now out of date, previous research established that the cost of weekly art therapy sessions for six years in the NHS was £7,915, which, at the time, was the equivalent of 26 days' psychiatric hospital admission (Greenwood, Leach, Lucock and Noble 2007). Considering the current economic climate, it is more than ever important to consider economic considerations and if art therapy does contribute towards recovery then it may well be a highly cost effective intervention.

Conclusion

I have presented the side-by-side approach in art therapy within groups and individual art therapy. I have proposed that art therapy group work has the potential to reverse negative effects of psychosis in line with current guidelines (NICE 2014) and also enhances the capacity for mentalising. Group therapy is more realistic, fosters less dependency and offers more equality than individual therapy (González de Chávez 2009). In my view, the needs met in either individual or group art therapy are different. It may be that group art therapy is most relevant where negative symptoms predominate, and individual art therapy particularly helpful when therapy is attempting to support a person in processing childhood adversity. My individual art therapy focused on witnessing the narratives of peoples' life histories which included serious abuse, deprivation and loss.

If we can develop more interest in a range of responses to trauma, then services in the UK might be configured so that the need for people to have the opportunity to speak of what has happened to them is given more importance than at present. Currently, there is often no easily accessible route to psychological therapies for people with psychosis. I fear that the presence of psychosis is in danger of remaining an exclusion criterion for certain types of therapy, such as psychodynamic therapies. At the moment diagnoses of personality disorder, post traumatic stress disorder or schizophrenia will result in very different interventions. In my experience the current situation is very inconsistent, and in any one care team the professionals that comprise it might hold quite different models of psychosis and different attitudes regarding underlying causes. I think that we have to listen carefully to our clients, and work hard to make their needs understandable to other colleagues and carers or family; failure to do so might compound the existing problem by leading to further isolation and marginalisation.

Art therapy, and the arts therapies generally, can be adapted to offer a form of psychodynamic therapy for people who experience psychosis, or psychotic thought processes, and who might also have suffered traumatic life experiences. This adaptation involves maximising opportunities for empowerment and reducing the experienced authority of the therapist. Aspects of creativity, play and humour make a significant contribution in the personal experience of vitality and power. Within this approach the therapist has an important role to facilitate the provision of a secure therapeutic relationship working with issues of trust and reliability, and also strengthening of boundaries. From an experience of containment (Bion 1962) anxieties can be made tolerable, a process of learning emerges and thinking develops. Similarly, from an attachment perspective a secure base facilitates empowerment through self-understanding (Holmes 2010).

If therapists refrain from exerting professional authority it becomes possible to empower those who are diagnosed with psychosis, and those abused or bullied in childhood who present with psychosis. Shifting emphasis from an insight orientated approach towards a side-by-side therapeutic relationship allows the therapist to reinforce adaptive defences thereby facilitating growth of the ego. Intensity of transference can be reduced and the goal of insight, which may heighten psychotic defences, can be shifted. I leave the final words to Koehler *et al.*, 'What is often more important is internalising a tolerant, kind, confused and stubborn therapist, who is there to help, can tolerate negative affect as well as not understanding and who doesn't quit.' (2013: 245)

Note

1 Mervyn Morris was the first co-therapist in the outpatient art therapy group in 1984. He has since become a professor of community mental health challenging stigma and focussing on alternatives to hospitalisation and medication. Service user inclusion and empowerment are central to his work in the area of psychosis.

References

American Psychiatric Association (1987). *Diagnostic and statistical manual of mental disorders,* 3rd ed. revised, Washington, DC.

Arman, Y. (1985). *Marcel Duchamp plays and wins,* New York: Gallerie Yves Arman.

Bateman, A. and Fonagy, P. (2006). *Mentalisation-based treatment for borderline personality disorder,* Oxford: Oxford University Press.

Beale, P. and Partridge, E (1984). *A dictionary of slang and unconventional English,* New York: Macmillan.

Bebbington, P. *et al.* (2011). 'Childhood sexual abuse and psychosis: Data from a cross-sectional national psychiatric survey in England', *British Journal of Psychiatry,* 199: 29–37.

Bell, D.L. (1995). 'Knowledge and its pretenders: Bion's contribution to knowledge and thought', in J. Ellwood (ed.) *Psychosis: Understanding and Treatment,* London: Jessica Kingsley.

Bion, W.R (1962). *Learning from experience,* London: Heinemann.

Brooker, J. *et al.* (2007). *The use of art work in art psychotherapy with people who are prone to psychotic states. An evidence based clinical guideline,* London: Goldsmiths University of London.

Crawford, M.J. *et al.* (2010). 'The MATISSE study: A randomised trial of group art therapy for people with schizophrenia', *BMC Psychiatry,* 10: 65.

Franks, M. and Whitaker, R. (2007). 'The image, mentalisation and group art psychotherapy', *Inscape,* 12: 3–17.

Garland, C. (1998). 'Thinking about trauma', in C. Garland (ed.) *Understanding Trauma: A Psychoanalytical Approach,* London: Duckworth.

González de Chávez, M. (2009). 'Group psychotherapy and schizophrenia', in Alanen, Y; González de Chávez, M; Silver, A-L. and Martindale, B. (eds.) *Psychotherapeutic Approaches to Schizophrenic Psychoses,* London: Routledge.

Greenwood, H. (1994). 'Cracked pots: Art therapy and psychosis', *Inscape,* 1: 11–14.

Greenwood, H. (1997). 'Psychosis and the maturing ego', in Schaverien, J. and Killick, K. (eds.) *Art Therapy and Psychosis,* London: Routledge.

Greenwood, H. (2000). 'Captivity and terror in the therapeutic relationship', *Inscape,* 5(2): 53–61.

Greenwood, H. (2012). 'What aspects of an art therapy group aid recovery for people diagnosed with psychosis?' *ATOL: Art Therapy Online,* 3(1). Available online at http://eprints-gojo.gold.ac.uk.

Greenwood, H. and Layton, G. (1987). 'An out patient art therapy group', *Inscape,* 10(1) Summer: 12–19.

Greenwood, H. and Layton, G. (1988). 'Taking the piss', *British Journal of Clinical and Social Psychiatry,* Autumn; reprinted in *Inscape* (1991), Winter: 7–14.

Greenwood, H., Leach, C., Lucock, M. and Noble, R. (2007). 'The process of long-term art therapy: A case study combining artwork and clinical outcome', *Psychotherapy Research*, 17(5): 588–99.

Herman, J.L. (1992). *Trauma and recovery,* USA: Basic Books.

Holmes, J. (2010). *Exploring in security: Towards an attachment-informed psychoanalytic psychotherapy,* London: Routledge.

Holttum, S. and Huet, V. (2014). 'The MATISSE trial—a critique: Does art therapy really have nothing to offer people with a diagnosis of schizophrenia?' *SAGE Open 2014 4.* 1–11. Available online at http://www.sagepublications.com/content/4/2/2158244014532930 (accessed June, 2014).

Killick, K. (1991). 'The practice of art therapy with patients in acute psychotic states' in *Inscape,* Winter: 2–6.

Killick, K. (1993). 'Working with psychotic processes in art therapy' in *Psychoanalytic Psychotherapy,* 7(1): 25–38.

Killick, K. (1997). 'Unintegration and containment in acute psychosis' in *British Journal of Psychotherapy,* 13(2): 232–42.

Killick, K. (2000). 'The art room as container with analytical art psychotherapy with patients in psychotic states', in Gilroy, A. and McNeilly, G. (eds.) *The Changing Shape of Art Therapy,* London: Jessica Kingsley.

Killick, K. and Greenwood, H. (1995). 'Research in art therapy with people who have psychotic illnesses', in Gilroy, A. and Lee, C. (eds.) *Art and Music: Therapy and Research,* London: Routledge.

Koehler, B., Silver, A-L. and Karon, B. (2013). 'Psychodynamic approaches to understanding psychosis. Defences against terror', in Read, J. and Dillon, J. (eds.) *Models of Madness. Psychological, Social and Biological Approaches to Psychosis,* 2nd ed., London: Routledge.

Kohut, H. (1966). 'Forms and transformations of narcissism' in *Journal of American Psychoanalytical Association,* 14: 243–72.

Lachman-Chapin. M. (1979). 'Kohut's theories of narcissism. Implications for art therapy' in *American Journal of Art Therapy,* 19: 3–9.

Marshall-Tierney, A. (2014). 'Making art with and without patients in acute settings' in *International Journal of Art Therapy: Inscape,* 19(3): 96–106.

Morrison, A., Hutton, P., Shiers, D., and Turkington, D. (2012). 'Antipsychotics: Is it time to introduce patient choice?' *British Journal of Psychiatry,* 201: 83–84.

National Institute for Clinical Excellence (2014). *Psychosis and schizophrenia in adults: treatment and management.* NICE clinical guideline 178.

O'Connell, W.E. (1976). 'Freudian humour, the eupsychia of everyday life', in Chapman, A.and Foot, H. (eds.) *Humour and Laughter—Therapy, Research and Application,* Chichester: Wiley.

Read, J. (2013). 'Childhood, adversity and psychosis. From heresy to certainty', in Read, J. and Dillon, J. (eds.) *Models of Madness,* 2nd ed., London: Routledge.

Read, J., Mosher, L. and Bentall, R. (2013). 'Schizophrenia is not an illness' in Read, J. and Dillon, J. (eds.) *Models of Madness,* 2nd ed., London: Routledge.

Romme, M. and Morris, M. (2013). 'The recovery process with hearing voices: Accepting as well as exploring their emotional background through a supported process', in *Psychosis,* 5(3): 259–69.

Sandler, J., Dare, C. and Holder, A. (1992). *The patient and the analyst,* London: Karnac.

Segal, H. (1975). 'Psycho-analytical approach to the treatment of schizophrenia', in M.H. Lader (ed.) Studies of Schizophrenia, *British Journal of Psychiatry. Special Publication*, 10: 94–97.

Springham, N. (2012). Editorial. *International Journal of Art Therapy: Inscape*. Nov.

Summers, A. and Rosenbaum, B. (2013). 'Psychodynamic psychotherapy for psychosis: empirical evidence', in Read, J. and Dillon, J. (eds.) *Models of Madness*, 2nd ed., London: Routledge.

Vaillant, G. (1993). *The Wisdom of the ego*, Cambridge, Mass.: Harvard University Press.

Waller, D. (1993). *Group interactive art therapy*, London: Routledge.

Wood, C. (1997). 'The history of art therapy and psychosis (1938–95)', in Killick, K. and Schaverien, J. (eds.) *Art, Psychotherapy and Psychosis*, London: Routledge.

Wood, C. (2013). 'In the wake of the Matisse RCT: What about art therapy and psychosis?' in *International Journal of Art Therapy: Inscape*, 18(3): 88–97.

7

THE THREE-HEADED GIRL

The experience of dialogical art therapy viewed from different perspectives

Mimmu Rankanen

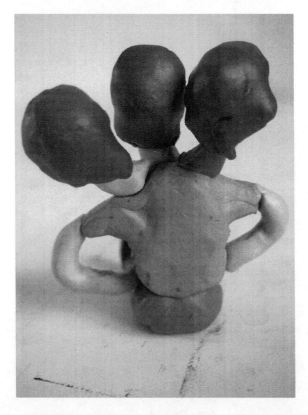

Figure 7.1 The Three-Headed Girl (Modelling clay, 12 cm × 10 cm × 8 cm).

> Every act of signification will always involve a three-term relation
> between two persons and the 'object' ... All meaning is generated
> within this developing, intercommunicative space, which unites
> that what is seen with what is not yet seen, which transforms
> practical, material transactions into signs, and which materializes
> symbolic and invisible forms of activity into practical acts and
> tangible objects. Everything that exists in the human mind ... is
> created within this living concrete and material space.
>
> Leiman (1992: 216)

This chapter explores how client and therapist experience an art therapy process by using a multi-method narrative case study (McLeod 2010). The research material consists of the therapist's notes, recorded and transcribed patient interviews and artworks. In the theoretical reflection on case narratives three layers of art oriented dialogical experiences are identified in addition to those interpersonal and intrapersonal dialogues inherent in verbal psychotherapy. These embodied, material and sensory dialogues are unique to art therapy experiences. This chapter has been read, commented on and accepted by the client during the writing process.

The story begins from my view as a therapist. First I aim to build a theoretical framework for dialogical art therapy by integrating the social notion of self derived from cognitive-analytic therapy with art-based art therapy. My specific focus is on the theoretical concept of multiple self-states, which is particularly useful for understanding experiences and problems classified as psychotic, traumatic and/or borderline. In the clinical case that follows, the client's and my experiences are explored and reflected on using the dialogical theoretical construct. Our stories are structured around four images that the client remembers from the course of the therapy. Each artwork is first recalled by the client, then viewed through my notes from the actual session, and finally observed together. These varying interpersonal and temporal perspectives aim to give a rich and manifold picture of the art therapy process, where layers of experiences cannot be reduced into one truth. Instead, at the core is my attempt to capture the differences between our lived experiences and to respect the client's view of the world as being as relevant and valuable for her as mine is for me.

The characters who explore their experiences in this article are a young woman, 'Kuura' (pseudonym), who has a history of multiple diagnoses including major depression with psychotic symptoms and borderline features and me, a middle-aged art therapist and cognitive-analytic psychotherapist. We have undertaken individual art therapy for three years, having twice weekly sessions during the first year, weekly sessions during the second year and one session every two weeks during the third year.

Art therapy tailored for psychosis

So far, there has been sparse process research on the working mechanisms, or quantitative research on the usefulness, of art therapy in psychotic disorders or symptoms (Hanevik *et al.* 2013; Killick and Greenwood 1995; Ruddy and Milnes 2005). One of the few quantitative studies was a recent large RCT study, 'MATISSE', which used non-directive group art therapy, did not indicate efficacy for patients with schizophrenia (Crawford *et al.* 2012). The treatment in 'MATISSE' consisted of non-directive art therapy in a group, undertaken by offering a range of art materials and encouraging patients to freely and spontaneously express themselves in a holding environment but without a structure set by a therapist or guidance for the art work or themes. Interestingly, the control groups where a leader guided patients' non-artistic social activities, such as games and themed discussions, gained some results in reducing positive symptoms of schizophrenia (Crawford *et al.* 2012). These results are not very surprising when considering the often high degree of impairment in cognitive and social functioning in chronic schizophrenia in relation to the great capacity for reflective and flexible thinking which non-directive group art therapy requires.

However, previous research does not prove that all kinds of art therapy approaches and methods are ineffective in treating clients with psychotic disorders or symptoms, and the analysis and assumptions of 'MATISSE' have also been critically reviewed (Holttum and Huet 2014). Many case studies and qualitative research studies show more positive outcomes (Brooker *et al.* 2006; Killick and Greenwood 1995; Killick and Schaverien 1997; Teglbjaerg 2009). For example, a more structured art-based group therapy, where a therapist guides the group with artistic warmups into chosen therapeutic themes or free art-making, values the real relationship and is present with her own personality, which Teglbjaerg (2009) and Hanevik *et al.* (2013), for example, have used in their multiple case studies, can be a more appropriate approach for clients suffering from psychotic disorders. As in all therapies, explicit sharing and overt negotiating of methods and goals builds a good working alliance and outcome (Goldfried and Davila 2005).

Similar conclusions can be drawn from the profound work which Brooker *et al.* (2006) conducted in developing evidence-based guidelines for clinical practices with people prone to psychotic states. Of special interest are the clients' views because clients' views of the therapeutic alliance have been shown to predict therapeutic outcomes (Duncan *et al.* 2003). In Brooker *et al.*'s (2006) guidelines, the users express their need for more explicit information on the art therapy process and its effects as well as more mutual negotiation of the aims and methods of both art-making and therapy. In addition, they criticise art therapists' tendency to over-interpret artworks and call for respect for their own understanding.

In addition to reduction of symptoms, another important aspect of the impact of art therapy is thus the nature of the art therapeutic relationship and the clients' experiences of it. Hanevik *et al.* undertook a qualitative study (2013) exploring clients' experiences and the working mechanisms of group art therapy for psychotic illnesses. They found that clients experienced art therapy as helpful in mastering or coping with their illness, and art-making enabled them to interact in a positive way and create a safe group. An additional important result was that the clients experienced feeling increasingly understood and valued. Art was experienced as a profoundly meaningful way to express themselves. At the beginning of art therapy, several participants had expressed fear of becoming labelled 'crazy' and becoming excluded from the social community, which in my experience is a common fear connected with many psychiatric disorders.

In contrast to group work, this chapter focuses on individual art therapy and aims to build a new perspective for understanding the working mechanisms of art therapy in the treatment of psychotic symptoms. Similarly to the participants of the art therapy group, Kuura, whose experiences are explored in this article, does not want to become identified as 'crazy'. The aim of this text is to respect and explore her unique experiences of psychic suffering as well as to better understand our shared process of art therapy, and to avoid 'labelling' her experiences. In contrast to her psychiatrist, Kuura did not recognise her experiences as psychotic. She could, however, acknowledge that the cognitive-analytic conceptualisation of multiple separate self-states matched the abrupt and uncontrollable nature of her experiences.

Cognitive-analytic theory and the dialogical self in art therapy

Kerr, Brickett and Chanen (2003) describe cognitive-analytic therapy (CAT) as an integrative interactive therapy which is based on a radically social notion of self and in which the main emphasis is on extending explicit self-reflective observing (Ryle and Kerr 2002). All mental actions are considered to be partly based on the sign-mediated internalisation of early interactive experiences and those social meanings which are associated with them. Self is based in this dialogical interaction, which can be described with Ryle's (1985, 2005) concept of reciprocal role procedures (RRPs) or Leiman's (1997, 2004) concept of dialogical sequences. These internalised patterns of relating to self and to others intertwine certain intentions, affects, procedural memory and action connected with each different internal role (Ryle 1975). Mental processes are thus always observed in a dialogically positioned interactive context constructed of different inner 'voices' and their relations (Stiles *et al.* 2006). I have proposed elsewhere that art therapy offers multilayered possibilities of exploring these 'voices' both during making art and observing the finished art object. Instead of using solely interpersonal verbal exploration, it enables concrete and embodied observation of emotional and cognitive experiences (Rankanen 2011, 2014).

Multiple voices in 'I' become visible

Kuura and I undertook a journey to familiarise ourselves in art and discussions with her repertoire of different internal figures and their dialogues. Visual art enabled the otherwise unrecognised figures to become concretely visible and observable through the senses, whereas our discussions explored the emotional relationships between them and built narratives for them. This is central work in developing a more coherent sense of self. When many self-processes are described as dialogues between internalised figures and voices, it is not always clear with which voice the 'I' is identified or if it is actually a 'federation' of many different voices instead of being a unitary 'I' (Ryle and Kerr 2002: 35). 'The therapist's task is to identify the restrictive and damaging voices and to encourage the emergence of a more reflective, independent, superordinate and complex "I".' (Ryle and Kerr 2002: 36). The repertoire of reciprocal roles defines the range of experienced possibilities and space for personal agency, and simultaneously shapes and limits the sense of self and others (Ryle and Kerr 2002).

Separate self-states restrict reflective observation

Anthony Ryle (1985, 1991, 1994) suggested that we can translate the concept of object relationships into cognitive language as largely unconscious reciprocal role procedures (RRPs). The repertoire of RRPs is internalised from real interaction during the course of life and, for example, significant experiences of separation or loss can affect the integration of procedures. Normally, we have quite a continuous experience of self in different situations, although at times everyone experiences some discontinuity. If the experiences are instead fragmented, uncontrollable, and vary in an extreme way from moment to moment, they can be described as separate self-states, which restrict or distort the capability to observe reality (Ryle 1985, 1997).

Absorbed in a particular self-state, the experience of reciprocity between internal roles is lost and one state of mind dominates the emotions, thoughts and actions. The current self-state rules the way in which one views and experiences self and others and how one responds to these experiences in action. Awareness of alternatives and flexibility of experience, perception and action have disappeared (Beard, Marlowe and Ryle 1990). A concrete dialogue with art materials and artworks has especial importance in those self-states where the internal dialogue is rigid, cruel or absent. It can aid in binding novel embodied meanings into previously stagnated mental and emotional views. Additionally, explicit dialogue with the artworks can aid in seeing the un-owned counter-position of the current self-state. Both embodied dialogue with materials during art-making and explicit discussion with the therapist can aid flexibility and build reflective distance into the damaging self-states.

Embodied artistic observation of un-integrated dialogues

In CAT, both personality disorders and psychotic symptoms are viewed as resulting from disruptions or failures in the integration of self processes and difficulties in achieving a subjective experience of continuous and integrated existence (Ryle and Kerr 2002). Certain unbearable reciprocal roles or dialogical voices can be dissociated into separate self-states outside conscious observing. In this context, many psychotic experiences can be described as amplified or distorted role procedures or as a total absence of dialogue (Kerr et al. 2003). The experienced discontinuity of self and sudden uncontrollable changes in self-states cause strong feelings of anxiety and difficulty in linking memories with feelings, actions and meanings. The narrative self, which binds together the sense of personal and social meaning, is fragmented. While in one self-state, the other states might be difficult or impossible to remember, resulting in amnesia between the different states. In therapy, the fragmented self-states and amnesia between them cause difficulties in attempts to integrate or create coherent narratives for experiences. Art offers a method for non-verbal expression, and for visually explicit sharing of many emotional states which would otherwise be too overwhelming and which have previously remained dissociated (Hughes 2007). By making the dissociated states externally visible, it is possible to increase distance from overwhelming sensations, which aids their explicit observation. Additionally, artworks document different self-states and enable a return to exploring otherwise forgotten states.

Unintegration of mental structures also impairs anxiety regulation skills and causes an inability to handle emotions without support from other people. Without the presence of the other and the dialogue with her, one is left alone with a frightening and uncontrollable inner dialogue or in a state of total emptiness and existential loneliness without any dialogue. When out of dialogue, the sense of self can dissolve, and this can be an even more intolerable experience than, for example, a self-destructive and hurting dialogue, which can thus form a defensive procedure against extremely confusing experiences of disappearing.

The concrete act of making art and handling materials is of special value with emotionally unstable clients. If a client's attachment system is hyperactive, strong emotions can restrict their ability to enter reflective dialogues and alter the client's self-state into developmentally earlier non-mentalising moods. This causes difficulties in connecting meanings with thoughts, whereas mental states can only be handled in concrete embodied and material actions (Koivisto *et al.* 2009). Art can become the channel for expressing and handling the evoked emotions in an adaptive way (Hinz 2009, Lusebrink 1990). Regulation becomes possible with the help of a material and tangible piece of art. Later, during another more reflective self-state, the implicit experiences can be remembered and meanings tied to the object being discussed. Embodied and emotional experiences can then become integrated with words and foster explicit cognitive understanding. Art thus enables the tangible sharing and understanding of dissociated self-states. Additionally, it offers an exit from helplessness in relation to the damaging self-state by enabling concrete acts of trying out, playing with and building a visible range of new possible ways to relate in it. Artworks can always be worked on over and over again, actively exploring and reformulating the meanings tied up within them. This process can initiate the integration of implicit embodied experiences and explicit reflection skills.

Exploration of case narratives

When we met for the first time, Kuura had left the hospital two days previously after being an inpatient in a psychiatric ward for over eight months. She was under heavy medication, including antidepressants and antipsychotics. She had physical experiences of both freezing and inability to move, as well as uncontrollable restlessness. These were in addition to distressing self-destructive thoughts and behaviour, which she experienced as impossible to ease by any means except taking strong medication and falling asleep. In some states her perception distorted and she heard disturbing voices. In spite of her overwhelming anxiety and uncontrollable experiences, Kuura was very determined. She made high demands on herself and conveyed grim expectations for coping. She was used to having excellent cognitive skills and was very annoyed by her amnesia. She could not find any reason for her psychological problems. Simultaneously with feeling too scared to be alone, she did not want anyone to know of her difficult state, be worried or take care of her. Currently, three years later, she is still anxious at times and needs on-going medication, but she has found other ways of coping when the anxiety is at a lower level, such as writing poems or listening to the lyrics of music. She is also able to study and enjoy learning. Art therapy has not been the only form of treatment: In addition, she has received normal psychiatric care in psychiatric clinic and has spent short periods in both psychiatric day hospital and in inpatient ward.

Diverse perspectives to artworks from different times

The first interview took place twenty-two months and ninety-six sessions after the beginning of the art therapy. I was interested in which artworks Kuura remembers from therapy and which emotions she connects with her memories of the images. After recalling each picture (The Three-Headed Girl, Making Music, The Map and The Girl with the Masks) we jump back in time and I present my original notes on the art-making situations and our discussions, which I wrote immediately after each session. Then we move to the second interview, which took place twenty-six months after the beginning of the therapy, and where we returned to look at and discuss those four artworks. This was the first time that we concretely observed earlier pictures from the course of therapy. I was interested in how Kuura now sees them and what kind of emotions or thoughts they awake in her. Additionally, I was curious as to whether the images would match her memories. I found it interesting that although Kuura stated she did not remember anything from the time she started the therapy, three of the four works she remembered were made during the first three months of therapy. Even the last one was made nine months after the beginning of therapy.

The Three-Headed Girl

In our first interview, Kuura recalled that she had made a girl with three heads out of modelling clay. She did not remember what the heads looked like, but she guessed one was good, the other was bad and the third was something in between. I asked what kind of feelings she connected with the Three-Headed Girl. Kuura remembered her inability to make anything out of the modelling clay. She recalled experiencing difficult feelings after making the clay model. It felt too revealing. The artwork depicted her state of mind too well. I asked if it still had the same meaning for her, but Kuura said she did not know. It was not nice to reminisce. When I now view Kuura's experiences evoked by modelling the clay, I see a dialogue between a demanding or critical position in relation to an inept and bad counter-position. At the same time, the Three-Headed Girl shows her negative feelings, which Kuura would not want to see.

Therapist's notes from the third session, in which Kuura moulded the Three-Headed Girl

Kuura came early and had made four small pictures at home. First there was a poor girl in fog under a rain cloud. We discussed how the girl experienced her situation and found out that she could not see anything outside the fog. The cloud was following her where ever she went—she could not step away from it. On the other side of the paper was the same girl in an endless circle of failures, blaming herself and feeling bad. On another sheet of paper, she had drawn a restless and scared girl in the middle of the night. She could not feel safe anywhere. Instead, she was very scared and anxious all the time. I saw many different dialogues within these pictures. The cloud was governing and restricting the helpless girl, but on the other hand the same girl was blaming herself and feeling bad. Another girl was threatened by uncontrollable nightmares or scary thoughts with which she engaged in a scared position.

I asked if Kuura wanted to create a picture, and she answered: 'Yes, gladly.' I was about to offer her some paper, but I saw the modelling clay, and asked if she would like to try it. She smiled and said: 'OK, it is really a long time since the last time I modelled.' We both began to mould our own pieces. We sat quietly for a while before we talked. We discussed how Kuura experienced being angry. I got to know that she never felt or expressed anger towards others. She was only angry and violent towards herself. I suggested that anger sounded like an important issue for us. Our aim would be to find and practice more constructive ways to express anger than hurting herself. During our dialogue, I experienced myself as curious and interested in relation to her genuine position. On the other hand, Kuura was expressing in her art-making her inner dialogue, where the angry side was hurting the emotionally dissociated wounded side.

Kuura moulded a girl with three heads (Figures 7.1, 7.2). The middle head had a smiling face which was visible to others. On the left-hand side was the irritated red head, which was angry and violent—kicking and hitting herself. The head on the right side was disgusted and felt nauseous. Her feelings were similar to those of the girl who stood in the rain. She felt like a loser and blamed herself. Currently I recognise that each of the figure's heads had a different inner dialogue. The angry figure head was out of dialogue with the invisible wounded side. The shaming loser was counter-positioned with the blaming voice and the middle head, which was performing happiness or gladness for others, was not truly seen for real.

Figure 7.2 The Three-Headed Girl (Modelling clay, 12 cm × 10 cm × 8 cm).

Observing the Three-Headed Girl twenty-six months later

I: What does the Three-Headed Girl look like currently?

K: Stupid. The angry is angrier than I thought at that time. The disgusted one could be even more disgusted—the expression is not so strong. The glad has calmed down. It is more like satisfied, not so very glad. How long ago did I make this?

I: Two years.

K: It doesn't feel like such a long time.

I: Does it remind you of the feeling you had at the time?

K: No, it does not. It has nothing depressed, melancholic or sad in it. I do not know if that angry face was angry then, or was it anguished? There are also a lot of holes, it is missing a lot. There should be more heads.

I: You mean it has changed in that way? You notice now that there is more variety and tones in her experiences—not just those three possibilities?

Playing Music and the Prosecutor General

We now return to the first interview, where Kuura remembered a picture of playing music together with her friends. It reminded her of friendship and pleasant cooperation. This image evoked both positive and negative feelings. She remembered the enjoyable moments of playing together. She recalled that the drawing was yellow, which depicted a good feeling for her. However, these moments were past, which instead evoked negative melancholic feelings in her. Currently, I see her relation to the artwork as containing two different dialogues—one where it is possible to be connected with others and experience being capable, and another where the connection to others is lost and where one feels helpless and unable to make contact with them.

Therapist's notes from the fifth session

Kuura was quiet and sat on the edge of the chair. She looked down at the floor. She had forgotten all of the previous days, because an unpleasant drama had taken place the day before. An employee in a day centre had shouted at her without any reason. Kuura's friend defended her and asked the employee to apologise. Still, she felt very ashamed of being the focus of attention and wished to sink under the ground. Her intolerable anxiety and restlessness had continued from there onwards.

I asked if she could make an image of the bad feeling. She wanted to draw with dry pastels, and I gave her a very large piece of paper. She asked if the image should fill the whole page, but I suggested to her to leave the other side empty for drawing another feeling later. She focused for a long time on drawing eyes with green pastel and returned at many points to make them more cruel-looking. Under the eyes she made a small crouched figure, which had her hands on her ears. At the top, she drew strong straight red lines, which she strengthened with black strokes. She made another little red figure down on the paper which sat cross-legged with her back to the viewer. Between the eyes and the small figures, she made a black mess and hands on both sides of it (Figure 7.3).

To me, the mess looked like a shouting mouth but Kuura said it was just a lump. She described how the hands were trying to push a glass wall in front of them and how all the characters were separated from each other in their own glass boxes. The harsh-looking figure told the small ones that they were bad and wrong. They did not deserve to even exist because everything in them was flawed. I asked what happened to the cruel figure if the small characters went away. Kuura said that they would always be replaced by new ones so that the cruel figure always had somebody to blame. I asked if the cruel figure then needed these small characters, but Kuura said it did not need anybody. I asked if there had been times in her life when the cruel figure had been smaller. 'It is me', Kuura said. I said that the cruel figure was not her, because she also has many other sides. Of course she could experience it as one part of her, but it was not everything she is. Kuura explained that the cruel side had always existed, but she had only begun to become aware of it during the last year. I asked if this figure had some similarity to the heads of the modelling clay figure, but she denied this. This figure was the worst of all—the Prosecutor General. He told everybody that they were somehow flawed lousy losers, which made the small figures feel ashamed and question their right to even exist.

Figure 7.3 The Prosecutor General (Soft pastels, 72 cm × 44 cm).

Next, I asked Kuura to recall and draw another moment, when she had felt good, enjoyed herself or felt comfortable. Her movements changed totally. She drew in an easy, fast and relaxed way three people who were playing music. She drew colourful lamps in each corner and above them a singing dream bird (Figure 7.4). When she had finished drawing, I described for her how different her movements and touch seemed to be. She smiled and described how fun it was to play music together. In the picture, she was happy and playing with her friends like she used to. Not only her inner dialogue but also her embodied dialogue with the art materials changed during making this picture.

Figure 7.4 Playing Music and the Prosecutor General (Soft pastels, 72 cm × 104 cm).

Observing Playing Music and the Prosecutor General Two Years Later

When we observe the picture twenty-six months later, Kuura is surprised. She had not remembered the Prosecutor General. However, she recognises now that she is not only the cruel person. The black lump and the small characters depict other parts of her.

I: You are the black messed lump, the obstructive person with angry eyes as well as those small cowering nice persons in the picture?

K: Except the small ones just look nice, they are not truly nice because they have turned away from others.

I: OK. And you remember the incident with which this was connected?

K: Yes.

I: How do you feel when you look at the other side of the picture?

K: A little melancholic. I feel bad, because I wish I could still make music with these friends. But I can't. And I cannot learn by myself—I need another person, who tells me what to do.

I: You mean you would like to have somebody guiding you?

K: Mm. And that person should also enjoy it and not only be a teacher. Because otherwise I become anxious and think I should be better or become better faster.

I: So the demands are there right away. Those others are expecting something from you.

K: Mm.

I: And you think you are not good enough?

K: Mm.

I: And then you feel disappointed or irritated, or?

K: No, it is not irritation. I feel like giving up.

I: So before you were capable of doing things you enjoyed but now you have lost it somehow finally—you cannot experience it again?

K: Mm.

I: Do you actually become sad looking at this picture?

K: Nods silently.

I: And if you compare this feeling with the three-headed girl?

K: The music playing picture awakes more emotions.

I: Now this modelling clay does not awake so much emotion any more?

K: No.

I: So these artworks, which at the time pictured bad feelings, are not affecting you in a similar way in the current moment?

K: Or then I myself have been more obstructive. But I do remember that rejection, and I will never go there again because they acted like that. It would be just the same if it was right or wrong. I feel so bad when I think about how they snubbed me there.

I: Yes—you should be angry with them.

K: Well, I should handle the anger and move forward, not be trapped in it for ever.

I: Mm. But are you allowed to be angry?

K: I should be angry.

I: But is it so that you cannot be, or it is too scary?

K: I cannot. I am sadder.

I: So the anger turns into sadness?

K: Mm.

I: And instead of directing the anger outside you, it somehow turns inside?

K: Yes.

Continuing discussion of the most important images—Playing Music and the Black Lump

I: Which of these pictures are most important for you currently?

K: Playing Music is most important and that black lump is also quite important.

I: You mean the black mess in the cruel picture, which you recognized as being a part of you?

K: Or it is like a lump in a throat.

I: Is the lump like a feeling in a throat? Which is somehow stuck and doesn't come out?

K: Yes.

I: Is it sadness or anger, or?

K: I don't know. Maybe it is all the emotions at the moment.

I: So, all the emotions are somehow packed in there?

K: Mm. But I found a good way to manage anxiety. We went on a rollercoaster which goes upside down and I thought 'Now I'm going to die!' It was a real adrenalin rush! I became straight away adrenalin junkie. I am going to travel around the world bungee jumping.

We laugh together.

The Taped Map

In the first interview, I also asked if Kuura remembered any of the homework. Kuura remembered the Map, in which she glued the pieces of her ripped picture back together. She experienced it as quite a groovy and nice task. She had not done anything like it before and the outcome turned out totally unlike the starting point. She found herself in a surprised and curious position in relation to the challenging art task. She made this homework between the eleventh and twelfth sessions.

Therapist's notes from the eleventh and twelfth sessions

Kuura painted a landscape which pictured an ideally good place from outside and an unbearable bad place from inside and a path which was between them. Inside the bad place was a deep darkness, a river and a path, which was not going anywhere and where you could only get lost. In the background were high mountains with snow peaks. During the year before, it had not yet been possible to even see the bad place, because it was invisible somewhere behind the mountains. The yellow bowl was the good place. It was not possible to enter the bowl, but it contained a warm, vivid and dazzling place, which was protected with coloured light, like a rainbow or aurora borealis. It was easy to fall down from the good place but the road from the bad place to the good place was long and difficult (Figure 7.5).

Figure 7.5 The Map (Therapist's copy of Kuura's original painting) Poster paints, 52 cm × 72 cm.

I asked where Kuura was in the image at that moment and she made a yellow fingerprint on the path between the good and the bad place. I continued by asking where she was last year, and she placed herself in the river inside the bad place. A year ago, she was lost and astray in the darkness. Two years ago she was on the path close to the good place and five years ago in the good place. For me it was possible to imagine these two places as picturing an ideally protected and safe self-state and an absolutely unsecure and needy self-state.

I asked if someone else could also enter this landscape. Kuura denied it. I took a toy dinosaur from the table and asked if this could enter there? She started to laugh and said no. I took a monkey and asked if that could be there? K: 'Maybe, somewhere far away behind the mountains.' I took a small turtle, 'how about this?' K: 'No, it cannot.' I: 'How about this small frog, can it enter there?' K: 'Maybe, somewhere far outside the bad place.' She looked at the point on the path where she had placed herself. I asked: 'I guess it must feel quite heavy to be right there?' 'Yes', she answered. Kuura smudged the yellow fingerprint on the path. 'This has begun to look really stupid', she said. I: 'You don't like it any more? Is it irritating?' K: 'Yes, it is ugly. Actually the whole work is stupid.' I: 'What would you like to do with it?' K: 'I could tear it up.' I: 'Well, go ahead.' Kuura tore the picture carefully into rectangular pieces. I felt calm. I thought how good it was to have a possibility of showing and handling anger in a manageable and symbolic way. After shredding the picture, she placed the pieces in a beautiful pile and handed them to me. I said: 'Well, now I also have homework for you.' I gave the pieces back to Kuura and asked her to use them for a collage. 'Oh no', she said. 'I shouldn't have shredded the picture. The work will be huge if I use all of these pieces.' I: 'You can place these on top of each other and use them as a base for your work. Please bring the work for me the next time we meet.' K: 'Well, you did give me a challenging task.' I: 'Yes, I feel quite nasty. I wonder when you will get angry at me.' K: 'Well, that you will have to wait for.' After the session, I felt I had failed and made a mistake. I thought that my reaction was not appropriate and this allowed me to experience how uncomfortable and guilty it felt to be inside the bad place. I experienced the inner dialogue between accusing and awkward positions within myself.

At the beginning of our next session, she took a taped-up picture out of her bag (Figures 7.6, 7.7). 'This was a really good and nice task' she said. 'It was just difficult to stick the pieces together, so I had to tape them.' She seemed pleased with the work. I examined the picture for a long time and read aloud some texts from it. The phrase: 'I hated the girl who spoiled her life' was important for Kuura. I wondered if that girl was able to like or feel sympathy for herself. 'No, she cannot,' Kuura said. On the other hand, the challenge of repairing the picture was counter-positioned with her experience of capability. In her dialogue with the valued artwork she could experience pride.

Figure 7.6 The Taped Map (Collage, 32 cm × 99 cm).

The ideal image on the right-hand side of the picture contained relaxation, love and joy. I asked if these could be her wishes, but she did not think so. She would have needed a miracle to experience happy feelings. They could only be reached by suddenly waking up and being an eight-year-old girl again, for whom everything was fine. I wondered whether she could care for that child, but Kuura said she was too far away in the past. It was not possible to experience the happy child as a part of her current self. In the middle of the picture there was a wall of fire and chains which prevented one from going further. I admitted that it must be very difficult to go through the fire and free oneself from the chains. When I observed the picture, I experienced deep sorrow in my dialogue with the image, which I saw as wounded and hurt.

Figure 7.7 The Taped Map (back) (Collage, 32 cm × 99 cm).

Observing the Taped Map two years later

I: This is the homework you remembered.

K: Yes, the map. (Reads texts from the picture aloud) '*Cried, disappointed and ashamed. I understand those who hang around violence*'—this is the adrenalin rush which makes you forget the anxiety!

I: Mm.

K:*'Hospital. Extreme trauma. Affected and crying. Died of worries. Embar-
rassed! Restless feet. Are you also worried? Secret role. I cried and was
frustrated.'* I should do these again! These were great!

I: Yes.

K: *'I thought I would become crazy.'*—Well, how strange. *'Abused girls. Help,
someone ... Hit. Not allowed to be afraid. I hated the girl who spoiled her
life.'*—Well that is quite a striking phrase. *'One has managed with medicines.
No warning about the catastrophe.'*

I: And here is some more.

K: *'Suddenly I woke up. I was eight years old again.'* That one I remember! *'No
need to be afraid. No need to be ashamed. New easy life. Feelings are not
killing you. It doesn't mean that one wouldn't love. Carefree. Happy souls.
Shared accepting air. Now the hope is not dying. New day. Relaxed.'* These
two phrases are the most important: 'I hated the girl who spoiled her life' and
'Suddenly I woke up. I was eight years old again.'

I: What is important in those?

K: It would just be so cool to wake up and start everything from the beginning—
in another way. And the other phrase—when you see yourself spoiling your
own life—you may hate that girl. If it had been someone else who spoiled
your life, but when you experience you have yourself caused it and spoiled
your own life ...

I: You mean there is some kind of blaming? It is not only anger, but somehow
blaming?

K: Yes. One is exasperated about being like this, for not doing better. But any-
way, it is an especially bad thing when you see from outside that someone is
spoiling her own chances.

I: And this would be a good thing. *'Suddenly I woke up and was eight years old
again'*. (Points to the work.)

K: Well, I would like to be a child. Then one could get away from everything.

I: Yes, one could get away from being guilty.

K: Yes. I could be a child forever. That would be quite nice.

I: But as an adult it is also possible to free oneself from the guilt and decide it
was not my fault, I didn't spoil it.

K: But if it feels like one spoiled it.

I: Yes, I understand it feels like that.

K: Mm.

I: But in principle, you could think like a child. You could in a way overcome
that blaming anger or free yourself from your own blaming and demands?

The Girl with the Masks

In the first interview, Kuura also remembered that she drew a girl with smiling
and sad masks. She experienced that the smiling face had started to crumble a

little bit since the time of making the picture. It was not so easy to keep it up any more, which she experienced as good, because she does not fake so much any more. In a way, she also experienced it as bad, because she could not fake any more, even if she would have liked to. Simultaneously, as she was a little bit more visible in a genuine way, she would not have wanted to show all the lousy feelings she had. She did not want to make other people worried. Instead, she at least sometimes wanted to fake how she felt and be less transparent. I experienced it as very positive that Kuura had become more visible as she is. I remembered our first session, when I had asked Kuura to pick a card which pictured her hopes and aim for the therapy. She chose a picture of a little red-haired Native American child who had black stripes painted on his skin. Kuura said that she would like to become more visible and explained she had been invisible too long in a wrong, harmful way. In that sense, I felt good hearing her becoming more visible, even if it did not always feel so nice for her. I now reflect that her dialogical relation into unpleasant and negative emotions had slightly changed and she was slightly more capable of tolerating them.

Therapist's notes from the forty-eighth session

It was the last session before our Christmas vacation. Kuura was worried about becoming anxious during the Christmas break. She was scared of being at home. I wondered what was so scary there. She said it was difficult to show anyone her bad feelings. Instead she wanted to behave as if everything was fine so as not to worry anyone. I said it must be very tiring for her to perform glad simultaneously with being afraid of becoming anxious in an unmanageable way. It sounded like a cage from which it is not possible to escape. Because she needs to use a lot of energy for performing and keeping the anxiety away, this just makes the fear and anxiety grow. Kuura recognised this experience. We discussed how she could relax and feel safe in those places, where she could also experience bad feelings and where her unpleasant feelings had become seen.

After our discussion, Kuura wanted to draw. The picture became quite truthful (Figure 7.8). There was a girl who stood and pondered which of the masks she should choose. She had one mask for each day of the week. She used the angry mask only for watching herself and the sad one had totally disappeared somewhere. The smiling mask was yellow and almost invisible. In the hospital, the girl could be without a mask or use the glad and apathetic ones in turns. In therapy, she could also be without a mask and feel more pensive. I asked: 'Is there something wrong with the girl's face because she wants to cover it? At least she is not ugly, or is she?' 'Well, it can happen that she is', Kuura said. 'But mostly she just tries to choose the masks according to others' expectations, because she is quite numb and does not feel anything. She is not very glad, sad or anything else she should be.' In the girl's dialogue, others were very demanding and she answered by performing something she supposed that others would accept. Simultaneously neither herself nor the others could see her real feelings, which became dissociated outside the dialogue.

Figure 7.8 The Girl with the Masks (Soft pastels, 104 cm × 72 cm).

Observing the Girl with the Masks twenty-six months later

I: You said the Three-Headed Girl should have more different heads or she has kind of holes in her. Do you think the Girl with the Masks has those heads she is missing?

K: Yes. Here are sad, anxious, angry-surprised, angry-enraged, glad and then this nauseous face. And that one is someone invisible. It has an unseen face.

I: You mean that yellow one?

K: Yes.

I: And that one is enraged?

K: Yes. It is angry-enraged.

I: What do you think about this picture now? Is it like you remembered?

K: I thought there were more of those heads.

Joint observation of the process

I finish our story at the end of the second interview, where we explore how Kuura has experienced art therapy, art-making and observing pictures in relation to her self-understanding.

I: How did you experience observing these pictures?

K: Some of them were useless and some of them were important. That homework was nice. It is the only one I am satisfied with. I like it because of the texts. 'I hated the girl who spoiled her life' and 'Suddenly, I woke up and I was eight years old again' are good. And most important is the picture of making music. I recognised that I sometimes drew again same pictures here which I did at home or when I was a child. I wonder if there was any sense in drawing them again.

I: Maybe it has been important because of being able to discuss them? Maybe you have not had the possibility to talk about them with anyone before?

K: Yes, that's true.

I: What is it like making pictures here? Is it like in other situations?

K: No. First of all, the pictures are ugly. They are stick figures and other lousy pictures. For some reason, I cannot draw here. Elsewhere I can draw.

I: Well, maybe it is part of the importance of this therapy situation. You can practise making mistakes and not being perfect. Maybe it is important to make ugly images somewhere? How do you experience art-making here?

K: I do not think anything when I draw. But almost every time, I first imagine the picture in my mind before I start to draw. Only later on, when we look at the picture, do I start to think again.

I: Does the picture look like you planned in your mind or is there something different?

K: It looks like I thought. The surprising thing is, when I supposedly discover what it means.

I: Supposedly?

K: Well, you know, the drawings don't think. They are just two-dimensional pictures. When you ask: 'What do you think that dragon thinks?' I need to make it up: 'ah, I guess it thinks like …' In that moment, there appears something else than I thought in the beginning. It is meaningful but it needs some guidance to happen.

I: Can you say more about that? How is it for you when I guide you?

K: Well, what you say is good guidance. Sometimes if I feel irritated to start with, it can of course feel irritating.

I: Have I noticed your reaction, when I have said something that irritates you or which you find stupid? Or have I just gone on?

K: No, you have noticed how I feel.

I: Can you tell more about how you experience our discussions of the pictures?

K: When we discuss, the pictures unfold more and that impacts the way in which I feel about them. I gain more views. If I didn't like the picture in the beginning, I might get over it.

I: How have you experienced the situation when I sometimes have the picture from a previous session on the wall?

K: It has been a little bit awkward, because I never remember what I have done. Again, if I remember, it is boring, and I cannot find anything new in it.

I: Can there be anything good about viewing a picture from a previous session?

K: No, nothing good that I would recall.

I: Does art-making always feel the same, or does it change?

K: It is not always the same. It is significant where the image has been made and how I have felt. Working in the presence of other people has been easier than drawing alone. In the hospital, I could not stand to be alone and draw; I needed somebody to stay with me in the room. Later, I drew alone a lot, but I showed the pictures to nurses and the psychologist. I could not describe how I felt but I could draw it.

I: Was looking at the pictures similar to how it is in here?

K: No, talking was different. We didn't analyse the pictures. They looked at the images and said: 'That is a great picture'. In the picture group, we did not look so much at one image at the time and we were asked: 'How did you feel making it?'

I: Can you tell more—what do you mean by analysing pictures?

K: Analysing pictures is positive. I like it when we observe my pictures. The more we discuss about my issues, the more I like it. My pictures and my issues become meaningful.

I: What is it like observing pictures here?

K: They become meaningful when we first discuss, then I draw, and then we discuss again. That gives me new insights. I can find such surprises in them.

I: Would it be different if we just discussed and you didn't make any pictures?

K: The images guide me towards new issues more than just talking. The pictures unfold issues which wouldn't come to my mind by only discussing.

I: I know you also visit a psychiatric clinic where you talk and don't make pictures. Have you noticed any differences?

K: I feel worse here. I cannot hide my bad feelings so much. I guess that is partly because I have been coming here quite a long time. But it is also because images unfold feelings that I wouldn't have noticed or shown otherwise.

I: Do you think that making images can be harmful on some occasions?

K: No, never.

I: Even if you feel bad when you make them?

K: No, they cannot be harmful even if I felt bad.
I: Is there anything more that you would like to say?
K: This has been a very good form of therapy for me.

Discussion

I end this chapter by reflecting on these narratives about Kuura's art therapy from the dialogical point of view. Within the triangular relationship of art therapy, there are multiple dialogues in comparison to those occurring in verbal therapy which I aim to discuss in the following conclusions. Instead of focusing on the verbal interpersonal dialogue between therapist and client and their intrapersonal dialogues—which cognitive analytic theory already elucidates—I describe and give structure to those three additional art oriented layers of embodied, material and sensory dialogues, which I have found from the narratives of our experiences: Dialogues between art maker and art materials, dialogues within artworks and dialogues between the viewers and the artworks.

1. Dialogues between art maker and art materials

First, art maker and art material have a counter-positioned dialogue. Art materials elicit and affect both internal and external dialogue, as in Leiman's (2004) example of a potter, who goes through a rapid sequence of different positions from excitement to frustration and disappointment in relation to the clay which she is trying to mould. The potter and clay have a counter-positioned relationship which undergoes constant changes. In Kuura's case the embodied and emotional dialogue between her and art materials changed visibly at least twice. First, in the fifth session, between making the Prosecutor General and Playing Music (Figures 7.3, 7.4), where her aggressive drawing movements towards either helplessly receiving or silently resistant paper changed into easy, fast and relaxed movements in cooperation with the smooth and accepting paper. Next, the changes in material dialogue were visible in the process of making the Map, tearing it in pieces and taping them back together into a new work (Figures 7.5, 7.6, 7.7). While painting the original map of her experiences, Kuura was using poster paints instead of dry pastels, which she normally preferred. At first she had an accepting position towards painting and the picture of her experiences was accepted. However, following our dialogue and my action—where I played with toy animals which tried to enter in the landscape—her relation to the painting suddenly turned into unaccepting and she experienced that it was bad or spoiled. Her dialogue with the art materials changed into an angry position towards the contemptible picture and she destroyed it. When I asked her to use the destroyed pieces for continuing art-making, she experienced an excited and curious relationship towards the challenging art material. She was capable of repairing and transforming the material into a successful new piece, which she respected and was proud of.

For the art therapy client, the interaction with art materials often feels a safer and more self-manageable way of expressing difficult self-states or un-owned 'voices' than focusing on relational work directly with the therapist. The client actively creates meanings and maintains ownership of the artwork and its significances, unless the therapist is eager to push interpretations or is otherwise intrusive. Kuura reflected about her relationship to art-making and care personnel that she was unable to describe with words how she felt, but she could draw it. She also felt worse in therapy than in other places and could not hide her bad feelings, for making images brought up feelings that she would not have noticed or shown otherwise. During art-making, her difficult experiences became expressed and their existence concretely witnessed. At that moment they were seen and not dissociated out of sight even if many of the images were afterwards forgotten by her.

2. Dialogues within artworks

Second, artworks contain different dialogical voices within a single piece as well as between two or more pieces. However, recognising the other party of the dialogue is often not easy for it can be invisible or emotionally cut off from awareness into a separate self-state. In Kuura's homework drawings from the third session, there were visible dialogues between different elements of the drawings. The compelling cloud and threatening nightmares were governing the girl, who was captured in a helpless and scared position. In contrast, the dialogues of the three modelling clay heads (Figures 7.1, 7.2), which each contained different counter-positions within them, were visually invisible and possible to find only by empathic imagination. One was enraged and violent towards the numb or dissociated wounded side. The other was a shameful loser who was blamed and despised by an invisible voice. The third was playing happy and ignoring the voice of unrecognised real emotions. The dialogue of the third head was similar to that of the Girl with the Masks (Figure 7.8), who tried to perform according to others' demands in order to feel accepted. At the same time the demand for performing caused dissociation of her authentic feelings. On the other hand, I experienced a connection between the inner dialogues of the second head and the picture of the Prosecutor General (Figure 7.3). Kuura, however, did not find the same. The second despised head was blamed by the contemptuous voice and the Prosecutor General was extremely judgemental towards the isolated flawed and shaming creatures.

In addition to dialogical counter-positions, an artwork can thus contain different self-states. In later reflections Kuura remembered only the image of happy moments of making music but not the cruel and judgemental state of the Prosecutor General from the other side of the same picture. In Kuura's original Map painting (Figure 7.5), the contrasting self-states of perfect safety and deserted loss could be viewed simultaneously in the same landscape even if the path between these places was very fragile and easily cut off. In the Taped Map (Figure 7.6), fire and chains were preventing the possibility of moving from traumatic state into accepting experience.

3. Dialogues between the viewers and the artworks

Third, both the therapist and the client can view the same artwork from different positions. The positions they take can reflect their own inner repertoire of accepted reciprocal roles and their flexibility or rigidity. Looking at the Taped Map evoked quite different positions in me and in Kuura. I looked at the back of the picture experiencing sadness in relation to the taped wounds I saw, whereas Kuura experienced pride and satisfaction in relation to her successfully reformulated picture. Exploring diverse views can enrich therapeutic observation and give understanding of the variety of possible dialogical positions.

At first, the position and meaning of a certain figure can often seem to be fixed. One can identify with one or more figures in the artwork and feel that it is 'just like me'. Kuura identified herself with the position of the Prosecutor General. On the other hand, the black mess was meaningless for her and not connected with other parts of the picture, whereas I saw it as an angry shouting mouth of the cruel person. However, two years later her view had changed and she experienced the black lump as important. It had changed from meaningless mess into lump of stuck emotions in a throat which caused anxiety. She could also recognise that she was not solely the cruel person but understood that the black lump and the small characters also reflected some parts of her experiences. Images are thus never unambiguous and linear.

Taking diverse stands in space and time can change experiences and open novel views. Those meanings which arise while looking at the artwork can be counter-positioned or set in contrast to meanings which were experienced during art-making. At the same time, one can integrate these contrasting experiences and meanings in one piece of art. In addition to the current moment they can also refer to experiences of the past and hopes for the future, which become simultaneously observable. In other words, artwork enables the simultaneous observation of different dialogues from outside and fosters the client's capability to reflect on what kind of dialogues the artworks contain. In her final reflection, Kuura described these changes in her observing awareness during the process of art-making and when looking at the picture later. She did not recall thinking anything while drawing but only later, while looking at the picture and discussing it with me. Even though the picture looked like she had imagined it beforehand, she was surprised to discover novel and unexpected meanings in it, when I asked her to take different positions in relation to the figures in the picture and when she imagined what they experienced, thought or saw.

It is thus possible not only to view the artwork from one position and experience a counter-position appearing in the artwork but also to take an observing position to it and see both sides of the dialogue. Reaching an observing position may be made possible by looking at the artwork in different emotional states or by taking distance from it physically, or in time. We can observe the piece from different angles and distances, which tangibly enables more flexible perspectives. If we place a new object—a toy, an earlier piece, a postcard or an imagined person—in relation to the artwork, a shift, reversal or change in dialogical position can also occur. In addition to the more abstract verbal reflection, art therapists and clients are equipped with tangible visual, spatial and artistic means for observing, organising and assimilating experiences (Rankanen 2011).

When Kuura returned to look at the Three-Headed Girl two years after it was made, she saw the emotional expressions were of different qualities than she had remembered. Additionally, she felt there were a lot of holes and the girl was missing heads. She recognised the three heads did not picture any of the sad and melancholic feelings that she experienced, and felt there should be more heads for absent emotions. When we then placed the Girl with the Masks beside the Three-Headed Girl, Kuura noticed it pictured many of those emotions, which had been out of dialogue.

Kuura described these changes in her final reflections by explaining how she could gain novel views and experience how new meanings unfolded in her pictures, when we looked at them and discussed. This again had an impact on her emotions towards the images and her feelings could change. 'If I didn't like the picture in the beginning, I might get over it then.' She found that looking at her pictures and discussing them increased her experiences of meaningfulness and gave novel insights.

Within the triangular relationship of art therapy, all these layers of concrete and dialogical art-oriented actions, reformulations and descriptions can thus be transformed into an increasingly reflective understanding of self and others.

References

Beard, H., Marlowe, M. and Ryle, A. (1990). 'The management and treatment of personality disordered patients. The use of sequential diagramatic reformulation', *British Journal of Psychiatry*, 156: 541–45.

Brooker, J. *et al.* (2006). *The use of art work in art psychotherapy with people who are prone to psychotic states*, London: Goldsmiths College.

Crawford, M.J. *et al.* (2012). 'Group art therapy as an adjunctive treatment for people with schizophrenia: a randomised controlled trial (MATISSE)', *Health Technology Assessment*, vol. 16, no. 8. DOI:10.3310/hta16080.

Duncan, B.L. *et al.* (2003). 'The session rating scale: Preliminary psychometric properties of a "working" alliance measure', *Journal of Brief Therapy*, 3(1): 3–12.

Goldfried, M. and Davila, J. (2005). 'The role of relationship and technique in therapeutic cahnge', *Psychotherapy: Theory, Research, Practice, Training*, 42(4): 421–30.

Hanevik, H., Hestad, K., Lien, L., Teglbjaerg, H.S., Danbolt, L.J. (2013). 'Expressive arts therapy for psychosis: A multiple case study', *The Arts in Psychotherapy*, 40: 312–21.

Hinz, L. (2009). *Expressive therapies continuum. A framework for using art in therapy*, London: Routledge.

Holttum, S. and Huet, V. (2014). 'The MATISSE trial—a critique. Does art therapy really have nothing to offer people with a diagnosis of schizophrenia?' *SAGE Open*, 4(2): 1–12. DOI:10.1177/2158244014532930.

Hughes, R. (2007). 'An enquiry into an integration of cognitive analytic therapy with art therapy', *International Journal of Art Therapy*, 12(1): 28–38.

Kerr, I.B., Birkett, P.B.L. and Chanen, A. (2003). 'Clinical and service implications of a cognitive analytic therapy model of psychosis', *Australian and New Zealand Journal of Psychiatry*, 37: 515–23.

Killick, K. and Greenwood, H. (1995). 'Research in art therapy with people who have psychotic illnesses', in Gilroy, A. and Lee, C. (eds.) *Art and Music. Therapy and Research*, London: Routledge.

Killick, K. and Schaverien, J. (eds.) (1997). *Art, psychotherapy and psychosis*, London: Routledge.

Koivisto, M., Stenberg, J-H., Nikkilä, H. and Karlsson, H. (2009). *Epävakaan persoonallisuushäiriön hoito*, Helsinki: Duodecim.

Leiman, M. (1992). 'The concept of sign in the work of Vygotsky, Winnicott and Bakhtin: Further integration of object relations theory and activity theory', *British Journal of Medical Psychology*, 65: 209–21.

Leiman, M. (1997). 'Procedures as dialogical sequences: A revised version of the fundamental concept in cognitive analytic therapy', *British Journal of Medical Psychology*, 70: 193–207.

Leiman, M. (2004). 'Dialogical sequence analysis', in Hermans, H.J.M. and Dimaggio, G. (eds.) *The Dialogical Self in Psychotherapy*, New York: Brunner-Routledge.

Lusebrink, V.B. (1990). *Imagery and visual expression in therapy*, New York: Plenum Press.

McLeod, J. (2010). *Case study research: In counselling and psychotherapy*, London: SAGE Publications.

Rankanen, M. (2011). 'The space between art experiences and reflective understanding in therapy' in Lapoujade, C., Ross, M. and Scoble, S. (eds.) *Arts Therapies and the Space Between*, ECArTE, European Consortium for Arts Therapies Education, University of Plymouth Press.

Rankanen, M. (2014). 'Clients' positive and negative experiences of experiential art therapy group process', *The Arts in Psychotherapy*, 41: 193–204.

Ruddy, R. and Milnes, D. (2005). 'Art therapy for schizophrenia or schizophrenia-like illnesses', *Cochrane Database of Systematic Reviews* 2005, Issue 4. Art. No.: CD003728. DOI:10.1002/14651858.CD003728.pub2. Retrieved 18.3.2014.

Ryle, A. (1975). 'The world's shortest account of object relations theory. Self-to-self and self-to-other', *New Psychiatry*, 24: 12–13.

Ryle, A. (1985). 'Cognitive theory, object relations and the self', *British Journal of Medical Psychology*, 58: 1–7.

Ryle, A. (1991). 'Object relations theory and activity theory: A proposed link by way of the procedural sequence model', *Brittish Journal of Medical Psychology*, 64: 307–16.

Ryle, A. (1994). 'Projective identification: A particular form of reciprocal role procedure', *Brittish Journal of Medical Psychology*, 67: 107–14.

Ryle, A. (1997). *Cognitive analytic therapy and borderline personality disorder: The model and the method,* London: John Wiley and Sons.

Ryle, A. (2005). 'Cognitive analytic therapy', in Norcross, J.C. and Goldfried, M.R. (eds.) *Handbook of Psychotherapy Integration,* Oxford: Oxford University Press.

Ryle, A. and Kerr, I. (2002). *Introducing cognitive-analytic psychotherapy. Principles and practice,* London: John Wiley and Sons.

Stiles, W.B. *et al.* (2006). 'What does the first exchange tell? Dialogical sequence analysis and assimilation in very brief therapy', *Psychotherapy Research,* 16: 408–21.

Teglbjaerg, H.S. (2009). *Kunstterapi i psykiatrisk behandling, med saerlig fokus på skizofreni,* Det Sundhedsvidenskabelige Fakultet, Aarhus Universitetet.

8

AN EXPLORATION OF ART THERAPY PROCESS WITH A DETAINEE DIAGNOSED WITH SCHIZOPHRENIA IN A CORRECTIONAL FACILITY WITH REFERENCE TO THE USE OF THE COMIC STRIP

Eleanor Hagert

This chapter is an art therapy case study describing work that the author undertook in a correctional facility located in an urban area of the United States of America. This case study explores the use of the comic strip format in art therapy, and discusses whether this format could provide containment for the detainee concerned, who had a diagnosis of schizophrenia.

As Day and Onorato (1989) and Fenner and Gussak (2006) have shown, inmates often employ defence mechanisms to maintain an experience of safety when adjusting to incarceration. I will explore some defensive strategies that can be observed among inmates and how these affect the use of art therapy. Riley (1999) and Fernandez (2009) have shown that the comic strip format has the potential to hold threatening emotions by providing a sense of security, and Liebmann (1990) has shown that this format allows the artist a feeling of control and agency.

The chapter proposes that the imagery that resulted from the use of this approach articulated the needs of this highly defended detainee, for whom I will use the pseudonym 'Jeremiah', who was adaptively surviving in an emotionally restrictive environment. It seems to me that through his attempts to avoid emotional states and libidinal impulses, Jeremiah used the comic strip template as a coping mechanism to explore his fantasies of controlling his experience.

Psychoanalytic theories of containment will be referred to in my discussions of the intentions of my approach in general and the use of the comic strip format in particular. Throughout our sessions Jeremiah's environment, his delusions and our therapeutic relationship required complex forms of containment, and these will be described. The concepts of 'holding' and 'containment' will be discussed to explain the intentions of my approach, with reference to the work of Ogden (2004).

Art therapy in the correctional setting

Research undertaken by the dual trained art therapists and psychologists Gussak and Virshup (1997) has suggested that correctional populations benefit from the art therapy modality. At the same time, the complexities of these settings present particular challenges to the therapist attempting to meet the therapeutic needs of the individuals therein. One of these is that correctional facilities are rarely considered therapeutic environments, in that from a managerial standpoint the primary purpose is penalisation, as discussed by the art therapists Day and Onorato (1989). Accordingly the therapist is required to adapt to the nature of the correctional setting while at the same time bearing in mind that many inmates[1] are still receptive and motivated for change. Fenner and Gussak (2006) recognise that adjustment to incarceration can result in resistance to therapy, because of inmates' distrust of verbal self-disclosure and voicing vulnerabilities. They state that: 'rigid defences, manifested through silence, lies, and aggressive acts, are built for basic survival' (2006: 414). Within this setting, survival becomes the priority, and enactments of 'survival of the fittest' challenge the presentation of vulnerabilities (Gussak 2009: 205). Day and Onorato (1989) suggest that through artmaking, inmates are enabled to 'voice their emotions' in a safe manner, while allowing them an experience of control. The process of creative expression can create experiences of containment and catharsis, and the finished product can contribute to an experience of holding, metaphorically containing potentially threatening emotions on the page (1989: 128).

As Day and Onorato (1989) have shown, the therapeutic alliance also has the important potential to provide validation of the inmate. They state that by regarding the inmate's creative process and artwork as valuable, the therapist fosters an emotional relationship with the individual, which can lead to validation and emotional progress. The acknowledgment of this research supports compassionate recognition of suffering within this population that might otherwise be ignored due to the stigma attached to its criminal status. The therapist can serve the individual by appreciation of their humanness, as a person who deserves relief from distress. Art therapy can serve as a vehicle, not only for mastery of the individual's experience, but also as an opportunity to create a healing bond with another human being.

Use of defence within the correctional setting

Awareness of how the setting influences inmate behaviour and identity can shape how the clinician works within the correctional system, especially in relation to how the individuals therein use defence mechanisms. Psychologist and psychoanalyst McWilliams (1994) discusses how defence mechanisms are utilised as protective measures, and describes their unconscious purpose as 'the avoidance or management of some powerful, threatening feeling, usually anxiety but sometimes overwhelming grief and other disorganizing emotional experiences' (1994: 97).

She further explains that defences are formulated from healthy and adaptive attempts at understanding and experiencing the world around us. These coping strategies are being employed to protect the self against what is perceived to be a threat.

Gussak and Virshup (1997) show that within the correctional setting, this threat exists on both internal and external levels. They suggest that because of the restrictive nature of the setting, inmates are constantly in avoidance of emotional states and 'real' human contact (1997: 29). They also remind us that 'rigid defence mechanisms' can be used in this setting to ensure survival, further emphasising this point by stating that: 'What may be considered maladaptive defences in the outside society are adaptive inside' (1997: 1). They argue the importance of the therapist's own ability to adapt 'to prison standards, not standards of the outside world' (1997: 2), and thereby encourage the inmates' notion of self, while allowing them to maintain their defences. Further, they propose that art therapy can circumvent the mechanisms employed to avoid uncomfortable emotions and impulses, enabling inmates to 'channel and discharge strong emotion', within an emotionally limiting setting (1997: 39). At the same time, because the inmates are generally unaware of the self-disclosure of their artwork, it also meets the requirements of their defences.

The comic strip as art therapy

In my opinion the use of the comic strip format has much potential as an art therapy modality. The art therapists Lucas-Falk and Moon (2010) propose that the comic strip can be defined as a 'narrative sequence composed of pictures and words', further developing into 'bordered panels that give structure to the narrative' (2010: 231). The art therapist Fernandez (2009) suggests that through examination of a structured illustrative narrative the artist becomes able to identify and control threatening emotions while examining the 'incongruity of reality and fantasy' (2009: 91). She describes the use of the comic strip as a process that allows for distance through its bordered containment of words and imagery. This distance occurs through the container that the comic strip border provides on the paper.

Gussak and Virshup (1997) discuss the concept of containment as a device that could be utilised to 'confront pain at a safe and manageable pace' (1997: 138). The art therapist Riley (1999) examines these ideas, describing the drawn border on a page as a container. She recognizes that resistance to artmaking can occur because 'patients who are not ready to deal with their primitive visual expressions can be deeply distressed by their own inner turmoil, emerging in the artwork' (1999: 101). When a client is decompensating she suggests using a border around the imagery, stating that the containment provided through the use of a border allows for 'suppression of the inner turbulence' (Riley 1999: 101). Riley's technique included her intervening in the artistic process if the client appeared distressed, and suggesting that the artist and art therapist create a border around the image together. In the approach that I took in my own work, I provided clients with a sheet of paper that had a border already drawn on the page, in my hopes that the border may provide some unconscious experience of containing the internal experience. Riley also proposes that the act of the art therapist physically holding the artwork signifies another layer of containment. In my mind, Riley's ideas reflect those of Winnicott's 'holding environment', to which Mitchell and Black (1995) refer and define as: 'a physical and psychical space within which the infant is protected without knowing he is protected' (1995: 126).

Although the container of the comic strip holds the imagery, the therapeutic relationship itself becomes another metaphoric container. Writing about the psychoanalytic setting, Mitchell and Black (1995) present this idea in their statement: 'The analyst and the analytic situation provide a holding environment in which aborted self-development can be reanimated, safe enough for the true self to begin to emerge' (1995: 133). McWilliams (2004) points to Bion's theories (1970) where the therapist also functions as a 'container' of intolerable emotions or imagery experienced by the patient (2004: 134).

At the time of undertaking the work described in this chapter, I comprehended the terms 'holding' and 'containment' broadly, as a similar emotional experience for the individual that was in accord with my wish to convey a feeling of safety towards Jeremiah that would allow for his emotional tolerance and psychological growth. I have since understood that these concepts are quite different and the psychoanalyst Ogden (2004) provides clarity in his definition and differentiation of these terms. He reminds us that Bion was not referring to the 'container' as an object but rather 'the processing (dreaming) of thoughts derived from lived emotional experience' (2004: 1362), whereas Winnicott's idea of 'holding' is more emotionally akin to the consistent 'arms of the mother' (2004: 1362). I wondered if the process of creating art within the safety of a border, as discussed by Riley (1999) and Fernandez (2009), could be a metaphor for creating a physical space for processing unconscious emotion, thereby giving substance to something unrealised. I saw this as being in line with Ogden's (2004: 1,362) discussion of the 'container-contained' and the processing of 'lived emotional experiences'.

Linking psychoanalytic theory with art therapy practice, Killick (1997, 2000) has discussed the containing values of the art therapy setting itself, and the use of concrete art materials. In reference to the art room functioning as a container Killick (2000: 105) states 'Initially the therapist's task was to establish a boundaried space which could be experienced as a safe place for the patient to be'. In addition, she recognises the value of using actual containers such as folders, boxes and notebooks to contribute to the sense of containment (1997). To me these actual containers, as well as the comic strip border, are resonant with the 'analytic frame' (Spuriell 1983), where the consistent rules and boundaries of the therapeutic space (McWilliams 2004) and the mutual exploration of unconscious material (Spuriell 1983) provide an experience of containment. Similarly, the border of the comic strip could make these experiences, of the 'analytic frame', 'holding' and 'containment' more tangible. Detailed discussion of the idea that these objects and rules support containment is beyond the scope of this chapter. However, I suggest that they could metaphorically create an internal experience of safety in the artist's mind that allows for the processing of unconscious emotions. In this chapter I discuss my physical holding of Jeremiah's artwork, which I see as being related to this suggestion. By placing his artwork into a folder and carrying it back and forth to him each session, I hoped that he felt that his work and identity was protected. I later wondered if my desire to protect him contributed to his ability to process his emotional experience with me.

The method

The art therapy process presented in this chapter consisted of open studio groups, held on the mental health observation units of a correctional facility. As discussed by the art therapist Malchiodi (2007), an open studio group refers to a setting in which clients are provided with a choice of materials and are encouraged to engage in self-directed art-making. Groups were structured in a way that allowed the detainees to come and go as they pleased and they were encouraged to work on 'whatever interested them'. All detainees were encouraged to participate; however, attendance was voluntary.

The therapeutic aim of the group was to facilitate the use of creative expression as a healthy coping skill while reducing aggressive or self-injurious behaviour among participants. Persons (2009) has described this as one of the benefits of art therapy in this setting. The group met weekly and consisted of ten to fifteen participants, and was held in the day room of a dormitory style unit. Due to the large size this group was quite hectic and emotionally charged, as detainees appeared to be vying for materials and attention. However, the overall mood of the group was usually positive and the participants were generally respectful of each other, the therapists, and the care and maintenance of the materials.

Jeremiah

Jeremiah was a 40-year-old man with a history of psychiatric hospitalisations, homelessness and substance abuse. He was charged with various rape and sexual misconduct offences. He had been given the diagnosis of schizophrenia. This psychosis was recorded in his chart by the staff psychiatrist as being revealed through 'delusional and disorganized thinking, internal preoccupation, and illogical nonsensical speech'. Jeremiah presented religious preoccupation and somatic delusions. These consisted of theories related to breathing processes, which he claimed to expel negative forces from the body and surrounding atmosphere. These delusions made it difficult to engage with him conversationally, as his preoccupation with his theories appeared to prevent human connection; however, he was a consistent participant in art therapy groups.

During my interactions with Jeremiah, he seemed to use me as a container by monopolising my attention with accounts of his somatic and atmospheric delusional experiences, which could be thought of as a discharge of affect into me. It was this behaviour that led me to consider whether Jeremiah would be receptive to using the comic strip format as a container, as discussed previously. I wondered if in a setting where verbal disclosure could be dangerous, as discussed by Gussak and Virshup (1997), I could provide an opportunity for him to communicate through imagery while providing an experience of supporting his defences.

Jeremiah's artwork was held securely and returned to him each week by myself, which in my view emphasised the experience of a holding environment and provided a nurturing experience of myself as a further container for his internal experiences. The material that I present here was gathered over ten group art therapy sessions. In addition to the images, examinations of the therapeutic alliance, and of transference and countertransference, materialised throughout the process.

The psychoanalytic lens

The perspective that I adopted in my effort to comprehend this complex individual in an untraditional therapeutic framework was psychoanalytic in nature. My viewpoint was based on psychoanalytical theories of mind, which influenced my thinking about the approach that I took to Jeremiah. Mitchell and Black (1995) describe some of the tenets of psychoanalytic thought that I identified with during my work with Jeremiah, such as the use of interpretations, the containment of libidinal impulses, and transferential work (1995: 250).

I believe that the defended behaviour and artwork presented by Jeremiah lent itself to what I would describe as an analytic approach in the broadest sense of this term. I chose this approach to gather information from process and product by non-verbal means, as Jeremiah's verbosity seemed to form a barrier to our potential therapeutic alliance. The humanising influence of the analytic lens helped me to appreciate Jeremiah as more than the sum total of his diagnosis and charges. My efforts to make sense of his communications felt hopeless, and I felt impelled to explore a language of symbols in order to find a way of understanding him. This was done through a close examination of the symbology that I found in each of his works of art as defined in ARAS (2010). I realised that these concepts of symbols could not be thought of as definite replications of meaning that exist in Jeremiah's mind. They were used as guides to my efforts to understand his internal experience that appeared guarded by rigid defences.

The therapeutic relationship and dialogues were built within the safety of the metaphor of his imagery, allowing his defences to remain intact, as recommended by Riley (1999). My perceptions of his work were never overtly expressed to him as he may have experienced them as intrusive and damaging. Searles (1961) in his work with individuals experiencing psychosis discusses how the patient's identity is based on his psychotic symptoms, and I feel that focussing on Jeremiah's symbols and delusions as aspects of his identity, instead of trying to relieve him of his symptoms, allowed our relationship to develop. In this way, art therapy and metaphor facilitated a connection with Jeremiah as an individual, and a means of respecting his individuality.

While in group, I would give Jeremiah space to create, checking in with him throughout the process or sometimes sitting near him and watching. Towards the end of the group I would ask him to tell me about his drawing. Usually he would read out loud the words written on the image. I often wondered what message he was trying to share with me. I felt unable to build a coherent understanding of his experience solely based on what he said. I began to scrutinise and ana- lyse every bit of information in his subject matter, colour choices and process of art-making, seeking any sources I could to translate his message. I wondered if I could interpret his symbols to glimpse his internal experience, hoping that we could communicate through an unwritten language of archetypal images. This process was driven by my wish to connect while maintaining my boundaries. I kept my distance emotionally and did not put much pressure on him to relate in a reality-based way as I feared that doing so would cause him to retreat. It was more important to me that he knew that I was seeing him and was holding his experience in mind. In retrospect, I wonder whether my drive to interpret the meaning of Jeremiah's work was itself a barrier to treatment, a metaphoric wall that I constructed to create distance between us. My understanding of the role that countertransference played in our work will be further explored in the dis- cussion section of this chapter.

Observation of sessions

I have attempted to categorise our work into sessions centred on specific images in order to provide an experience of progression for the reader. Jeremiah worked on various images simultaneously, sometimes revisiting images from previous sessions. I have indicated when this happened so that his art-making process can be as understandable as possible.

During my first interaction with Jeremiah he attempted to monopolise the group's attention with descriptions of his somatic theories. As Jeremiah ex- plained his philosophy I asked him to draw a picture of his theories. The result of the first session was a colour pencil drawing expressing his process of expelling and controlling anger (Figure 8.1). He explained how he manipulated his breath and facial orifices, which controlled the surrounding environment.

In my opinion, the first compartment labelled 'uncontrolled anger' presented Jeremiah's fear that anger has the power to transform the human into an animal form. The animal seems to greet the viewer in a confrontational manner, appear- ing to provide a territorial warning. The red emanating from the orifices seemed to allude to the intensity of his anger. The border of this section seems to be anx- iously drawn, for example in the outline being corrected, presenting his difficulty in containing such intense emotions. The vapour that surrounds the ears could

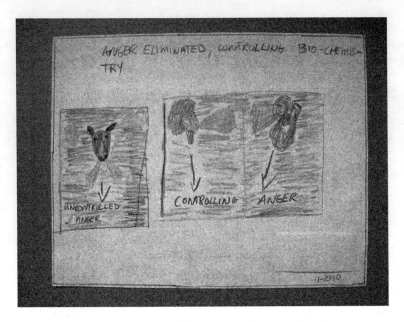

Figure 8.1 Anger Eliminated; Controlling Bio-Chemistry.

be seen to be entering the orifices from the surrounding environment, which could point to the presence of auditory hallucinations influencing the internal emotional state as described by the psychologist Hammer (1958).

Through the section 'Controlling Anger', I perceived the potential that Jeremiah's somatic processes had for him as a means of soothing his emotional state. On examination of these heads, the quality of the hair could allude to the effect of emotions. In the yellow section, the hair appears to overwhelm the head, and in the following profile after the anger has been expelled, the head is completely devoid of hair. The blue section suggests to me a soothed state as the anger has been expelled through the ear. The muscular looking arm seems to reflect Jeremiah's compulsion to control his emotions by means of actions. The merging of yellow, which is seen as energizing in ARAS (2010), and blue, seen as calming in ARAS (2010), suggests a complex progression of emotional states that could indicate that he oscillates between different states of mind.

Jeremiah was able to force visible vapours out of his mouth, which he claimed were evidence of his theories. He showed this to me, stating, 'See this here (pointing to a blemish on his face as evidence of negative forces in the body)?' then proceeding to hold his nose closed while he expelled a whitish vapour from his open mouth, thereby physically demonstrating his theory. Throughout our work together, Jeremiah would employ these actions at times when he appeared anxious or distressed.

Figure 8.2 The Three Curses Lifted by the Immortal Keys.

In the second session I presented him with three different comic formats, asking him to 'tell a story' through the boxes. This specific wording was important, as distinct from 'tell a story for me'. I consciously refrained from adding the words 'for me', because I felt that I would be influencing his process, and that this would be experienced as an attempt to merge, or otherwise interfere, with Jeremiah's ability to formulate a sense of mastery. Jeremiah chose a template and spent the next two sessions on this image (Figure 8.2). For those sessions he

189

worked quietly, seemingly absorbed in the process, and barely interacting with the other group participants.

I perceived that the use of pencil and absence of colour could be an attempt to control his emotions, suggesting defensive strategies of repression and avoidance such as those described by Hammer (1958). Hammer (1958) proposes that thorny branches imply the existence of aggressive impulses. He further states that if the individual presents a mild manner (as Jeremiah usually did), the thorns could suggest repression of these inner tensions. The need to fill in and divide more space within the compartments could reflect a compulsive need to fill time and space with words and actions to avoid emotions. The small eyes on the figures seem to deny an emotional connection between the internal experience and the other, as Hammer (1958) suggests. The eyes appear to be dysfunctional, which suggests to me that the ability to see and experience reality is overtaken by mental thought processes, possibly indicating internal preoccupation.

Upon beginning the fourth session, I presented Jeremiah with a new comic strip template, on higher quality paper. I believed that the higher quality would be appealing and would reflect to Jeremiah that I saw his work as valuable. I provided him with a three-inch long pencil (long pencils are contraband in this setting as they can be used as a weapon) and eraser. While drawing, he worked meticulously, making many erasures and corrections. Upon completion, I asked him to title his drawing, which he named, 'Curse of the Devil' (Figure 8.3). I told Jeremiah that I would hold his artwork until the following week to guard its safety as sometimes Corrections Officers searched the unit and personal items would be taken. While handing me the drawing, Jeremiah said: 'In case you get confused about where it comes from, it was an army of a thousand bridegrooms'. At the time, I found it difficult to attach any meaning to this, but over time it gathered more significance for me as I came to understand his transferential desires towards me. In reference to this drawing, I asked, 'What comes next?', to which his reply was, 'The first drawing was about man and woman (Figure 8.2), the second was about God and Devil (Figure 8.3). Next will be fields and orchards, fertile soil'.

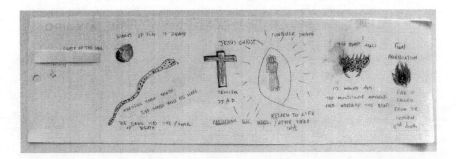

Figure 8.3 Curse of the Devil.

In 'Curse of the Devil' (Figure 8.3), the symbols initially appear disconnected. In my view, following ARAS (2010), 'sin' was equated to masculine and feminine principles that are reflected in the apple (feminine) and snake (masculine). I noticed that the snake is facing away from the apple and towards the cross, suggesting an avoidance of sexuality, and possibly emphasising Jeremiah's religious preoccupation as a coping mechanism for sexual compulsions. This work implies to me cycles of death and rebirth. This could be seen through death on the cross in contrast with the round shape surrounding Christ's return, which could also suggest a displaced vaginal opening (ARAS 2010). I wondered whether these cycles of life could reflect Jeremiah's cyclical state of mind.

Jeremiah had asked me to write "Jesus Christ" above the cross in this drawing. I told him 'I do not want to draw on your picture and I will bring it back to you next week for you to add it yourself'. During the fifth group session, I returned it to him and he added the statement 'Jesus Christ' to the drawing. He asked me about 'correct' wording and colour choices, and I reminded him that it was his decision to make. He then asked me what colours he should use for the apple. I said, 'Sometimes apples are red or yellow or green, but it could be any colour that you wanted'. He said, 'That's perfect' and then proceeded to use all three colours in a striped manner.

These are examples of how Jeremiah would attempt to draw me into his art-making process, and he became agitated when I refused to write on his work as requested. My refusal in these moments was based on clinical theories that suggest that gratification of the client's requirements interferes with 'an opportunity for insight' (Mitchell and Black 1995: 241). He continuously asked me for my opinion with regard to his work. At one point, I reminded him that it was 'most important whether he liked it as it was for him'. He then stated, 'No, it's for us', and I replied, 'You're right'. I was hesitant to reply in this way because it suggested my willingness to merge with him; however, he was aware that to an extent it is indeed 'for me', as I had explained to him that I would be writing about him when I gained his consent to use his material for publication.

Despite my attempts to establish and maintain separateness, inevitably a level of merging occurred as the therapeutic relationship progressed. Although the apprehension that I felt about merging did have a clinically considered basis, I recognise that it was also influenced by my self-protective boundary setting and fear of allowing myself to know how vulnerable I felt as a female in such a masculine environment. There was a level of detachment on my part, which was more of a dissociative response to the 'survival of the fittest' mentality of the setting, than to Jeremiah himself. However, I later acknowledged that there was some denial and repression of my own emotions in regard to my relationship with Jeremiah, which Searles (1959) has found to sometimes occur in therapists working with patients who are struggling with psychosis.

During the fifth session an interest in atmospheric processes emerges. While drawing, he described that one side of the mountain is not exposed to light, causing the 'temperature drops', which cause rain. He then went on to describe that 'the

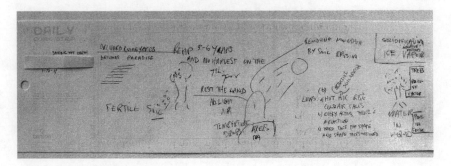

Figure 8.4 Saving the Earth.

equilibrium' of the rain turns 'the axis of the Earth ("axels")'. Jeremiah then stated that, 'We need the equilibrium'. I agreed, suggesting that, 'Equilibrium needs a mix of positive and negative and that they can not exist without the other'. He described the 'solidification' of water into ice and circled the word 'ice', which he later erased. He stated, 'Water in liquid form can be used. When the ice comes, the mountains will flatten out', and then proceeded to draw a straight line starting from the mountain and leading to the fields. He next stated, 'That is when man can farm orchards and vineyards'. He drew more horizontal lines that appear to be rows of fields. He then wrote 'fertile soil', stating, 'Earth cannot exist without fertile soil'. To this comment I asked, 'How does the soil get fertile?'. He replied, 'That's a good question', yet gave no answer. Noticing that he had written 'orchards and vineyards becomes paradise', I asked him 'What does paradise look like?'. He replied, 'No tears, no pain, no sorrow, no death, eternal day, no day, no night'.

During this session, Jeremiah seemed anxious, presented by his constant talking and the disorganised manner of production and line quality. While reviewing the image, I saw indications of decompensation.[2] Examples of this are that the trees are disjointed reflecting a possible fragmentation of self. The roots and branches are sparse, suggesting additional disconnect from surroundings and others, whereas their phallic appearance, and the fact that they appear to be fertilising the soil could indicate sexual preoccupation along the lines that Hammer (1958) proposes. The large and chaotic lettering further suggests decompensation when compared to his previous handwriting.

Towards the end of the group, he said, 'I had a vision of this'. I assumed that he was referring to his drawing, so I said 'Isn't it nice to see on paper the visions that we have in our heads'. His reply was: 'No, I had a vision that you came to the door of the other mental health unit I was on. You came and were sitting and drawing and the noise was forcing the art'. I asked him 'What noise?' and he said: 'the sound you were making'. This vision will be addressed further in my discussion of my subsequent thinking about our transferential relationship, as it seems especially meaningful in the development of our therapeutic alliance and Jeremiah's progress.

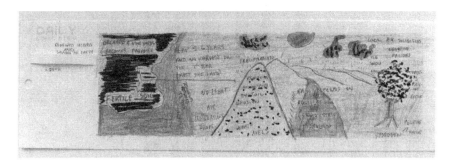

Figure 8.5 Renewed Heaven and Saving the Earth.

During the sixth session he placed the previous drawing (Figure 8.4) above a new sheet and began to reproduce it in a more organised manner (Figure 8.5). In Figure 8.5 he coloured the black on the clouds first, calling them 'dark clouds'. Then he coloured the sun yellow and the tree green, then added orange to the tree, and finally coloured rows of 'field' brown. Next he drew the dot-like markings on the mountain and used a blue pencil to colour in the water. He then asked me if he could 'tear up' the drawing presented in Figure 8.4. Jeremiah expressed dislike of this image, which I thought was possibly due to the uncontrolled manner of its execution. I discouraged this (wanting to preserve it an indicator of decompensation) and suggested that I keep it so that later we could see the progression of his story.

I noticed in Figure 8.5 that the landscape looked more realistic due to the execution of a background and foreground, which suggests a more grounded sense of reality to me. Following the ideas presented in ARAS (2010) I wondered whether the sun was labelled to confirm it as a source of nurturance, and the orchards and vineyards could be a reflection of hope. The rain could refer to cleansing and growth, whereas the dark clouds appear ominous, suggesting threatening emotions. I believe that Jeremiah created a state of tension between the life sustaining and destroying aspects of atmospheric forces.

The repeated outlining of mountains and green hatch-marks between the mountain and river interest me and may be evidence of anxiety in relation to sexual feelings. Interpreting the image with reference to ARAS (2010), I wondered whether the river flowing between the mountains could be a reflection of a displaced vulva that produces a potential rebirth. Additionally, I wondered about the wedge-like form of the central mountain and river, bearing in mind that research undertaken by Spring (2004) has suggested that this shape suggests entrapment, pointing to "active dynamics of fear, anger, confusion, and conflict" (2004: 201). Despite these possibly threatening emotions, I noticed that the tree trunk appears stronger, suggesting more integrated ego strength than the previous decompensated image.

During this session, Jeremiah said: 'When I was in school, my teacher asked me to draw a new school logo. I drew the number 60 with some snakes under it. The teacher put it up in a store window where everyone could see it.' I asked

'How did it feel to see your work up there?' He replied, 'I felt like part of me was gone'. I then said, 'It may have felt that way to you, but maybe seeing your art made other people feel good'. He said, 'Yeah I think it did, you're right'. I stated, 'Don't worry about these drawings being gone, that is why I suggested that I hold onto them and keep them safe for you. Then later we can look at them all together'. This was the first time I experienced his recognition of an emotive response and memory. He then stated, 'Take a string and put a pebble on it, hold it up in the air and go like this (swinging his hand in a circular motion)'. I asked him 'What will that do?', He said, 'The sounds cause vibrations, every action causes a reaction, like the mountains (Figure 8.4)'.

During the seventh session, Jeremiah wanted to make a poster of butcher paper approximately two feet by three feet (Figure 8.7), which he said would be 'paradise'. He told the group that 'It was coming soon', in reference to his paradise. He began looking at his drawings that I had laid out for him. He asked me in reference to 'Saving the Earth' (Figure 8.5), 'Does it look finished? Should I add more colour?'. I told him that it was 'up to him', and he still seemed unsure, stating, 'I don't want to cover up the inscription'. I reminded him 'In artmaking, if we don't like the way something turns out we can change it or start another image'. I also said I was 'excited to see where his story would go next'. He replied to this by pointing to the blank poster on the wall (Figure 8.7) and said: 'Paradise, New Earth and New Heaven'. He then got out a new piece of the comic strip paper and started to draw a new image with graphite pencil (Figure 8.6).

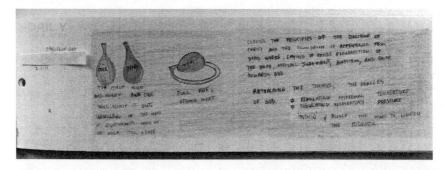

Figure 8.6 Oracle of God.

In Figure 8.6, I perceived sexual preoccupation reflected in the vessels of milk (maternal secretions) and honey (sexual secretions), as well as 'meat'. It is possible that the sexual implications of these images caused Jeremiah to revert to verbal language for the remainder of the template. The written references to his somatic processes seem to me to be an avoidant defence against his fear of instinctual drives. I wonder if the references to milk and honey inducing vomiting are reflections of the intensity of his emotions towards me that began to surface and therefore may need to be bottled and regulated by Jeremiah. This reminded me of Searles' (1963) descriptions of the intense emotional experiences of his patients who were diagnosed with schizophrenia. During this session I asked; 'Why would too much milk and honey make someone vomit?'. He replied, 'Because if it is too much it is undigestible [*sic*]. Like when a new baby drinks too much milk and then spits it up, too much of a good thing is bad'. Therefore, 'vomit' could be seen as a caution against excess, and possibly a purging of his sexuality and of his feelings towards me.

During the eighth session, Jeremiah continued to colour in 'Oracle of God' (Figure 8.6) from the previous session. First he coloured the honey jar a reddish brown, and then began to lightly colour in the background with a blue pencil. He then coloured the meat and plate, followed by the milk jar and the yellow rims of both jars. He then added stars next to the words 'regulating', after erasing and then re-executing them.

At the end of the session he looked at Figure 8.4 and asked me, 'What should we do with this one? Should I tear it up?'. I replied by stating, 'You can do whatever you want with it'. Previously I had encouraged him to keep this drawing; therefore, I was glad that he brought this issue up again, so that I could reinforce the idea that it was his choice. He stated, 'I want to tear it up', however he seemed unsure, seemingly looking at me for my approval. Before I could respond he said in a firmer voice, 'But this message is really important, so I am going to keep it'.

Figure 8.7 Oracles of God (Poster).

During the ninth session, Jeremiah was primarily working on his poster (Figure 8.7). He stated that he wanted to colour in the stars with white, and I suggested using a white pastel, as it would show up nicely on the brown paper. He was singing and dancing for most of the session while colouring. He called me over to him by asking: 'Come here, which star are you?' I replied, 'I don't know, which one do you think I am?' He picked the star closest to his name at the bottom-right corner, and said, 'This one, this one is you, and this one is me'. I asked him 'Do you think that one looks like me?', to which he replied: 'It is illuminated, the white is illuminated'. Although we should consider whether this is simply a reference to our difference in skin colour, it could also suggest his transferential urge to include me in his celestial world. This was further emphasised when upon my departure he was singing: 'I love you, I love you, I love you, and you love me too'. For the last three sessions, he had started singing right as I was departing, and I wondered if the singing was another avoidant defence against the anxiety brought about by my leaving.

Jeremiah described his poster as 'Paradise'. I found the presence of dichotomies, such as references to 'alpha and omega, kings and queens, princes and princesses' interesting. These dualities could reflect his possible concerns with good and evil. When I asked him if I could document his poster, he said: 'Of course, just make sure that you know that this (pointing to phrase 'alpha and omega') is the beginning and end of sin'. I perceived that the use of the white stars, suggesting 'illumination', contrasted the use of black for the sky, which, according to ARAS (2010), could suggest depression, as representation of the duality that he experiences in regards to life and death that was featured in earlier works. It is important to note that each section of this poster is contained, which I felt mirrored the comic strip templates.

When I entered the group room to begin the tenth session, a verbal therapy group had just ended, and Jeremiah said that he did not participate 'because they bring up too much emotional stuff'. At that point he showed me photographs of some of his children, which was surprising to me, as he had never mentioned his family before. When Jeremiah signed in on the group log sheet, he wrote his name backwards like a mirror image, and he seemed agitated when I asked him how he was, replying: 'Good, good, same to you' in an aggressive tone. He worked quietly on his poster (Figure 7), not interacting with any of the group members. At one point another detainee asked if he could use some pastels. I told him that Jeremiah was using them but that he could take a few at a time. Jeremiah immediately jumped into the conversation and said 'No, don't take them, I'm using them'. A few minutes later he seemed angry with me that the black pastel was missing. I then pointed out to him that it was in the box and not missing at all.

Jeremiah spent this group re-emphasising the outlines that separate the phrases on his poster. He also re-outlined the stars with the white pastel, and used the black pastel to fill in the background. I approached him and stated, 'You are putting a lot of time and effort into this'. His reply was, 'Always. I use a lot of concentration as there is no room for errors'. I then stated, 'Don't you feel like everyone makes mistakes?', to which he said, 'No, I am very calculated so that I don't make errors'. My reply was, 'Never? I know that sometimes in my life I have made mistakes and then I have ended up learning from them. I see it as kind of the same as when you say "every action causes a reaction" (mentioned in Figure 8.4)'. He seemed excited by this connection and exclaimed 'Exactly!'. He then said, 'I can tell you specific examples of when that happened, like the Titanic'. My response was, 'What about your life? Do you feel like there were times in your life that you made mistakes?'. He replied, 'No, I didn't develop skeletally and biologically until I was full grown, and this is when I started (reference to his breathing processes). I used to wear all velvet and leather to make myself perspire to create the (breathing processes)'. I then asked, 'How old were you when this happened?', and he said: '12'. This conversation interests me because after working closely with him for ten sessions, this was my only attempt to challenge his defences. I was trying to see if he could connect to the reality surrounding him, but ultimately found that he was not ready to leave the fantasy that he created and could control.

Discussion

In my opinion, Jeremiah's delusions enabled him to avoid the experience of his internal and external realities. His apparent desire to manipulate the external world suggested to me that fantasy was being employed as a defence to avoid anxiety and emotions. Jeremiah seemed to be attempting to control his internal emotional state by manipulating his external atmosphere. Although he existed in an environment where much was out of his control, he seemed to employ his somatic delusions in the service of controlling his internal tensions. Jeremiah's compulsive detail, constant corrections and use of a pencil in his artwork also presented attempts to control. Hammer (1958) suggests that this type of behaviour can maintain defences protecting against anger, anxiety and mental instability. I thought that the use of the comic could offer him control of his reality in a contained and communicative format, functioning as an alternative to his defences against the feelings of powerlessness brought about by his experience of incarceration.

Jeremiah was possibly controlling the emotions that stemmed from his libidinal drives, and I wondered if part of him was aware that they were reflected in his artwork. Perhaps he felt at risk of being overwhelmed by the emotions presented in his comic strips, especially his vessels of potential erotic and maternal transference in Figure 8.6. The significance of his overwhelming emotions is further emphasised by his statement of 'too much of a good thing is bad' in reference to the 'milk' and 'honey' in that image. By focusing on the safety of the poster (Figure 8.7), he could create a future where sins will be absolved. He indicated that in 'paradise', there would be 'no tears, no pain, no sorrow, no death'. This statement could suggest an urge to achieve freedom from the internal conflict that drives his preoccupations. I saw this poster as a place where contrast becomes balanced, and internal struggles of good and evil are erased. It appears that through his connection with religion he felt that he would be given an opportunity for rebirth in 'paradise', where he will be free from internal conflict. It is possible that the process of resolution of this conflict would have been intolerable, and that the pain of his reality necessitated his defensive strategies.

The prevalence of symbols that suggest fertility and nurturance in Jeremiah's artwork could reflect a longing for connection with an other. I wondered whether his desires for nurturance were triggered by our therapeutic alliance, as his statements to me indicate a transferential experience. The art therapist Allen (1988: 113) defines transference as 'a client's unconscious projection of feelings onto the therapist, who has come to represent a significant person or an aspect of that person, from the client's past'. Mitchell and Black (1995: 234) refer to Freud's ideas of transference feelings towards the analyst as 'forbidden impulses and fantasies'. His 'vision' of me, inclusion of me on his poster, and love songs allowed me to witness his positive feelings for me and the anxiety that these may have caused. Searles (1963: 338) discusses this kind of experience in his work with patients diagnosed with schizophrenia. He shows that ambivalence often occurs towards the therapist, as the patient begins to experience 'positive feelings' and the fear of these needs being unfulfilled.

The 'vision' could have been Jeremiah's attempt to invite me into his fantasies; however, I wondered whether he also felt that I was 'forcing his art'. That moment became a turning point in our relationship as he acknowledged a desire to connect with me outside of the group process. This vision was relayed to me during a session when the image produced appeared to present decompensation, and it could have been this vulnerability and my tolerance of his decompensation that allowed him to disclose his fear and desire. The reference to his 'teacher', who put his work on display, may indicate fears that I will expose him or destroy him through sharing his artwork. Most importantly, in my opinion, it indicates the importance that my holding of his work had for him, because he seemed so deeply identified with his art. These instances seem to indicate the ambivalence that predominated in his relationship with me.

I felt that Jeremiah wanted to merge with me, and at the same time he seemed to fear the threat to his individuation, as well as the potential loss of our relationship. As previously mentioned, this type of emotional response has been explored by Searles (1963) in his work with patients diagnosed with schizophrenia. It is possible that his references to 'equilibrium' and nature as being life sustaining and destroying (Figure 8.4–8.5) could also reflect his ambivalent feelings towards me. Further, while interpreting his images of 'milk' and 'honey' that cause vomiting in Figure 8.6, I saw a connection to Mitchell and Black's discussion of Melanie Klein's theories of the complexities of the analytic relationship. They explain this by stating 'At times, the analyst is a good breast, magically transformative; interpretations are good milk, protective, nurturing, restorative. At times, the analyst is a bad breast, deadly and destructive; interpretations are poisonous, destroying from within if ingested' (1995: 106).

Fenner and Gussak (2006) have raised the question as to how the correctional setting influences the process of transference. They suggest that the environment may be 'too primitive to take advantage of the transferential relationship that would develop' (2006: 420). They propose that this relationship may be overwhelmingly regressive to the inmate, which could be detrimental to the emotional state and subsequent survival. Further research could explore whether therapies that work with transference could also be advantageous in this setting, especially in regards to those individuals who are actively presenting signs of psychosis.

If the correctional setting restricts the full development of transference, the art therapy process may be even more relevant in that it offers the potential for transferential material to be discharged into, and held in, the artwork. Allen (1988) suggests guiding the client to use the art for this experience of containment as distinct from forms of therapy involving greater reliance on the person of the therapist. I believe this approach allows for transferential material to be expressed even if the setting discourages it.

In retrospect, I wonder whether the comic strip template may have provided both Jeremiah and myself with holding and containment. It is possible that I needed to manage his fantasies so that they did not overwhelm me. My focus on the symbolic meanings of his imagery may have interfered with my ability to hear his fears and desires in relation to working so closely with me. At that time my limited experience with transferential work caused me to instead become preoccupied with understanding him through interpretation. I believe that both of us were experiencing ambivalent feelings towards our relationship, thereby contributing to each other's conflicting emotions.

I often felt emotionally flooded while I was researching the symbology of Jeremiah's imagery. Alternatively, I felt guarded in relation to my internal experience in his presence, so as to protect myself from being overwhelmed by his discharge of affect into me. Searles (1961: 265) discusses the possibility of the therapist unconsciously defending his or her own 'deeply ambivalent feelings' towards the patient. My countertransferential longing involved a desire to merge with him through his internal experience and simultaneous fears of this occurring, because he was so profoundly ambivalent. I perceived him as striving to merge with me and fearing that I would destroy him as Searles (1965) has discussed in his exploration of maternal transference.

In hindsight, I question whether I was unconsciously inviting him to merge and also denying our relationship. Was I being seductive by giving him my attention, only to ignore his feelings of 'love'? Did this contribute to his ambivalence towards our relationship? It is important for me to question my own limitations in attempting to provide a containing experience for Jeremiah. I now acknowledge that I unconsciously denied our relationship as being emotional, and instead focused on intellectualising it, as described by Searles (1959). As mentioned previously, my emotional boundaries may have been avoidance of my own experiences of vulnerability and 'love' as a young woman in a setting that was often aggressively and sexually charged. In retrospect, I wonder whether my focus on the comic strip as an actual container disregarded the significance of the transference and countertransference, and I think that more familiarity with working with transference and countertransference might have provided additional containment through an emotional relationship.

Conclusions

Although I do believe that my work with Jeremiah allowed for an emotive release through metaphor, I also recognise that the comic strip alone was limited in its ability to contain his experience. His artwork appears defended through metaphoric symbology, as if he needed to contain himself within the container. He repeatedly threatened to destroy the image reflecting his decompensation (Figure 8.4), suggesting an awareness of the possible discomfort of emotional states occurring during its execution. However, it appears that it became tolerable; especially because he expressed that it may be meaningful to others. This could indicate an acceptance of feeling states, and suggests a sense of reality and strength, in that the self can be fallible and emotional, instead of all 'good' or 'bad'. Also, because I suggested holding his work, he may have begun to learn that I was accepting of his conflicting emotional states.

Though Jeremiah's work is shrouded in defence, what it illustrates is human emotional experience. This experience was witnessed in his attempt to express loving feelings and possible rejection in regards to our relationship, while incorporating the need for safety in his environment. Searles (1963) describes the complexity of his patients' feelings towards him in his own work, which provided much insight into my own relationship with Jeremiah. It could be considered progress in therapeutic terms for a highly defended individual such as Jeremiah to reveal and tolerate these aspects of him- or her- self through symbol and metaphor. Despite certain pathologies and alleged crimes, the artwork allows a stigmatised detainee to be humanised. Although this validation may be in conflict with the stereotypic notion of the correctional system, in that it provides empowerment for individuals who are physically confined and penalised, it may point to the benefit of the art therapy process for those inside.

Jeremiah's delusions eventually overflowed out of the comic strip templates onto the poster (Figure 8.7). This caused me to wonder if the use of the comic strip was ineffectual, as it was ultimately unable to contain and hold Jeremiah's fantasy. However, I witnessed emotional progress through his communication and connection with myself. Therefore, I see the comic strip as a tool that worked in tandem with our therapeutic relationship. It may have made a specific contribution to what was achieved, although it is impossible to draw firm conclusions about this. The containment that it provided offered a safe space for his conflicts and delusions to be accepted and held by me, without challenging his defences.

Exploring the limitations of the actual comic strip template as a container became a learning experience for my own practice as an art therapist. It became an exploration of symbolism, containment, and relationship based on my interest in psychoanalytic principles. It also indicated to me how much containment is necessary for a detainee struggling with psychosis to experience being "safely held". What has emerged through this process is my awareness of many levels of containment. This is witnessed through the ideas of the defended mind as a container for threatening impulses, the correctional setting as a container for the individual's mind and body, artwork as a container for un-expressed emotion, the comic strip as a container for fantasy, and the therapeutic alliance as a container for the dualistic experience of fear and hope.

Through his poster "Oracles of God" (Figure 8.7), Jeremiah seemed to express the hope of good conquering evil in his internal struggle. Furthermore his escape through the fantasy and creative process signifies what Day and Onorato (1989: 131) describe as a 'psychic escape' from the prison walls, as well as an escape from the internal dichotomy of self. The concentric layers of containment within containment that occurred though Jeremiah's use of defence, the setting, the art therapy process, the comic strip template and our therapeutic relationship encouraged a meaningful emotional experience. I felt that this experience allowed Jeremiah to be to some extent reborn as an artist and complex human being, 'the true self' (Mitchell and Black 1995: 133) surfacing beneath his delusions.

Notes

1 When addressing research that pertains to the prison population, the legal term 'inmate' is used. However when addressing Jeremiah the term 'detainee' is used, as at that time he was awaiting sentencing for his alleged crimes.

2 With regard to Jeremiah, I use the term *decompensation* to refer to an increase of his psychotic symptoms and a decrease of the maintenance of his defences.

References

Allen, P. (1988). 'A consideration of transference in art therapy', *The American Journal of Art Therapy* 26, 113–118.

Archive for Research in Archetypal Symbolism (ARAS) (2010). *The book of symbols: Reflections on archetypal images.* Cologne, Germany: Taschen.

Bion, W.R. (1970). *Attention and interpretation*, New York, NY: Jason Aronson.

Day, E.S. and Onorato, G.T. (1989). 'Making art in a jail setting' in Wadeson, H., Durkin, J. and Perach, D. (eds.), *Advances in Art Therapy*, New York: John Wiley and Sons.

Fenner, L.B. and Gussak, D.E. (2006). 'Therapeutic boundaries in a prison setting: A dialogue between an intern and her supervisor', *Arts in Psychotherapy* 33, 5, 414–421. doi:10.1016/j.aip.2006.08.002.

Fernandez, K.M. (2009). 'Comic addict: A qualitative study of the benefits of addressing ambivalence through comic/cartoon drawing with clients in in-patient treatment for chemical dependency' in Brooke, S.L. (ed.), *The Use of Creative Therapies with Chemical Dependency Issues*, Springfield, IL, USA: Charles C. Thomas.

Gussak, D. (2006). 'Effects of art therapy with prison inmates: A follow-up study', *Arts in Psychotherapy* 33, 188–198. doi:10.1016/j.aip.2005.11.003.

Gussak, D. (2009). 'Comparing the effectiveness of art therapy on depression and locus of control of male and female inmates', *Arts in Psychotherapy* 36, 4, 202–207.

Gussak, D. and Virshup, E. (1997). *Drawing time: Art therapy in prisons and other correctional settings*, Chicago, IL: Magnolia Street.

Hammer, E.F. (1958). *The clinical application of projective drawings*, Springfield, IL: Charles. C Thomas.

Killick, K. (1997). 'Unintegration and containment in acute psychosis' in Killick, K. and Schaverien, J. (eds.), *Art, Psychotherapy and Psychosis*, London, New York, US: Routledge/Taylor and Francis Group. Available online at https://play.google.com/books/reader?printsec=frontcoverandoutput=reader&id=ox9QVRdE_SQC&pg=GBS. PT61 (viewed 28 April 2014).

Killick, K. (2000).'The art room as container in analytical art psychotherapy with patients in psychotic states' in Gilroy, A. and McNeilly, G. (eds.), *The Changing Shape of Art Therapy: New Developments in Theory and Practice*, London, Philadelphia: Jessica Kingsley. Available online at https://play.google.com/books/reader?printsec=frontcover&output=reader&id=RbACFxmVtp0C (viewed 16 January 2015).

Liebmann, M. (1990). 'It just happened: Looking at crime events' in Liebmann, M. (ed.) *Art Therapy in Practice*, Bristol, PA: Jessica Kingsley.

Lucas-Falk, K. and Moon, C.H. (2010). 'Comic books, connection, and the artist identity' in Moon, C.H. (ed.), *Materials and Media in Art Therapy: Critical Understandings of Diverse Artistic Vocabularies*, New York: Routledge/Taylor and Francis Group.

Malchiodi, C. (2007). *The art therapy sourcebook*, New York: McGraw-Hill.

McWilliams, N. (1994). *Psychoanalytic diagnosis: Understanding personality structure in the clinical process*, New York: The Guilford Press.

McWilliams, N. (2004). *Psychoanalytic psychotherapy: A practitioner's guide*, New York: The Guilford Press.

Mitchell, S.A. and Black, M.J. (1995). *Freud and beyond: A history of modern psychoanalytic thought*, New York: Basic Books.

Ogden, T.H. (2004). 'On holding and containing, being and dreaming', *The International Journal of Psychoanalysis* 85, 1, 349–364.

Persons, R.W. (2009). 'Art therapy with serious juvenile offenders: A phenomenological analysis', *International Journal of Offender Therapy and Comparative Criminology* 53, US: Sage Publications. doi:10.1177/0306624X08320208.

Riley, S. (1999). *Contemporary art therapy with adolescents*, London: Jessica Kingsley.

Searles, H.F. (1959). 'Oedipal love in the countertransference', *International Journal of Psychoanalysis* 40, May–Aug 1959, 180–90.

Searles, H.F. (1961). 'Phases of patient-therapist interaction in the psychotherapy of chronic schizophrenia' in Buckley, P. (ed.) (1988) *Essential Papers on Psychosis*, New York: New York University Press.

Searles, H.F. (1963). 'Scorn, disillusionment and adoration in the psychotherapy of schizophrenia', *Psychoanalytic Review 49C*, 39–60.

Searles, H.F. (1965). 'The evolution of the mother transference in psychotherapy with the schizophrenic patient' in Searles, H.F (ed.), *Collected Papers on Schizophrenia and Related Subjects*, London: Karnac.

Spring, D. (2004). 'Thirty-year study links neuroscience, specific trauma, ptsd, image conversion, and language translation'. *Art Therapy: Journal of the American Art Therapy Association* 21, 4, 200–209.

Spuriell, V. (1983). 'The rules and frame of the psychoanalytic situation', *Psychoanalytic Quarterly* 52, 1–33. Available online at http://www.analysis.com/vs/vs83b.html (viewed 28 April 2014).

INDEX

Dr Laurence Errington